Anonymus

History of the Brooklyn and Long Island Fair February 22. 1864

Anonymus

History of the Brooklyn and Long Island Fair February 22. 1864

ISBN/EAN: 9783741144455

Manufactured in Europe, USA, Canada, Australia, Japa

Cover: Foto ©ninafisch / pixelio.de

Manufactured and distributed by brebook publishing software
(www.brebook.com)

Anonymus

History of the Brooklyn and Long Island Fair February 22. 1864

HISTORY

OF THE

BROOKLYN AND LONG ISLAND FAIR,

FEBRUARY 22, 1864.

Fair is a bargain, when 'tis made
According to the rules of trade;
Fair is the maid who sells these rhymes,
You've called her so a thousand times;
Fair are the speeches—false as fair—
That oft to Congress [illegible] come;
Fair are the [illegible] that throng Broadway
On every [illegible] opening day;
In [illegible] as Job sets forth, (xxxvii. 22,)
"Fair weather cometh from the North;"
Fairmount by Schuylkill's watch is fair;
Fairfield is famed for wholesome air;
Fair winds propel Fairhaven's sails,
Bidding in Arctic seas for whales;
Fair was the fight at Naseby, when
Stout Fairfax beat King Charles' men;
And fair with ornament rich and rare
Is Brooklyn's Sanitary Fair.

Boston, Feb. 16, 1864. John G. Palfrey

Prepared and Published by Authority of the Executive Committee.

BROOKLYN.
"THE UNION," STEAM PRESSES, 10 FRONT STREET.
1864.

HISTORY

OF THE

Brooklyn and Long Island Fair.

THE Brooklyn and Long Island Fair, in aid of the United States Sanitary Commission, was the first great act of self-assertion ever made by the City of Brooklyn. Previous to that we had contented ourselves as a community with believing that for beauty of local position, Brooklyn was rarely surpassed; a claim generally admitted. She had also, with remarkable unanimity, been allowed the sobriquet of the "City of Churches," although never exceeding the proportion of one church to two thousand persons. The census was an indisputable witness to the fact of the wondrous ratio in which her population had increased, till she was equally, beyond denial, the third city, in that respect, in the Union. Among the merchants of New York most prominent for intelligence, wealth, and consequent influence, were found many who resided within the walls of Brooklyn; while the crowds crossing her ferries to and from the Great Metropolis at morning and evening, showed how largely the entire business and labor of the latter were performed by our citizens.

Nevertheless, Brooklyn was but a suburb, overshadowed by her mighty neighbor. Travellers, foreign and native, in vast numbers, visited the chief commercial city of our country on errands of business or pleasure; but if not called to Brooklyn through personal claims of kindred or friendship, rarely sought it except to visit the great Navy Yard of the nation, or the most beautiful Cemetery in the world; severally so placed, on what was once her northern and what is still her southern boundary, that either could be reached while the City itself was practically ignored. The visitor came and went, having seen little or nothing of it except its unattractive outskirts, and with no longing awakened to see more. Meanwhile she had gathered to herself Public Schools, which had grown to rank among the best of the kind in the land; private or corporate institutions of education for either sex, which in their entire equipment, management, and efficiency would do honor to any community; a body of clergy, as a whole, and for their numbers not surpassed in character and gifts by those of any of our cities; great institutions of charity, too largely dependent, however, on annual contributions rather than permanent endowments; courses of lectures, delivered by the ablest men of the country, or by savans from abroad, travelling or resident in America; a well appointed Philharmonic Society, amply patronised and appreciated; an Academy of Music, the beauty and value of which the Fair has made to be more widely and palpably known; a Mercantile Library, which for seven years has met, in a measure, which we could wish vastly greater, an inevitable want of every progressive community; and an Historical Society, recently formed for the City and Island, which has started on its course with remarkable vigor. And yet withal, Brooklyn, till the Fair, had no status before the country beyond that of a remarkably quiet suburban town, where, after a hard day's labor, weary men found comfortable lodging places till the next day's work began. An account of the inception, prospects, and results of the Great Fair just closed, may serve to open the popular eye to the fact that it was nothing less than a Great City which inaugurated, sustained, and carried it through.

A similar course of remark is applicable to Long Island. The Battle of Long Island and Washington's masterly retreat, great connected facts in our Revolutionary History, attracted to the Island the anxious eyes of that generation, and made its name famous in the national annals. But aside of being one of the great fruit and vegetable gardens for the supply of our city markets, it has been since that period known abroad chiefly for the fine watering places on the Bay and along its Sea-side, of great summer resort; and for numerous lovely villages on the Sound, where wealthy residents both of Brooklyn and New York have built elegant villas on some of the choicest rural spots of the vicinity. But a new era seems to have opened upon the Island since the beginning of the war. The spirit of the War Fund Committee and of the Woman's Relief Association became evident very early far beyond the limits of the City, or of the County of Kings. Associations like the latter came into existence in various places very soon after the outbreak of the Rebellion. Ninety miles down the Island, almost at the eastern extremity of its coast, the "Ladies' Relief Union" of Southold is coeval with the moment when our armies first took the field; and no sooner had the Sanitary Commission announced itself in being, than it began to receive the bounty of the loyal women of that remote village. We mean nothing invidious to the rest of the Island when we thus single out Southold. Here is merely one example of what has been doing by other towns and villages all the way on its territory between itself and Brooklyn. The sequel will show how nobly and generously, when the Fair was proposed for the City and Island, the whole Island came up to the work. The generous spirits of both were hand in hand throughout. A large-hearted unity of plan and work was established through sympathy and interest in a grand common object, which it was delightful to witness, and more delightful to share. In our Appendix will be found, in full, the names of those of either sex who were actively engaged in arranging and managing the Fair, and a list of the contributions from all quarters to its Treasury. There it will be seen that the City vindicated her claim to be a "power" in the land by something better than the mere numbers of her population. She stood forth for once apart from New York, to help to the utmost of her means the noblest charity of the world, and proved herself alive to her proud position, her abundant wealth, her great privileges and opportunities. She summoned Long Island to her side, and she came. Together they carried through the work to a result far beyond the expectations of the most sanguine; and the thousands and tens of thousands thus gathered into the Treasury of the Fair, will be dispensed by the wise and faithful hands of the Sanitary Commission, for the relief and comfort of our heroic and suffering brothers in the field and the hospital.

THE SOURCES.

The Brooklyn and Long Island Fair was the creation jointly of the "War Fund Committee of Brooklyn and County of Kings," now consisting of one hundred and thirty of its prominent active citizens, acting through its Sanitary Committee, or "Committee on the U. S. Sanitary Commission and Hospitals;" and of the "Woman's Relief Association of the City of Brooklyn," recognized by the Commission as its "Brooklyn Auxiliary," to which the Sanitary Committee of the War Fund is Advisory, without whose concurrence none of its measures can be carried into effect. To show how excellent a working basis for the Fair already existed in these two organizations, consider the common objects had in view, and the machinery for operating on our community which they already had running when that was in contemplation.

The War Fund Committee grew in part out of the appointment, in the Summer of 1862, by the State Executive of New York, of Two Committees in the Second and Third Senatorial Districts, for the purpose of raising each a Regiment of Volunteers, to serve for three years, or during the war. The Board of Supervisors of this County appointed almost simultaneously a large Committee to aid in all measures for the increase of the Army and Navy. These several committees appear to have united in the conviction that a large central committee was indispensable to the work devolved on them; and at their suggestion and request the "War Fund Committee" was organized in September, 1862, and soon after confirmed and appointed by an immense public meeting of the citizens. This committee has among its special duties "to promote the objects of and to aid the Sanitary Commission;" and besides, "to do all in their power to aid in procuring Recruits; to do what may be needful in behalf of the sick and wounded; to aid discharged soldiers, and the families of deceased soldiers and sailors in procuring the pay or pensions to which they may be entitled; and to assist the Allotment Commissioners in their philanthropic work, and generally to use their efforts and influence in aiding the Government to suppress the Rebellion."

In its efforts in behalf of these objects the committee has made hundreds of applications for and secured pensions, bounties, pay in arrear, and prize money. Information and aid to a very large extent have been given to families of soldiers belonging to Brooklyn and other regiments; grants have been made from time to time in aid of the work of the Sanitary Commission, and considerable sums have been advanced to help forward the organization of Volunteer Regiments.

The "Woman's Relief Association" was fully organized December 9th, 1862; at which time, composed as it was intended to be of female delegates from the several churches of the City, thirty churches were thus represented; and by the end of April more than fifty had joined it and were in active co-operation. This Association has also for its objects "to stimulate, concentrate, and direct the philanthropic efforts of the community in behalf of the sick and wounded soldiers of our armies; to obtain and distribute reliable information concerning their immediate and prospective wants; to collect supplies of hospital stores and medical comforts of all kinds, and generally to advance the views and objects of the Sanitary Committee, as appointed by the 'War Fund Committee of the City of Brooklyn and County of Kings,' to which it shall be distinctly and permanently auxiliary, and to whose disposal all receipts, of whatsoever nature, shall be subject."

Thus it will be seen that with these common objects before them, and among which aid to the U. S. Sanitary Commission stood so prominent; representing as they did the loyal population of the City of either sex; actively engaged in, habituated to, and almost by a moral necessity profoundly interested in, the specific work of the Commission itself; with the most cordial and intimate relations to the Commission, cemented and confirmed by frequent and large contributions of hospital clothing and comforts to its stores; they were the prepared and natural agencies for inaugurating and carrying on the Fair.

In May, 1863, an appeal was made by the War Fund Sanitary Committee to the churches of Brooklyn, asking cash contributions for the purchase of materials for hospital clothing, to be made up by the families of our soldiers in the field through the agency of the Female Employment Society, one of the best benevolent organizations in the City; and which, though created long before the war for the object its name intimates, has rendered itself, as in the case before us, a most efficient co-laborer with those special organizations which had their origin in the war. The response placed about six thousand dollars in the hands of the Committee, which was an ample provision during the Summer, when many of the ladies of the City connected with the management of its charities were away, for aiding the soldiers' families and keeping up our quota of supplies to the Sanitary Commission.

In the following Autumn it was found that the Woman's Relief Association, through the Sanitary Committee of the War Fund, and during the first year of its existence, had turned into the depot of the Sanitary Commission supplies of hospital clothing to the value of about fifty thousand dollars. It became a serious question with the Committee whether fresh appeals should be made to the churches, or whether some new plan could be devised by which the citizens of Brooklyn could be brought into active and efficient sympathy with the work of the Woman's Relief Association for the Winter of 1863-4. Early in October the plan of a great Fair for the City, was suggested by Mr. James H. Frothingham, of the Committee, and he and the Chairman, Mr. Dwight Johnson, conferred with the President of the Sanitary Commission, Dr. Bellows, and corresponded with friends in Boston, where great Fairs had been held with eminent success, on the best mode of conducting them. Dr. Bellows was not at first impressed very favorably by the suggestion; and when, on the 6th of November following, the Sanitary Committee brought the matter before the stated meeting of the Woman's Relief Association in the form of a general plan for a Great City Fair, expressing their conviction that if undertaken with unanimity and zeal by them, seventy to eighty thousand dollars might be realized for the Sanitary Commission, it met with no marked favor by the Ladies assembled. It was feared that our local charities, whose annual fairs were already being prepared for, would suffer too seriously by such an undertaking. The Ladies, however, after further deliberation, suggested that the Great Fair might perhaps be postponed to some day in February, and the subject was laid over by common consent till the next meeting.

Meanwhile, on the 14th of the same month of November, the Ladies of New York, under the auspices of the U. S. Sanitary Commission, announced by a circular the project of a Great Metropolitan Fair, to begin in that city on the 22d of February, 1864. The circular was sent to ladies in Brooklyn, inviting their presence and co-operation at a meeting in New York; when it was proposed to assign a department of the Fair to Brooklyn, but the Fair still to be held in New York.

On the 20th of November, the Woman's Relief Association of Brooklyn decided to unite in the effort, as the Brooklyn Division of the Metropolitan Fair, leaving open the question in which city the Brooklyn Division would carry on their work.

On the 21st inst. the Brooklyn Sanitary Committee had an interview with Dr. Bellows upon the subject. They represented to him the great advantages already possessed in the City through the Woman's Relief Association, for bringing into active effect the sympathies and energies of our whole loyal population in behalf of a Fair to be held in our own City; and the inevitable disadvantage and inconvenience to our Ladies, of instituting and keeping up a Brooklyn Division of the Fair at the distance of at least four miles from many of their homes. At the close of the conference there was the most cordial concurrence of opinion that to the Woman's Relief Association should be left the decision of the question. On these facts being reported to the War Fund Committee they met the warmest reception.

THE INITIATORY STEPS.

A special meeting of the Woman's Relief Association was held on the 24th of November, when with full knowledge of the above facts, the Ladies, in anticipation of a great Fair, decided to increase the representation from the respective churches, the better to inaugurate the work.

On the 4th of December a very large meeting of the Association was held in the Chapel of the Packer Female Institute.

The meeting was called to order by the President, Mrs. J. S. T. Stranahan. Miss Waterbury, acting as Secretary, read the minutes of the previous meeting, which were approved. Mr. Dwight Johnson, Secretary of the Sanitary Committee, was introduced and made an interesting statement of the objects of the meeting. He stated that New York had incorporated a movement for a great Metropolitan Fair, which was to be opened on the 22d of February next. "It is to be an attempt to revive the great Market Fairs of the old world, and will be continued for two weeks, for the benefit of our sick and wounded soldiers. Every branch of trade or industry, of art or skill, every kind of ability—mechanical, ornamental, artistic, useful, amusing, instructive, humane—will be expected to contribute to the result. Every workshop, house, or store, every heart and hand, will be asked, and will be glad to give something, great or small. It was at first contemplated to invite Brooklyn, Jersey City, and surrounding towns to take part in this great demonstration. But it had been thought better for this City to make an independent effort in the same direction, especially as it would have the aid of an important auxiliary association, now in active operation, and numbering among its members representatives of nearly every church in the City. They would be able to invoke the aid of every influence—the Fire Department, the Philharmonic Society, and other organizations, which would insure the success of the movement, and enable our City to make a demonstration that would redound to its credit throughout the country, and give comfort to our sick soldiers. Ours is a City of three hundred thousand inhabitants, and we should make ourselves felt and appreciated, and accomplish as much relatively as the City of New York."

Mrs. Stranahan said the design of the Woman's Relief Association was to expand itself. Some resolutions had been prepared which would be read. Mrs. Dr. Duffin then read the following resolutions, which were adopted:

THE RESOLUTIONS.

Resolved, That the name of the Executive Committee be changed to Executive Board, and that it have power to add to its number.

Resolved, That the Executive Board be empowered to add to the present members from each church. Also to appoint members from outside church organizations, the whole number not to exceed one thousand.

Resolved, That the War Fund Committee be requested to appoint an Advisory Committee of twenty-five or more to assist us in carrying out the object and plan of the Fair.

Addresses were also made by Rev. Drs. Buddington, Farley and Spear; and Dr. Spear in his enthusiasm ventured a prediction, which doubtless most of those who were present thought very extravagant, that one hundred and fifty thousand dollars would thereby be realized.

On Saturday evening the 5th of December, a meeting of the War Fund Committee was held at their rooms, to which the Sanitary Committee invited a large number of citizens, that they might "unite in making arrangements for the Brooklyn Division of the Metropolitan Fair." The meeting was attended by about a hundred persons of recognized influence in the community. After it had been addressed at length in a thrilling speech by Rev. Mr. Hatfield, and by others both of the clergy and laity, it was resolved "that a committee of sixty Gentlemen be named by the Chair, who shall have power as a General Committee to add to their number at their discretion, to co-operate with the Ladies of the Woman's Relief Association in arranging for and conducting the Brooklyn Division of the Great Metropolitan Fair." For this Committee see Appendix.

Immediately after the meeting adjourned, the Committee thus appointed met and organized, electing Mr. A. A. Low its President. On motion, a Special Committee of five was appointed, who with the Sanitary Committee shall, at a future meeting, nominate an Executive Committee of Gentlemen and form and propose a plan of operations by which most efficiently to aid the Ladies in the arrangement and conduct of the Fair. This Committee, besides the Sanitary Committee, consisted of Messrs. Stranahan, Mills, Buckley, Benson, and Snow. The Committee of Ten thus constituted went industriously to work. They met every evening for a week; and on the 17th of December issued a call to the General Committee to meet them on Saturday evening the 19th, to deliberate on a final plan of operations then to be submitted.

A meeting of the Woman's Relief Association was held in the chapel of Packer Institute on Friday morning, December 18. An address was made by Dr. Farley, in which he gave an account of the great Fair then in progress in Boston, which Brooklyn, having set out with the hope of equalling, if possible, has immensely surpassed. Dwight Johnson, Esq., Secretary of the Sanitary Committee of the Brooklyn War Fund, also made an interesting statement of the progress thus far in the preparations for the Fair. At this meeting Mr. Johnson stated that, when it was first suggested as possible to raise $100,000 to $150,000, he did not think it could be done; he had now changed his opinion, and thought even the *larger* sum might be reached, if not exceeded. The spirit was rising. It soon ran up to fever heat. Rev. Henry Ward Beecher also made some glowing remarks, in which he proposed that Brooklyn should give New York a good run for the precedence.

Notices were now sent to the Sewing Societies of the several Churches, and to the towns and villages of Long Island, asking their co-operation, and inviting them to send hospital stores to the Brooklyn Division of the Fair; promising that they should be credited in the final result to the full amount and value of their contributions. In response, articles were sent from various places to the value of nearly twenty-seven hundred dollars. Thus early was the active co-operation of the Island secured.

It is very certain that, had the two Fairs been held simultaneously in New York and Brooklyn, the latter *would* even then have run the Metropolis hard. But the division of the plan helped the cause amazingly. Brooklyn was put upon her mettle to show a proud record, while New York has been spurred to redoubled efforts to make her Fair worthy of her metropolitan fame and resources. It cannot be questioned that at least quadruple the sum will be realized to the Sanitary Commission from the two Fairs, that would have been yielded by a single Fair held in New York.

THE MEETING WHICH DROVE THE NAIL AND CLINCHED IT.

On Saturday evening, December 19th, a meeting of the War Fund Committee was held pursuant to the call of the Committee of Ten, above noted. This meeting was held at the chapel of the Polytechnic Institute, and proved to be of the most marked character for its enthusiastic spirit and action. Mr. Low presided, and Hon. Edward A. Lambert acted as Secretary. The nominations which the Committee of Ten presented of the Executive Committee and its officers were confirmed. Hon. J. S. T. Stranahan reported to the meeting the progress that had been made, stating that the Committee on Organization had had a number of meetings to perfect a plan. They had consulted with the Woman's Relief Association, who had requested them to assist in raising a fund for the benefit of our sick and wounded soldiers.

Mr. James H. Frothingham, the Treasurer of the Advisory Board, said that the consideration of the question by the board had led to the adoption of the three following resolutions:

Resolved, That in accordance with the request conveyed in a resolution adopted by the Woman's Relief Association of the City of Brooklyn, at their meeting of December 4th, 1863, the following gentlemen are appointed an Advisory Board, to co-operate with them in the conduct of the Brooklyn Division of the Metropolitan Fair, to be opened on the 22d of February, 1864, in aid of the work of the U. S. Sanitary Commission.

ADVISORY BOARD.

Dwight Johnson, Chairman.
Fred'k A. Farley, D.D., Corresponding Secretary.
Walter S. Griffith, Recording Secretary.
James H. Frothingham, Treasurer.

Hon. Jas. S. T. Stranahan,	Thomas Brooks,
Samuel B. Caldwell,	Ethelbert S. Mills,
Ambrose Snow,	James D. Sparkman,
Thomas T. Buckley,	Henry E. Pierrepont,
A. A. Low,	Arthur W. Benson,
Henry Sheldon,	S. B. Chittenden,
Charles A. Meigs,	J. D. McKenzie,
Wm. H. Jenkins,	George S. Stephenson,
Joseph Wilde,	Archibald Baxter,
H. B. Claflin,	Luther B. Wyman,
Elias Lewis, Jr.,	W. W. Armfield,
Hon. Edward A. Lambert,	Peter Rice,

E. J. Lowber.

Resolved, That the Advisory Board are empowered to adopt such measures as they may deem best to give effect to their appointment, and shall apply the proceeds of the Fair to the use of the U. S. Sanitary Commission under the direction of the Sanitary Committee of the Woman's Relief Association of the City of Brooklyn.

Resolved, That the Advisory Board be empowered to add to the members of the General Committee.

Dr. Farley, here, by request, made a report of his visit to the Boston Fair, made by authority of the General Committee. The method of organization and operation of that Fair for the first two days was detailed in aid of the present deliberations. Dwight Johnson, Esq., Rev. T. L. Cuyler, A. A. Low, Esq., and Walter S. Griffith, Esq., also made brief and earnest speeches. Then rose Mr. John D. McKenzie, who made a speech effective and emphatically to the point. We quote from a report of his remarks in the Brooklyn *Daily Eagle*, of December 21:

Mr. McKenzie said, referring to the language used by Mr. Johnson in introducing him, in commendation of his efforts in behalf of the poor colored people of New York after the great riots:

Mr. Chairman—I had supposed that the New York riots and the woes of the wronged and oppressed people who suffered in them were things of the past. Henry Ward Beecher, (I wish he was here to-night), referring to these disturbances and the good which had grown out of them, alluded to me in his speech at London as one who had "hated him with Christian hatred for the last sixteen years." Well, sir, if I did so, I was as Saul of Tarsus when he held the clothes of the men who stoned the martyr Stephen; I knew not what I did. But, sir, God educates men fast if they submit themselves to His teaching, and He is educating all of us up to the point where we should have been long ago; to the determination that, when this Rebellion is put down, the blot and the shame which has disgraced our nation so long shall be wiped out at once and forever.

The speaker then alluded to the special object of the meeting. In coming up to this place, and thinking of the circumstances of comfort which surround us all—our bright fire-sides, the sweet faces and voices of our children—and then of the poor soldier, outlying and watching in the darkness and the cold, suffering all manner of exposure and privation, engaged in deadly strife, or lying disabled after the struggle, and all to secure and perpetuate these fire-sides, and these altars—his heart was stirred within him. He spoke of the blessed influence of the Sanitary Commission. He wished the gentlemen could have been with him in passing through the hospital tents after the battle of Antietam. When he saw those suffering heroes—suffering for him, and those dear to him, and thought how hard it was that now neither mother, nor sister, nor daughter, nor friend could be near them and minister to them, he rejoiced to think that this heavenly agency of charity was there to perform the part of mother, and sister, and daughter and friend.

He congratulated the audience on the catholic feeling among ourselves which this effort was bringing about. Here were men of all persuasions in politics and religion, working together cheerfully in a holy cause, and feeling more and more of the spirit of brotherhood every moment.

During Mr. McKenzie's admirable speech the enthusiasm rose very high, and when he closed by calling attention to a paper which he laid upon the table, and from which the Secretary read the name of John D. McKenzie, heading a form of subscription with a contribution of one thousand dollars, it knew no bounds, and the applause was tumultuous.

It is certainly not invidious to say that this splendid opening made the Fair the grand thing it proved to be. Straightway a rivalry of generosity began which had never before been equalled. Mr. Low took the paper, and made a few remarks, in which he pleasantly said that the only fitting response he could make to Mr. McKenzie's speech was to do likewise. He should put down his name for $2,500. Great applause followed this second liberal contribution. We give, from the *Union* of December 21st, a report of this grand meeting, which gives but a faint idea of the enthusiasm and spirit which pervaded it to the close:

Mr. S. B. Chittenden subscribed $1,000.
Mr. Peter C. Cornell wished to subscribe $1,000.
Mr. Henry E. Pierrepont subscribed $1,000.

As each name was called the hall rang with plaudits.

Mr. Henry Sheldon subscribed $1,000.

Another gentleman expressed his desire to take $1,000 worth of Sanitary Commission stock, as it was a sound concern.

The President said that this was a very good beginning.

Mr. George B. Archer subscribed $1,000.

The President expressed the extreme pleasure he felt in presiding over such a meeting.

Then came some $500 subscriptions, among which were the names of Messrs. J. W. Frothingham and Stranahan. There were at least a dozen gentlemen on the floor at one time, each waiting to have his name put down.

The President, beaming with jollity, said, with a twinkle in his eye, that he did not think the preliminary proceedings in Boston were any better than these. [Immense applause.]

Rev. Dr. Farley spoke at some length in regard to the merits of the Sanitary Commission, which he said stood forth as the acknowledged instrument of healing for the men who had gone forth to fight our battles.

Ex-Mayor Hall moved that a committee be appointed to call on every citizen in Brooklyn for a dollar subscription.

The President said that a committee for the purpose had already been appointed. He suggested the appointing of ward committees.

Mr. Frothingham spoke in favor of Mr. Hall's suggestion and **moved that it be referred** to a committee. A motion was made to adjourn.

Alex. Wallace said that he hoped the President would not allow the meeting to adjourn, as there were a large number of gentlemen present who wished to contribute.

Mr. Seymour L. Husted contributed $1,000. [Long-continued applause.]

Mr. W. H. Lyon subscribed $250, and was followed by a number of other gentlemen.

Some other gentlemen then went into the $500 business again.

A gentleman at the lower end of the hall stated that he was authorized to say that a gentleman present wished the Secretary to put him down for $1,000.

Immense excitement and cries of "Name him." "Who is it?"

The Gentleman—"E. T. H. Gibson." [Long-continued applause.]

The use of the hall of the Polytechnic was tendered by I. H. Frothingham, Esq., free of cost.

He was followed by a gentleman who made the same offer in regard to the Packer Institute.

Mr. Chittenden said he had, in Connecticut, a pair of Devon steers in tolerable condition, which he would make as fat as possible on Yankee corn, and present to the Fair.

A motion was made to adjourn, but withdrawn.

The subscriptions then commenced again.

After a number of gentlemen had subscribed, remarks were made by various gentlemen, and the meeting adjourned till Tuesday evening, at the Academy of Music.

The following is the full list of the subscriptions at the meeting on Saturday night:

1. J. D. McKenzie	$1,000	21. S. M. Beard	$500
2. A. A. Low	[illegible]	22. Sidney Green	500
3. S. B. Chittenden	1,000	23. R. H. Manning	500
4. G. S. Stephenson	1,000	24. E. T. H. Gibson	1,000
5. Peter C. Cornell	1,000	25. Jas. P. Wallace	500
6. H. E. Pierrepont	1,000	26. Cor. J. Bergen	500
7. Henry Sheldon	1,000	27. Cyrus Adams	500
8. Josiah O. Low	1,000	28. Amos Robbins	500
9. Geo. B. Archer	1,000	29. J. B. Wellington	500
10. Joseph Ripley	500	30. John Bullard	500
11. S. B. Caldwell	500	31. Jas. C. Wilson	500
12. A. W. Benson	500	32. Chas. Storrs	500
13. R. W. Ropes	500	33. S. E. Howard	500
14. J. W. Frothingham	500	34. Jas. Humphrey	500
15. J. S. T. Stranahan	500	35. H. O. Reeve	250
16. Richard P. Buck	500	36. Thos. T. Buckley	250
17. S. L. Husted	1,000	37. E. D. Place	250
18. Henry Sanger	500	38. H. K. Worden	250
19. Rev. E. Sheldon	500	39. W. H. Lyon	250
20. Ambrose Snow	500	40. C. R. Marvin	250
Total			$[illegible]

During the day, 21st, the following additional subscriptions were published:

Journeay & Burnham	$500	Alex. M. White	500
E. H. R. Lyman	1,000	Chas. A. Meigs & Son	250
Edward Dodge	500	Cash	500
Wm. Aug. White	500	Chas. S. Bayliss	500

Making the total amount twenty-nine thousand seven hundred and fifty dollars.

We have given a report of this meeting at some length, because it was, as has been remarked, the meeting which made the success of the Fair a certainty. The enthusiasm of the proceedings was delightful to witness. From this point the progress of the Fair was like rolling a snowball down hill. It gave the enterprise an immense momentum, and thenceforward it gathered as it went.

On the 21st of December the Ladies' Executive Committee gave public notice that one member of the Board would be in daily attendance at the depot of the Woman's Relief Association, No. 30 Court street, between 10 A. M. and 3 P. M., to give information upon the subject of the Fair.

Before the end of December the subscription which Mr. McKenzie had started had reached a point of more than fifty thousand dollars, through the activity of the chairmen of the several special committees who had been appointed from the Executive Committee.

Towards the end of the month the managers of the Metropolitan Fair, on the part of the New York Division, had decided that it must be postponed from the 22d of February to the 28th of March.* The Ladies who represented the Brooklyn Division, the Gentlemen's Committee coinciding, felt on the contrary that it would be entirely bad policy to accede to such a postponement. The enthusiasm in Brooklyn was at its height; the 22d of February was hallowed and heart-stirring in its associations, and they could not afford to ignore or lose them. That must be the day for the Fair in this City. Accordingly, as we shall see, a cordial separation took place; the new policy was everywhere on this side the river greeted with

*It was so postponed; but at a subsequent day in March it was deferred to the 4th of April on account of the impracticability of an earlier date.

immense satisfaction by our citizens; and the event justified its wisdom to the full.

On Saturday evening, December 28th, a meeting of the Executive Committee was held at the rooms of the War Fund Committee, at which it was announced that arrangements had been made for holding a public meeting at the Academy of Music on Saturday evening, January 2d, in behalf of the Fair. At this meeting interesting reports were made of the progress of the work. It was announced that the Catholic Clergy were taking an interest in the matter, and had promised to urge it upon the attention of their parishioners. Mr. A. A. Low made a generous proffer of ground for the location of the Fair buildings. The meeting showed that a spirit of generous rivalry was rapidly developing itself among all classes of our citizens.

BROOKLYN CUTS ENTIRELY FREE FROM LEADING-STRINGS.

The regular weekly meeting of the Woman's Relief Association, held at Packer Institute on Wednesday morning, December 30th, was an occasion of peculiar interest. The President, Mrs. J. S. T. Stranahan, explained that in consequence of the Ladies of New York having postponed the time of opening the Metropolitan Fair from February 22d to March 28th, the question arose whether Brooklyn should proceed now without regard to the arrangements of New York. Resolutions were unanimously adopted to open our Fair on the 22d of February, in the Academy of Music and adjacent grounds; changing the name of the Executive Board to that of "Executive Committee of Ladies," and requesting the Gentlemen of the Advisory Committee to assume the name of Executive Committee of Gentlemen. The Executive Committees were authorized to perform all the duties necessary to carry out the objects of the Brooklyn and Long Island Fair.

Thus, promptly and fearlessly, Brooklyn cut her leading-strings, asserted her full grown manhood, (and womanhood) and started boldly to walk alone. She not only walked, but ran, and soared, and amazed even herself by the development of a truly gigantic strength.

Colonel Hawkins, of the famous Hawkins' Zouaves, was then introduced, and made a powerful and brilliant address, in which he spoke of the noble work done in this war by the Sanitary Commission. He commended the loyal women of our country very highly for the efficient part they had taken in this struggle for national life, and took occasion to urge upon them a renewed and higher consecration of their time and efforts to the great work. The gallant Colonel closed his truly thrilling address amid great enthusiasm.

Rev. Mr. Foss, of the South Fifth Street M. E. Church, also made a forcible address in behalf of the cause.

This meeting gave a fresh impulse to the work. Additions were made to the committees from persons out of the city for the purpose of operating upon and concentrating the interest and efforts of our Island population upon the Fair. A general circular, with full lists of the entire organization of both sexes, was prepared by the Corresponding Secretary, (vid. Appendix,) and sent forth far and wide. The Special Committees, besides, sent forth their own circulars in their respective and special walks or departments of effort. The Academy of Music was engaged; and arrangements were instituted and rapidly matured for other buildings, as the case might require; and the City became, throughout all classes of the people, intent, energetic, enthusiastic to the highest degree, in preparation for what all felt was the People's work, the People's pride, the People's duty.

PUBLIC MEETING AT THE ACADEMY OF MUSIC.

On Saturday evening, January 2d, a public meeting in behalf of the Fair was held at the Academy of Music. The night was one of extreme bitterness; so cold, in fact, that it was impossible to warm any large building so as to be comfortable, and the consequence was, that, so far as numbers were concerned, the meeting was not what was anticipated.

Still, a goodly number of ladies and gentlemen, who depended upon the warmth of their hearts in the cause to overmatch the frigid atmosphere, were present, and a great impulse was given to the work.

Mr. A. A. Low presided, and made some happy remarks in opening the meeting, upon the propriety of the step which Brooklyn was now taking to have a Fair in her own borders. He said he hoped that the effect of the meeting would be to quicken noble purposes into noble deeds, and that all would be able to leave with the conviction that it was good for them to have been there.

Rev. Henry Ward Beecher was then introduced, and made a speech of characteristic power. He spoke of the confidence he had in the Sanitary Commission, and remarked:

I should be proud to have Brooklyn stand, if not first, at least high upon the roll of honor, and still farther should be proud to have my own people stand highest among you; but local pride, though it might have a subordinate place, is not that to which I would appeal. It is to that common to you and all the people of New York and the whole land, our common love of humanity, our common love of country, our common love of God, who, in the person of his Son, our Saviour, went about doing good, healing the sick, and comforting the suffering. It is to these higher motives that I would appeal, and I know I would not appeal in vain; and when Brooklyn shall have accomplished her labor of love, I know there will be not one thing to be ashamed of, but much to be proud of, and that God shall be pleased with the offering we shall bring.

Rev. Dr. Porter, of Williamsburg, was next introduced, and made a few remarks as the representative of the Eastern District. In conclusion the reverend gentleman pledged himself that in the Eastern District the people would be in nowise behind those of any part of the City.

Hon. M. F. Odell, the able and patriotic representative in Congress of the IIId. District, Brooklyn, then made a strong appeal for the Sanitary Commission, which he said was the best charity on earth. Mr. Odell related a large number of incidents of his personal experience in testing the benefits of the Commission on the battle-field, which had a powerful effect in opening the eyes of the people of Brooklyn to the full value and importance of the great charity whose hands they were laboring to strengthen.

Mr. Odell in his peroration said:

> There is a class of men at the North who do not feel any sympathy for this movement. I see them in prospective, and feel sorry for them. By-and-bye this war will be over, our flag will wave in triumph over every foot of territory in the thirty-four States, we shall have obtained the boon we fought so well for, and our country will be worth more than she ever was before—and I am one of those who believe she is worth more to-day than when Sumter was assailed, worth more because we have given much more for her, and in consequence we prize her more dearly—but to-day the men who are standing in our defence, and giving their lives for us, have claims on every man, woman and child in this city and country; and I am sorry for that man, when this Rebellion is passed, who will have disregarded these claims. Sad will be his case who has not given his mite of aid to help crush it out. I hope sincerely that from this meeting, and from other gatherings of this kind, shall go out an influence which shall extend and widen; and that when this Fair shall have ended, it shall be found that Brooklyn is first of all the cities of the country in her munificence to the Sanitary Commission, and through them to the soldiers who are fighting our battles.

Rev. A. A. Willitts was the next speaker, who was followed by S. B. Chittenden, Esq.; both these gentlemen spoke with feeling and power.

Rev. R. M. Hatfield and Mr. George B. Lincoln added a few words, and the meeting then adjourned.

MUNICIPAL PERMISSION.

The Board of Aldermen, at their regular meeting Monday evening, January 17th, gave the managers of the Fair permission to erect the buildings necessary for the Fair.

On the 19th of January, the Committee on Internal Arrangements and Reception of Goods, gave public notice that they were prepared to receive donations of goods, produce, &c., and receipt for the same, at the following places:

SMALL PACKAGES OF DRY OR FANCY GOODS.

H. P. Morgan & Co., 245 Fulton street; Husted & Carll, 205 Fulton street; C. J. Oppenheim & Brothers, 285 Fulton street; Academy of Music; U. S. Sanitary Depot, 60 Court street; Nassau Bank, 8 Court street; Brooklyn City Gas Co., 136 Remsen street.

GROCERIES, WET AND HEAVY GOODS.

Ford's Stores; Pierrepont's Stores; Thomas's Stores; Woodruff & Robinson's Stores.

PUBLIC MEETING AT GREENPOINT.

On Tuesday evening, January 19th, a spirited public meeting was held in the Reformed Dutch Church, at Greenpoint, in aid of the Fair. The meeting was addressed by Rev. H. J. Eddy, Chaplain of the Thirty-third Illinois Regiment, who gave a thrilling and graphic account of the siege of Vicksburg, and the battles in its vicinity, and the prompt and efficient aid afforded the sick and wounded soldiers of General Grant's army by the U. S. Sanitary Commission.

Rev. E. S. Porter, of Williamsburg, also made one of his strong, eloquent, and convincing appeals in behalf of the soldiers and the Fair.

MEETING OF COMMITTEE ON INTERNAL ARRANGEMENTS, ETC.

On Saturday evening, January 16th, at a meeting of the Committee on Internal Arrangements and Reception of Goods, an important report was received from a sub-committee, appointed January 9th, to apportion space, &c., to exhibitors, which was adopted.

On the 23d of January, Mr. Stephenson in behalf of the Gentlemen's, and Mrs. Archer of the Ladies' Committees on Internal Arrangements issued the following circular, which was placed in the newspapers, and widely distributed through the Island in a separate form :

TO ALL WOMEN INTERESTED IN AND WORKING FOR THE BROOKLYN AND LONG ISLAND FAIR:

In order to meet and answer as far as possible the many questions asked relative to the arrangement and appropriation of the tables at the approaching Fair to be held in aid of the Sanitary Commission, the Joint Committee "On Internal Arrangement and Reception of Goods" beg leave to submit herewith the following plan as the one in their judgment best calculated to promote the general interests of the Fair.

After careful and mature deliberation, it is the firm conviction and belief of the committee that we can best serve the cause we are all aiming to promote by having no tables of religious or other organizations distinctly as such.

In the judgment of the Committee it is much to be desired that our citizens on this occasion, ignoring all party or sectarian lines, should all unite as with one heart in aid of the noblest charity which has ever been presented to our people.

As it is, however, the disposition of the Committee to meet as far as may be the wishes of all interested as contributors, should there be any religious or other organizations desirous of a separate table, and willing to assume the responsibility of furnishing and maintaining such table during the continuance of the Fair, such organization, by making official application in writing to the Chairman of the Gentlemen's Committee, George S.

Stephenson, 16 Court street, on or before the first day of February next, can have table room assigned to it, as far as the same may be possible and consistent with the other arrangements of the Committee.

The Committee beg leave to assure all contributors that, by sending their donations to this Committee at the time and place of which due notice will be given, they will be carefully arranged for display and sale; and that donations from churches, societies and individuals will be accredited to them respectively, and formally acknowledged.

Religious or other organizations which may be represented by separate tables, will be expected to appoint two ladies for each table, to be their responsible heads; such ladies to select such assistants to act as saleswomen during the Fair as may be necessary, subject, however, to such regulations as the Committee may deem it proper to prescribe.

All other appointments of ladies to act as heads of departments and saleswomen, and the arrangement and designation of tables, will be made by the Committee at the earliest practicable moment, from the different denominations, and due notice given of the same.

The report was accompanied by diagrams, etc., showing the general plan adopted by the Committee. The excellent results of the system adopted, are spoken of elsewhere. The Sub-Committee above, consisted of Messrs. Isaac H. Frothingham, Alex. M. White, and James O. Morse.

MEETING AT FLATBUSH.

On Thursday evening, January 21st, a large meeting was held in the Reformed Dutch Church, in Flatbush, to concentrate the efforts of that suburb in behalf of the Fair. Revs. S. Street, of York, Pa., and A. A. Willitts, of this City, severally made addresses. The meeting was a source of abundant good.

THE LONG ISLAND TOWNS.

Meanwhile the good people of the Island were not behind in preparations for the Fair. Public meetings were held in most of the towns, large and efficient committees appointed, and every energy used to bring out a handsome representation from the Island on the occasion.

THE BUILDINGS.

It was determined to erect two temporary structures for the Fair; one on a lot, the use of which was loaned by A. A. Low, Esq., adjoining the Academy of Music, on the west, to be 68 by 100 feet, and two stories in height, and the other to be located on a lot opposite the Academy, loaned for the purpose by Mrs. Packer, to be 100 feet square, and one story high. The first of these buildings was to be occupied by the restaurant, and was called Knickerbocker Hall, and the latter by the Hall of Manufactures and the New England Kitchen. This building was to communicate with the Academy by a covered way, or bridge, elevated above Montague street at a sufficient height not to interfere with public travel. Ground was broken on the 23d of January, and under the energetic management of Arthur W. Benson, Esq., Chairman of the Building Committee, they were completed in ample season. A committee of builders, consisting of Messrs. E. L. Roberts, P. F. O'Brien, and D. S. Voorhies, took charge of the practical part of the work, and to the skill and assiduity of these gentlemen the prompt completion and excellence of the work is due.

The large building on the northeast corner of Montague and Clinton streets, known as the Taylor Mansion, was also engaged for the use of the Fair. In this the Museum of Arts, Relics, and Curiosities was located, and also the editorial rooms of the *Drum-Beat*.

From this time onward the work of preparation progressed space. The Executive Committee and various sub-committees held frequent meetings, always reporting satisfactory progress. Donations of all kinds began to flow in, and the public prints teemed with acknowledgments of contributions. The warm interest which the people at large took in the Fair was manifested by numerous communications to the papers, containing suggestions, wise, or otherwise, to the managers concerning the arrangements making. Everything was discussed; some matters, such as prices, and the propriety or policy of permitting the sale of wine, and raffling at the Fair, were discussed warmly. The Executive Committee gave careful heed to all these suggestions, adopting the good with cordiality, and rejecting the bad without compunction. On the whole, it is believed, their decisions gave general satisfaction. At all events, it is certain that the good of the cause was the sole and all-compelling spring of their action.

The Academy was opened for the reception of goods from February 15th to 18th, inclusive, and the vast influx astonished even those who were best informed of the progress of the work.

THE OFFICIAL PROGRAMME.

On Friday, February 19th, all being ready for the announcement, the Official Programme was promulgated, the features of which, not already noted, were as follows:

On Monday, the 22d of February inst., the Birth-day of Washington, the Fair will commence in this City. The Committees hope that all business will, as far as possible, be suspended, and the day made a holiday for all classes of the population.

In the afternoon there will be a grand parade of the entire military force of the City, passing the Academy in review at three o'clock precisely, including, it is hoped, the soldiers of our regiments in the army on furlough, and the United States Marines from the Navy Yard.

At seven o'clock P. M., the various departments of the Fair will be thrown open.

Dodworth's full band will be in attendance on Monday, Tuesday, Wednesday, and Thursday evenings of the first week, and on those of Friday and Saturday the band of the U. S. Receiving Ship North Carolina, kindly detailed for the service by Captain Meade.

A large corps of Marshals to aid the Ladies at the tables, and the Committee on Internal Arrangements, have volunteered for the purpose, and a sufficient Police force will be on duty.

PRICES OF ADMISSION.

1. Tickets admitting one person, on Monday evening only, the opening night of the Fair, to all its departments, two dollars.

2. Season ticket, not transferable, admitting the holder at all times to all the departments of the Fair, at its opening and to its close, four dollars.

3. Season ticket, not transferable, admitting the holder to all departments of the Fair, at all times on and after Tuesday, the 23d inst., two dollars.

4. Single tickets for the remainder of the first week after the opening night, to the Auditorium, fifty cents; to each of the other departments, twenty-five cents.

5. Single tickets for the second week, to the close of the Fair, to each of all the departments, twenty-five cents.

On Tuesday, the 23d inst., and thereafter during the Fair, the hours of business will be from 11 A. M. to 10 P. M. each and every day. A signal for the company to retire will be given each night precisely at the last named hour.

The prices, and hours of business were subsequently modified; the price of admission being fixed at seventy-five cents to the Auditorium, and twenty-five cents to the Museum. The hour of opening was changed to twelve o'clock

THE OPENING DAY.

THE MILITARY PARADE

MAJOR-General Dix, Commander of the Eastern Department, and his staff, General Stannard, Admirals Paulding and Gregory, Acting Master C. G. Haaffe and the officers of the Navy Yard, His Honor the Mayor, Mr. Johnson, Chairman of the Executive Committee, accompanied by Mr. Stranahan, Judge Reynolds, Judge Lott, Judge Dikeman, Dr. Farley, John H. Bergen, and a number of ladies, were stationed on the platform erected for the occasion in front of the Academy. The procession passed the Academy prompt to the hour of three, and in the following order: First came a detachment of Policemen; then a squadron of mounted men from the Seventieth Regiment of Light Artillery; then

Battalions of United States Marines under command of
Lieutenants Higbie, French, and Peet,
preceded by the Band of the
Ship-of-the-Line North Carolina.

Major-General Duryea and Staff.

General Crooke and Staff, of the Fifth Brigade, accompanied by Colonel Brewster, of the
Excelsior Brigade.

Band.

Thirteenth Regiment, Colonel John B. Woodward.

As the latter passed the stand they were greeted with cheers and waving of handkerchiefs.

Next came the Fourteenth Regiment Veterans, commanded by Major Baldwin, and followed by a carriage containing disabled soldiers. As they passed, the air was filled with cheers, and the great crowd from the pavement, the balconies, and the windows, hailed them with fluttering handkerchiefs and waving hats.

Band.

Twenty-eighth Regiment, Lieut. Col. David A. Bokee, commanding.

Seventieth Regiment, Cavalry, with mounted Band, followed by the Artillery.

A Company of Veterans, preceded by a Banner, borne by a Zouave, bearing the inscription

"Veterans of the Union."

Brigadier-General F. B. Spinola and Staff, of the Volunteers.

Brigadier-General Jesse C. Smith and Staff, of the Eleventh Brigade.

Band.

Twenty-third Regiment, Colonel C. E. Pratt.

Band.

Forty-seventh Regiment, Colonel J. V. Meserole.

Band.

Fifty-second Regiment, Colonel M. Cole.

Cadets of the Polytechnic Institute.

Band.

Fifty-sixth Regiment, Colonel John Q. Adams.

After passing the Academy the division marched through Court, Joralemon, Clinton, Atlantic, Nevins, and Livingston streets, Flatbush avenue, Lafayette avenue, Adelphi street to Myrtle avenue, where the parade was dismissed.

The Regiments were all in fine condition, and displayed an accuracy in marching, a readiness and thoroughness of discipline, and a soldierly appearance every way creditable to them. The young Polytechnic Cadets, too, won high honors.

ALL READY.

At a few minutes before seven o'clock, P. M., the doors of the several departments of the Fair were thrown open. We shall now proceed to take up each department in order, and give a sketch of their arrangements, and the prominent incidents which occurred in them during the Fair, noting, as space will permit, the principal features of interest in each.

THE GREAT CENTRAL BAZAAR.

The great central Bazaar, for the sale of articles for the Fair, was held in the Academy of Music, the entire building, with the exception of the "Assembly Room"—which was occupied as an Art Gallery—being used for the purpose. The ground floor of the Academy was boarded over, level with the stage, making a magnificent hall, with an area of 10,570 square feet. The second floor and lobbies, added an area of 9,730, making the total area devoted to the sale of goods in the Academy of Music, 20,300 square feet.

THE DECORATIONS.

The decorations of the Academy were very beautiful, and their patriotic nature was in fine keeping with the character of the great enterprise. From the centre of the Auditorium ceiling was suspended a mass of brilliantly colored bunting, giving the graceful effect of a swinging column. From the bottom of this was suspended, by invisible wires, an American eagle, which seemed to hover in mid-air over the majestic scene below. From the apex of the column of drapery sprung radiating bands of red, white, and blue bunting, which, stretching in graceful curves until they touched the pillars of the amphitheatre, were thence twined, and drooped, and festooned around the whole circle of the building. Above the arch of the stage, in letters formed of tiny jets of gas, blazed the inscription, "In Union is Strength."

The back wall of the stage was completely screened by a mammoth painting of a Field Hospital Tent of the U. S. Sanitary Commission, with nurses, wounded soldiers, etc. The rough wood-work above the side scenes was skilfully concealed by draperies of white and colored muslin, and flags were everywhere displayed in profusion. The huge crimson drop-curtain was caught up and stretched along the ceiling of the stage, thus entirely hiding its rude surface, and giving at the same time a brilliant effect. Many elegant paintings were also displayed in the Auditorium, while the superb afghans, and many-colored quilts, with which the vast building was fairly tapestried, added their vivid splendors to the effect of the *toute ensemble*. When the magnificent building was flooded at night with the splendor of a thousand gas jets, it presented a spectacle which was nothing less than enchanting. The fairy garden of Aladdin, blazing with its fruitage of gems, could not have been more brilliantly beautiful. To the fine taste of Messrs. Benson and Degrauw, aided by the skilful corps of Mr. William Paine, the well-known decorator, of 300 Fulton avenue, who loaned much of the material, and gave his personal services in the most generous manner, the public are indebted for the complete success of the decorative department.

Dodworth's Band, or the Band of the North Carolina, stationed in the Family Circle, furnished exquisite music every night, as long as the Fair lasted.

THE INTERIOR ARRANGEMENTS OF THE AUDITORIUM.

If the reader will now make the tour with us of this vast and splendid Bazaar, we will endeavor to point out the localities of the principal departments, and to reduce this great and dazzling mass to the elements of which it was composed.

ARRANGEMENT OF THE TABLES.

There probably never was an enterprise of the vast proportions of this Fair, which was so admirably systematized, considering the brief time that was permitted to perfect and carry the system of organization into execution. From the opening of the Fair, to its close, not the slightest indication of confusion in the workings of the machinery was visible to the observer, although no one but those who had the complicated arrangements in charge can estimate or appreciate the amount of thought, energy, and labor which were required to keep everything moving on with such delightful harmony and precision. But this was all below the surface. To the public, everything proceeded from day to day with as much order and regularity as if the Fair had been a vast business establishment wherein years of experience had been devoted to systematizing its operations.

The plan adopted after careful deliberation, by the Committee on Internal Arrangements and Reception of Goods, and which is more fully explained in the circular of the Committee heretofore published, was to have as few tables as possible under the exclusive control of societies or individuals. This plan, which was cheerfully acceded to except in a few cases where for special reasons churches desired a separate table, enabled the Committee to regulate the internal economy of the Fair upon a comprehensive system which should be under their entire control. To this wise decision, doubtless, much of the wonderful order and success of the Fair are to be attributed. The goods were separated into *classes*, as far as was practicable; and thus after a single glance around the Fair, the purchaser could tell just where to go to find the particular kind of goods wanted. Thus the necessity of visiting a dozen different parts of the building in order to ascertain what the extent and variety of the stock of that kind of goods in the Fair might be, was completely obviated, and the care and labor of selection very greatly lessened. If worsted goods were wanted, there was a department especially for that description of articles. If glass-ware, silver-ware, childrens' goods, perfumery, stationery was the object of search, they could be found each in its appropriate place.

The stalls of the ground floor were arranged in concentric arcs of circles, the space between each line of stalls being about four feet. The advantage of such an arrangement as this, in a building like the Academy, is obvious. A large space in the centre of the building was left vacant (with the exception of a platform for pianos,) for the accommodation of the people. On the whole, we do not see how the arrangement of the stalls could have been improved. The system of ushers was also admirably effective, and too much praise cannot be awarded to the gentlemen who performed that office with so much patience, prudence, and gallantry. The plan early adopted, and rigidly enforced, and which we are happy to say was acceded to by the public with the utmost good humor as a recognized matter of necessity, was to make the visitor enter the Auditorium by the centre door, and leave by one of the two side doors. This prevented all confusion at the entrance.

To begin in order: Entering the Academy by the grand entrance, on the right was the ticket office; next to this was the Police head-quarters, under charge of Inspector Folk, and Sergeants Cornell and Mathews. There probably will not be a better place than here to pay a just tribute to the police force charged with the preservation of order at the Fair. Perfectly gentlemanly, always attentive, and sleeplessly vigilant, they won golden opinions from everybody. The police had little occasion to make arrests, as there were no disturbances to quell, and few rogues about. They were of great service in restoring lost articles to their owners, and at all times a trunk full of handkerchiefs, furs, etc., awaiting claimants, was to be found at the Police head-quarters. Articles worth thousands of dollars were in this way returned during the Fair.

Mr. A. R. Frothingham, the Chief Marshal, was indefatigable in his attention to his duties, and his energy and skill assured the thorough carrying out of the various rules adopted for the conduct of business, and the preservation of order in the Fair.

Proceeding, we come to the turnstile, which admits to Knickerbocker Hall, and keeps the crowd constantly entering and emerging from that popular place in their relative positions. Flanking this is the Hat and Coat Room. We next come to the door of the "Directors' Room," over which is a sign, "General Executive Committee." The front room was the head-quarters of the very important Committee on Internal Arrangements and Reception of Goods, and hence proceeded the "Vermillion Edicts" which energized the whole enterprize.

We now enter the lobby of the ground floor of the Academy. Just inside the door, we find an elegant soda-water fountain, set up by Mr. D. G. Farwell, druggist, of No. 17 Court street. This was provided at all times with the refreshing beverage, together with a variety of the choicest syrups, all, with the polite attendants, being freely contributed to the Fair. This fountain was first erected in Knickerbocker Hall, but the restaurant being closed at stated hours, it was removed to the lobby, where it could refresh the thirsty multitude at all times. A portion of the lobby was also devoted to the exhibition of Clothes-Wringers, a very large number of which, both of the "Putnam" and "Universal" variety were presented to the Fair. On the extreme right of the lobby was the department of glass-ware, where Messrs. Dorflinger & Co., of Greenpoint, exhibited many exquisite specimens of American manufacture, fully equal to the best imported. The lustrous flashing of the crystal wares was a beautiful sight. At the opposite extremity of the lobby, and completing its objects of interest, was the "Skating Pond." This very curious and beautiful exhibition was justly regarded as one of the most interesting things in the Fair. By the aid of mirrors, upon the principle of the kaleidoscope, a very striking optical illusion was presented, being apparently a field of ice, thousands of acres in extent, crowded with skaters in brilliant and picturesque costumes, all in rapid and graceful motion. This interesting toy was the invention of Mrs. Edward Anthony, who generously exhibited it for the benefit of the Fair.

We will now enter the great Sale-room, or Auditorium. At once a vision of splendor breaks on the eye, before which few fail to stand in mute admiration and amazement. We see, as in some gorgeous dream of fairy-land, a world of beautiful creations rising before us. Our eyes are dazzled with vivid colors, and our ears stunned with the clamor of thousands of tongues. It is night. A myriad of gas-lights pour floods of radiance on the wonderful scene. The vast room seems wainscoted and ceiled with rainbows. Glass and silver flash back the blaze in streams of iridescent light; silks and satins shimmer softly, brilliant colors shine everywhere—gold, and crimson, and green, and blue, and rose, and purple; perfumes of rarest flowers scent the air; a melody from the piano tinkles through the tumult like the piping of birds in the pauses of a storm, or a burst of sumptuous music from the powerful band rolls out of the balcony and charms the clamor to a breathless hush. Above, the colors of our Union hang their glorious folds; the blazing legend, "In Union there is Strength," tells the story of the war in a word, while over all hovers the majestic eagle, fit emblem of a land which, while it aims to soar nearer to the sun of prosperity and power than any nation on earth, can yet sweep with unchecked wing and undaunted heart through the strongest storm that ever blew.

The departments in the interior of the Auditorium were disposed as follows: The tables immediately on the right were devoted to the worsted department. This was one of the most interesting, as it was naturally one of the most brilliant departments of the Fair. Here all the wonderful things that had ever been dreamed of before in the shape of worsted work were to be seen, together with many that it had not before entered into the imagination of any woman to conceive of. Sofa pillows, pin-cushions, mats, tidies, comforters, muffs, dolls, landscapes, hoods, nubias—but the line would stretch out "to the crack of doom." The richness, vividness, and variety of colors, of the thousand articles which heaped the tables, fluttered from the pillars, or glowed from the walls, gave one the impression of a bevy of rainbows playing hide-and-go-seek in the room. The irises of one's eyes for about five minutes after leaving this brilliant corner, resembled their etherial prototype as well in their rich play of colors, as in name.

Then there were tables devoted to the sale of baskets, of all kinds, among which were great numbers of the most exquisite nursery baskets ever seen, any of them good enough to hold the outfit of an embryo Emperor of France, who is, after all, no better than any infantile red republican of American. Then there were tables for pin-cushions, and numberless were the styles and shapes; there were tables for bead-work, shell-work, infants' clothing, milliner's goods, etc., on this side the Academy. Table No. 25, under the charge of Messrs. Hart & Aise, was appropriated to the sale of silver-ware, and a tempting variety was displayed, the cool white glitter of which was most refreshing to the eyes after the bewildering experiences of the preceding tables. Tables 33 and 35 were covered with the most exquisite French imported fancy goods, and articles of vertu, in bronze, Parian ware, glass, etc. These goods were imported by the ladies of St. Ann's Church expressly for the Fair, being admitted free of duty by Secretary Chase, after some correspondence had passed between Mr. A. A. Low and the Department. The Managers of the Fair were much indebted for this remission of duties to the urgent solicitations of Hon. M. F. Odell, and Senator Morgan, whose services in this behalf were gratefully acknowledged by the Executive Committee. These goods realized $3,380 to the Fair.

We now come to the Post Office, which was a very interesting and successful department of the Fair. It was under the special care of Mrs. J. P. Duffin, assisted by Mrs. St. John, Mrs. Humphrey, Mrs. W. E. Robinson, Miss Hattie Gladwin, Miss Kate Hillard, and Mrs. and Miss Newbold.

Mrs. Newbold, and Mrs. Gordon L. Ford, each contributed a large number of letters, of their own composition, for the office.

The price of postage was 15 and 25 cents. A list of letters, carefully revised each day, was displayed outside the office. Many of the letters were in poetry, and not a few of a high order of merit.

The Post Office occupied the Proscenium Box, on the right of the stage.

Then came in order the Department allotted to Ladies', Gentlemen's, and Children's White Goods, located in the recess to the right of the stage. Here was exhibited all manner of articles in this line that ever were, or probably ever will be designed. The display included Children's suits of every fabric and style, woolen, worsted, silk and cotton, embroidered, braided or plain. There was an immense assortment of Ladies' under clothing, comprising outfits for the most fastidious, while the gentleman who could not here find a dressing-gown, pair of slippers, or smoking-cap to suit him, might as well abandon the search at once and forever. The walls at the back of these tables were hung to the ceiling with elegant carpets and rugs. The tables at the back of the stage were appropriated to the contributions of

THE TOWNS OF LONG ISLAND.

These responded most nobly, hardly a town in Kings, Queens, or Suffolk Counties failing to send in generous donations of money or goods, or both, in response to the appeals of the indefatigable Committees on Long Island, and Kings County Town Contributions. The following towns were represented in the Fair, by goods or cash, or both.

KINGS COUNTY.

New Lotts, East New York, Gravesend, Gravesend Neck, Flatlands, Flatbush, Windsor Terrace, Greenfield, New Utrecht.

SUFFOLK COUNTY.

Huntington District, Northport, Cold Spring, Babylon, Islip, Sayville, Patchogue District, Smithtown, Fresh Pond, St. James, Stony Brook, Setanket, Port Jefferson, Miller's Place District, Riverhead District, Wading River, Baiting Hollow, Northville, Franklinville, Upper Aquebogue, Mattituck, Cutchogue, Southold, Greenport, Orient, Mariches, Quogue District, West Hampton, Atlanticville, Southampton, Bridge Hampton, East Hampton, Sag Harbor, Shelter Island.

QUEENS COUNTY

was represented by Newtown, Astoria, Ravenswood, Flushing, Jamaica, Queens, Woodhaven, Cypress Village, Hempstead, Rockaway District, North Hempstead, Manhasset District, Great Neck, Herricks and Lakeville, Roslyn, Westbury, Oysterbay, Oysterbay Cove, Glen Cove District, Brookville, Farmingdale, Amityville, Norwich and Syosset.

(For a more detailed acknowledgment of the contributions of the towns of Kings, Queens, and Suffolk, see Appendix.)

It will thus be seen that nearly every town on the Island sent its little rill, and many its copious stream of benefactions, to swell the rich tides which were to flow from this Fair into the Treasury of the Sanitary Commission. All honor and thanks to the noble and loyal men and women of Long Island.

The contributions from the above towns, as will be seen from the formal acknowledgment, were very largely in cash, but nevertheless enough goods were sent to supply the tables allotted to the towns of Long Island with a most brilliant variety, among which were some of the most elegant and tasteful of the fancy goods presented to the Fair.

We have now completed the tour of the right and rear of the Auditorium, and turn to the other side. As we leave the Long Island tables we find ourselves in front of a wall-tent, fitted with cots, etc., an exact copy of a field hospital tent of the U. S. Sanitary Commission. In the economy of space which the enormous affluence of contributions rendered necessary, this tent was put to excellent use for the sale of photographs of war scenes, and rings, and other articles of interest and curiosity manufactured by the soldiers, both Rebel and Union. It is here perhaps, as good a place as any to remark upon the interest taken in the success of the Fair by our gallant soldiers. From all quarters the managers of the Fair received evidences that the soldiers appreciated the labors of those who were building up this splendid tribute to their fidelity and patriotism, and many were the curious and valuable tokens sent to the Fair from hospital and field, for sale for the benefit of the cause. Not a few of these were of priceless value to their donors, from their associations; and their parting with them so freely, showed that from the bottom of their hearts they were grateful for the help which this Fair was intended to bestow upon them and their comrades. Most of these articles were offered for sale in the Sanitary Tent above alluded to, and it is a pleasant fact to chronicle that they were among the most eagerly sought of all the unique and valuable things with which the Fair abounded. The Soldier's Hospital in Burlington, Vt., contributed a box of charms, rings, crosses, and picture-frames, of curious material and design, enriched with patriotic mottoes, many of them relics of some of the most glorious battle-fields of the war, and every one with a history of its own. Of one of the rings sent, the soldier who made it, wrote, "This ring was worn in ten different engagements, being made by myself while on picket duty." From the hospital at Brattleboro, Vt., was received a box of picture-frames, of cone and leather work, and wood, some of which held photographs of their makers. The box also contained many rings, charms, etc. This invoice was exhausted very rapidly. From the Lowell General Hospital, Portsmouth Grove, R. I., was received a box, containing, among other very curious things, an elegantly carved bracket, with the following inscription: "Made by John Thatcher, U. S. Invalid

Corps, out of wood from the house in Portsmouth, R. I., in which Gen. Prescott, of the British Army, was captured during the Revolutionary War." The De Camp General Hospital, on David's Island, also sent numerous and beautiful articles. Among other articles in the tent were photographic copies of several beautiful and spirited original drawings, by a private soldier named J. B. Geyzer, entitled, "Moses smiting the Rock in Horeb," "Hunting in old Virginia," "Bringing in Contrabands," and "Marching Orders." There was also on exhibition a "Soldier's Scrap-book," being a collection of war-verses, culled from various sources, and all copied in a neat hand-writing, with incredible pains and patience, by some unknown young lady patriot. The idea was conceived from a hint contained in a letter from a wounded soldier that such a book would cheer the tedium of hospital life. It was bound in quarto form. After the Fair it was sent to Chaplain Merwin, to make such disposition of as he should deem fit. This was justly regarded as one of the most touching of the labors of love which on every hand throughout the Fair bore testimony to the devotion, the patriotism, the deep and strong ardor for the Great Cause which burns in the hearts of the women of our land.

At the back of the Sanitary tent, a fine specimen of the Southern Palmetto stood, scowling truculently down upon it. As the visitor saw this emblem of the State in whose heart of treason was conceived this accursed Rebellion, mounting grim and thorny guard over the tent from which flew the flag of the Union, he could not help seeing in the eye of fancy many a real scene of which this was the faithful type, of tents standing afar off under the blazing Southern sky, beneath the palmettos, in which the soldiers of the Republic lie shattered by shot and shell, or stricken down by rebel bullets as they stood under the glorious Banner of the Stars. And he could not but thank God for the inspiration which gave birth to so grand a purpose as the United States Sanitary Commission, which, with the tender care of a father for his children, seeks out every one of those white tents, whether among the war-blasted fields of Virginia, the clouds of Lookout Peak, the distant everglades of Florida, or the thorny wilds of Texas, and makes them shine with the golden light of patriotic love. Few passed this tent, without breathing a benison, warm from the inner heart, upon THE UNITED STATES SANITARY COMMISSION.

Passing the Sanitary Tent, we come to the entrance of the covered bridge leading to the Hall of Manufactures, and the New England Kitchen. Hard by this stands another elegant soda fountain, erected by Mr. H. H. Dickinson, druggist, corner of Atlantic and Henry streets. The beverage, with all kinds of delicious syrups, was furnished without cost to the Fair, as were also the services of the gentlemanly attendants. We have now reached the

TREASURER'S OFFICE,

into which, day after day, as long as the Fair remained open, flowed the bounteous benefactions of the citizens of Brooklyn and Long Island. Here books were provided for the reception of cash donations, and every day, over the front of the office, in full view of all, was displayed a bulletin showing how the volume of receipts was rolling up. It was interesting to watch the successive steps which the tide reached, from the $10,000 pointed out as the receipts of the first night, to the $400,000 proudly displayed before the Fair closed. Mr. James H. Frothingham, the Treasurer of the Executive Committee, was assiduous in his attention to the arduous duties of his office. He received most efficient co-operation from Mr. S. H. Farnham, General Cashier, and Messrs. Valentine H. Seaman, of the Dime Saving's Bank, Edgar S. Jones and Edward Smith, of the Nassau Bank, of Brooklyn.

Next to the Treasurer's Office stood the tables allotted to wax-work, flowers, etc.; some of the most elegant and elaborate works of art of this description ever exhibited were here offered for sale, and at prices noticeably moderate. Indeed, it may here be said that the moderate prices of the goods was one of the peculiar features of the Brooklyn and Long Island Fair. The principle adopted from the start was to ask no "fancy prices." Everything was marked quite as low, and in many cases very much lower than the article could be purchased in open market. It was considered better to *sell* the goods at even a low price than to *keep* them at a large one. Nevertheless, there was no disposition to sacrifice the stock, and, fortunately, no need of it. The principle aimed at was simply to charge a fair market price for everything.

But to return to the wax flowers. Some perfect triumphs of this beautiful art were shown. There were water-lilies startlingly natural in their superb and regal beauty. There were passion-flowers, that seemed to be exhaling from their purpled hearts a pure and fragrant grief and pity. Who can look upon the passion-flower without a melting heart, telling, as it does, the story of that awful night in Gethsemane, when the adorable Redeemer of the world, the Lord of glory, in his bitter agony sweat great drops, as it were blood? The superstition of an elder time saw folded among and pictured upon its petals the scourge, the crown of thorns, and the cruel and ignominious cross—the purified faith of this brighter age still deems it not an inappropriate symbol of the love and suffering of the Lamb who was slain on Calvary. On the table above noted was a fuller and more speaking illustration of the august symbolism so widely accepted, in a Cross, which a spray of passion-flowers tightly clasped, while their beautiful heads drooped low. Thus the tendrils of woman's love clasped the shameful tree, while her heart was bowed in unspeakable bitterness at its foot. Immortal constancy! Immortal grief!

On this side the Auditorium, also, were the stands of the dry-goods department, more of the horticultural tables, assortments of stationers' and druggists' fancy goods, combs, brushes, pocket-books, perfumery, soaps, etc., etc. On the left of the main entrance several stalls were appropriated to the Ladies' Fancy Goods Committee, under charge of Mrs. Henry Sheldon. On these tables a very large assortment of fancy goods of every possible variety, was exhibited. This department, presided over by Mrs. Sheldon and ladies of her Committee, was the largest in the Fair, and its receipts were of proportional magnitude. For the results of the labors of this efficient Committee, the reader is referred to the list of acknowledgments from them, printed in the Appendix.

THE SUPERINTENDENTS OF TABLES.

We give, so far as it has been possible to obtain them, the names of the ladies who had charge of the stalls.

Numbers 2 and 4 were appropriated to the churches of Messrs. Cuyler and Rockwell; 6, South Presbyterian Church; 8, Christ Church, Mrs. Shaller; 10, St. Paul's; 12 and 14, Mrs. Griffin and Mrs. McCoy, to the Associated Clinton avenue Churches; 38 and 40 were in charge of Mrs. Wempel and Mrs. Dominick; 42, Mrs. Jessop; 44, 46, 48, Mrs. C. H. Frothingham, Miss Alice B. Cary, and the Farmington, (Conn.,) School girls, who were represented by Miss Kent and Miss Rodman; 49 to 53, Mrs. Benson and Mrs. Wm. Sheldon; 55 to 59, Mrs. White Cornell, Mrs. Wyckoff, Miss Barton, and Miss Morton; 37, 39, 41, Mrs. Camden Dyke and Mrs. Kellogg; 43, 45, 47, Mrs. Morton and Mrs. Whitney; 26, 28, 30, 32, Mrs. Nesmith, Mrs. Watkins, Mrs. Ch. E. Davis, and Miss A. M. Farley; 25, 27, 29, 31, Mrs. Welsh, Mrs. Wheeler and Mrs. Edwards; No. 1, Mrs. Unkhardt; No. 3, Mrs. Malone; 5, Mrs. Greenwood; 7, Mrs. Reeves; 9, Mrs. Bergen; 11 and 13, Mrs. Tisdale and Mrs. Kelley; 15 and 17, Mrs. Curtis and Mrs. Bliss; 19, 21, 23, Mrs. Lukens, Mrs. Taylor, and Mrs. Brownell. The reader will bear in mind that the stands numbered "even" were on the left, and "odd" on the right.

The ladies having charge of the White Goods Department

were Mesdames French, Jackson, Pomeroy, Sandford, Buckley, Fowler, Beach and Hutchinson; Mrs. Capwell and Mrs. Beach superintended the Toy Department, and Mrs. Silleck, Mrs. Nichols, Mrs. Bartlett and Mrs. Moulton the Miscellaneous Department, opposite the tent. 73 and 75 were waited upon by Mrs. Justin Edwards, Mrs. Welsh, Mrs. Moses S. Beach, Mrs. J. B. Hutchinson, Mrs. J. Howard, Jr., and Mrs. John Hutchinson; 77 and 79 by Mrs. Pomeroy and Mrs. Sandford; 83, 85, 87, 89, (Flushing tables) by Mrs. Fuller and Mrs. Cox; 86, 88, 90, (Kings County tables) Mrs. Vanderbilt, Mrs. Lefferts and others; 68, 70, 72, perfumery, soaps, etc., Mr. H. Prentice; 32, 34, 36, (Horticultural) Mrs. T. F. King; 28, (Wax Flowers and Phantom Plants) Mrs. Benj. I. Nesmith, Miss J. Nesmith, Mrs. Watkins; Bouquet table, Miss Waterbury, Miss Starr.

We have now completed the round of the Auditorium, and have but to notice the few objects of interest in the centre of the floor. Here, on a raised platform, was exhibited an elegant piano from Messrs. Steinway & Son, which was sold early in the Fair for $500, being speedily replaced by a superb instrument from Messrs. W. B. Bradbury, of New York, valued at $700. Upon this platform, also, was exhibited a superb cut glass epergne, three feet high, contributed by Gould & Hoare, glass cutters. This was sold to Mr. A. A. Low for $225. There were also, after the first day or two, several tables in this part of the hall to receive the overflow of the White Goods Department, the accommodations for which, heretofore noted, proved entirely inadequate. One of the interesting features of the Fair at this point was "The Old Woman that lived in a Shoe." She was impersonated by a succession of pretty little girls, who sat from four to six hours. The Old Woman was "got up" with mob cap and spectacles, and seated in a huge shoe, filled and overrunning with dolls of all sizes and descriptions, which found a ready sale. The ladies of one of the City Churches were responsible for this very successful and lucrative illustration of the old nursery rhyme. In this part of the Auditorium also stood one of the tables of the Horticultural Department, which was kept constantly supplied with the choicest flowers by our professional and amateur florists.

We now leave the lower floor of the Academy, and make our way to

THE SECOND FLOOR,

or "Dress Circle." This from below presented a spectacle of wonderful brilliancy, completely tapestried as it was with afghans, quilts, and spreads, of the most vivid colors. The first four tiers of seats here, were left in their places for the accommodation of visitors, and from no point of view could a better *coup d'oeil* of the bewildering scene below be obtained. These seats were crowded at all times, as well as those in the tier above, which last was not occupied for the sale of goods. The Dress Circle was divided into five compartments of about two hundred and fifty square feet each. Here were sold afghans, quilts, etageres, screens, fancy chairs, chess tables, desks, campstools, toys, and hundreds of other articles of a miscellaneous character. The tables to the right of the central entrance to this gallery were occupied by the young ladies of the Packer Institute, who exhibited a great variety of fancy articles, valued at nearly $1,000. Among the young ladies in attendance at these tables were Misses Wright, E. J. Brown, E. W. Brown, Waterbury, Thompson, Thalheimer, Winslow, Hathaway, Hedden, Gallagher, Wells, and Harrison. The stalls in this gallery were under the charge of Messrs. Thomas Brooks and S. W. Smith.

DEPARTMENT OF BOOKS, PUBLICATIONS, ETC.

The lobby of the second floor was devoted to one of the most interesting departments of the Fair, namely, that for the sale of Books, Photographic Albums, etc. This department, through the generous liberality of the publishers of Brooklyn and New York, was kept stocked with as large and choice a variety of goods in the line of Books and Stationery as any first-class book store, and quiet as was the nook in which it was situated, it was at all times thronged with appreciative purchasers. Among the elegant Albums offered for sale, was one holding not less than 800 pictures, and valued at sixty dollars. The publishers of Webster's Quarto Pictorial Dictionary sent twenty-five copies of that valuable standard work. Another elegant Dictionary was a copy of Worcester's Quarto, bound in Russia leather, and valued at $12; Darley's Illustrations of Margaret, in Turkey Morocco, and another in antique, were among the books. Then there were the "Dusseldorff Gallery" in Turkey Morocco, full-gilt binding, $40; the New York Gallery of Pictures, $40; seven volumes of Harper's Illustrated Weekly, half Morocco, $40; Harper's Pictorial Family Bible, $25; Appleton's Encyclopædia, 16 volumes, in Sheep, $64, and another set, half Morocco, for $80; Johnson's Universal Atlas, $25; Ure's Dictionary, Appleton's Dictionary of Mechanics, Irving's Washington, Life of Henry Clay, Robinson's Songs of the Church, British Essayist, Spectator, and hundreds of other choice and standard works, besides an infinite variety of smaller miscellaneous books. In this department was exhibited a manuscript speech of Hon. Edward Everett, delivered at Faneuil Hall, Boston, Feb. 10, 1864, in introducing Col. N. G. Taylor, of East Tennessee, who came to plead with the true men of the East in behalf of the war-scourged loyalists of that region, faithful unto death.

A very pleasant and noticeable feature of the business of this department, was the demand for substantial, valuable books, and religious books were also much inquired for. During the last three days of the Fair, in response to an appeal for "reading matter" from Beaufort, S. C., in behalf of the wounded men just from Florida, a placard was hung up in the Book-room, addressed to the public: "Buy a book and leave it to be sent to the Hospital Library, Beaufort, S. C."

A member of the Book Committee writes:

"This card was read by many who gladly responded to the appeal. Three young soldiers were among the first of these. They each purchased a volume, wrote their name and regiment, and smilingly presented the gifts, while one said with an earnestness that brought the color to his cheek: 'You are doing a good work here ladies.' Another donation to this object came from a young lady shut up within her sick room. She heard of the opportunity, and, through a friend, selected 'The Autobiography of Dr. Lyman Beecher,' to go in her name to some weary invalid lying on his bed in a Southern hospital. As the result of this plan, over 150 volumes were received for Beaufort, which are already on their way, while a direct gift was made by the Committee, at the close of the Fair, of two packages of books for David's Island and Hart's Island."

On Tuesday evening, March 8th, the night of the formal closing of the Fair, an auction sale was held in the Book Room, of all the articles undisposed of. Mr. Leavitt, auctioneer of the Book Trade's Sales, of New York, officiated in a happy manner. There was not much left of value, but what there was went off briskly, at satisfactory prices.

In the third circle, as before stated, there were no stalls. There was, however, a scale, under charge of Mr. and Mrs. Schoonmaker, on which thousands tested their weight, in strolling through the upper regions.

SCENES AND INCIDENTS IN THE AUDITORIUM.

The main business in the Grand Bazaar being to dispose of the goods for sale, of course no great variety of incident could be expected to take place there. No time whatever was lost in irrelevant proceedings. There were no speeches or glorifications of any sort, men and women, managers and managed, bent their entire thoughts and energies from the opening hour to the closing, to the securing as large a sum as possible for the great Cause. Amusement was provided for in other departments of the Fair, but here, all was serious, systematic *business*. To be sure, the visitor might wander delightedly for hours together among the various attractions presented by the Bazaar, and nowhere could more real enjoyment be obtained than here, but there was on the part of all interested a faithful and rigid attention to duty which told effectively when the results were figured up. Indeed the business men and women who gave their time to the Fair, without exception devoted themselves to it with far greater faithfulness than they are accustomed to bestow upon the details of their customary business affairs. Many, during the progress of the Fair, gave their entire time to it, and all gave a very large proportion. It would be impossible to individualize all who distinguished themselves for unremitting labor, and untiring energy. They have their reward in the approval of their own consciences, which is but the approving voice of God.

But rare as were the incidents of extraordinary interest which occurred in the Auditorium, there were a few events of a pleasing character, during the progress of the Fair, of which it is proper to preserve a record here. The music, which was furnished every evening from the Dress Circle, the first four nights by Dodworth's celebrated brass and reed band, of thirty pieces, and during the remainder of the Fair by the band of the U. S. receiving ship North Carolina, was an ever charming feature. The programme of the opening night, which is here appended, will give an idea of the gems to which the visitors to the Fair were treated. Of course there was a change in the programme every night.

PROGRAMME OF OPENING NIGHT:

PART I.

1. War March, from "Athalia" .... Mendelssohn.
2. Mazourka, "Il Profeto" .... Meyerbeer.
3. Aria and Chorus, "La Favorita" .... Donizetti.
5. Divertissement, from "Lohengrin" .... R. Wagner.

PART II.

5. Overture, "Euryanthe" .... C. M. Von Weber.
6. Grand Selection from "Faust," introducing the celebrated Waltz and Soldier's Chorus .... Gounod.
7. Trab Trab Gallop .... Sonerlatt.
8. Grand Selection, "Don Pasquale" .... Donizetti.

PART III.

9. Quickstep, "Parade's Dismissed" .... Downing.
10. Linnet Polka .... Bousquet.
11. "Fair Star" Waltz .... Laurent.
12. Union Railroad .... Downing.

On the afternoon of Thursday, March 3, a pleasing incident occurred. Ten little girls, whose ages are between ten and twelve years, who had been holding a Fair of their own in South Brooklyn (see reports of entertainments auxiliary to the Fair, in Appendix,) visited the Academy together, to present the proceeds, amounting to $164. Of this little episode, the *Union*, of March 4, says:

"Mr. Stranahan introduced them to the audience with a few pleasant and pertinent remarks, stating that they, determined to do what they could for the Fair, made a quantity of small articles for it, which they sold, and thus netted the neat sum we have mentioned. Those within hearing loudly applauded the earnest little workers, and those at a distance, nothing doubting that the applause was for something meriting it, took up the echo until the great Academy rang again."

SWORD PRESENTATION.

One of the most interesting incidents of the Fair took place in the rooms of the Executive Committee on Monday evening, March 1, where a number of ladies and gentlemen assembled for the purpose of presenting a sword, sash, and belt, to Lieut. Col. J. Harris Hooper, of the 15th Mass. Volunteers, who recently escaped, with some brother officers, from the Libby Prison at Richmond. These equipments were purchased by a few of his friends and admirers, from a collection given to the Fair by the house of Messrs. Miller & Co. of 9 Maiden Lane, New York. The friends of Col. Hooper in this city heard in the morning of his safe arrival in Brooklyn, and of his presence at the Fair, and in a very brief space of time the subscription was complete. At 9 o'clock, James H. Frothingham, Esq., the Treasurer, and a personal friend of Col. Hooper, introduced him to the company gathered before him; after which A. A. Low, Esq., President of the General Committee, made the presentation in a neat address.

Mr. Low's remarks were received with warm applause, and expressions of profound interest in the young hero. Colonel Hooper, taken wholly by surprise, responded in a few graceful and modest words, fresh from a noble heart. At the suggestion of Mr. Low, he afterwards gave a thrilling account of the manner and incidents of his escape, and of the generous and careful spirit in which the negroes they encountered gave guidance and aid to himself and companions. At the close of his narrative, Col. Woodward, of the Brooklyn 13th, one of his comrades in his first campaign, proposed "three cheers for Col. Hooper," which were given with a will; and amid general congratulations to him, the meeting dissolved.

The evening the Fair was formally closed, Tuesday, March 8th, an interesting scene took place in the Auditorium. Not long before the hour of closing the Treasurer hung out his last bulletin, announcing to the noble people of Brooklyn and Long Island that their generous benefactions in behalf of the United States Sanitary Commission had reached the magnificent sum of

FOUR HUNDRED THOUSAND DOLLARS,

being nearly twice as much as the most sanguine had ventured to hope for. This proud announcement was greeted with the liveliest sensation by the multitude which packed the Academy. At a few minutes before ten o'clock, Mr. A. A. Low, Chairman of the General Committee, mounted an improvised rostrum in the centre of the floor, and begged the attention of all present. Mr. Low, then in a few well-chosen remarks stated the general results of the Fair, and proposed that the great "broom" which the managers of the Cincinnati Fair had sent us, challenging us to beat the $240,000 which they had swept up, be sent to the New York Fair with our $400,000 attached. The proposition was adopted by acclamation.

Rev. Dr. Farley then being called upon, said that as this great enterprise was now closing, he could think of nothing more appropriate than to request the band to play the "Star Spangled Banner," and he would beg the audience to join in the chorus. He also would request the band to play the more homely, but stirring music of "Yankee Doodle."

Loud applause followed this request, which was responded to by the band, who played in their best style the grand national hymn, in which the audience joined their voices. "Yankee Doodle" followed, to the lively strains of which the assemblage retired.

THE END OF THE FAIR—THE AUCTION SALE.

It was announced that all the goods remaining unsold at the close of the Fair would be disposed of at auction. The number was much less than was expected, not more than two or three thousand dollars worth being left on hand in the Auditorium, while the Museum and Hall of Manufacturers were also pretty thoroughly cleaned out. On Wednesday evening, March 9th, the auction was held, commencing with the unsold goods in the Auditorium. Those in the Book Department had been sold the previous night.

It should be premised that most of the purchasers of the choicest goods very kindly consented to allow them to remain until the close of the Fair, so that the spectacle presented to the visitor on the last days of the Fair was nearly as brilliant as it was at the opening, as the abundant supplies that kept coming in, enabled the ladies to replenish the stalls with the smaller articles and fancy goods, and to keep their attractions from flagging. After the formal close of the Fair on Wednesday night, the work of removal commenced, and in a very few hours the splendors which had made the Academy of Music seem a veritable fairy palace, full

> "Of jewels rare, and carved and gilded things
> More lovely than a dream's imaginings,"

were scattered in ten thousand homes, to remain as mementoes of the great Brooklyn and Long Island Fair, and the Academy was left looking, in its blank spaces, and bare walls, doubly desolate from the bright contrast of a few hours before.

The goods for auction were arranged on a few tables in the stage portion of the building. Mr. Joseph Hegeman, of corner of Willoughby and Pearl streets, commenced the sale, assisted by Mr. E. Sintzenich, of the firm of Ives & Co. The skill of these two gentlemen, aided by their ready wit, very soon disposed of the stock, which consisted of shaving soaps, stationery, perfumery, and toilet articles, combs, jewelry, wax-work, thread, sewing-silk, toys, Japanese and Chinese engravings, rebel trophies, relics of antiquity, Japanese opium pipes, canes, coins, pictures, vases, photographs, fans, autographs, autumn leaves, engravings, etc., etc. Several of the pictures in the Art Gallery were sold at prices very much below their value.

An assorted lot of plain photographs, some three hundred in number, went off for $10.

At 9 o'clock, the hour for selling the house and lot No. 540 Atlantic street, donated by Messrs. Scranton & Co. to the Fair, Mr. Sintzenich made his way through the crowd to the central stand. He announced the terms of sale to be, "Ten per cent. to be paid at once; the rest at the office of C. & S. Condit, on or before the 30th of March—the purchaser to sign a memorandum of the sale at the time of its purchase; full warranty deed to be executed, with exception of the mortgage of $2,000, on which interest was paid to date."

These terms being generally understood the sale was started by a bid at $3,000, which rapidly ran up, by hundred dollar bids, to $3,300. Then the bids ran up to $3,325, $3,350, $3,400, $3,450, $3,500, $3,550, $3,650. Here a competition arose between two persons on opposite sides of the stand, and the auctioneer became brilliant in his appeals to the one "not to be bluffed down," and the other "not to allow the property to be sacrificed to his adversary," each appeal bringing out a $50 bid, and the hearty applause of the now excited audience, until finally bidding ceased, and the property was knocked down to W. R. Tice, of No. 297 Fulton street, for the sum of $3,850.

In the meantime Mr. Hill had been selling off the stock of the Manufacturers Department, which was all, however, composed of small articles.

The buildings and lumber which had been used for the Fair were sold at auction on Friday, March 18th, for $1,487 50.

THE ART GALLERY

WAS located in the Assembly Room of the Academy, the entrance being from the lobby of the second floor, and on either side the Book Department, and was one of the most charming departments of the Fair. The Committee on Art comprised some of the most eminent artists in the country, residents of Brooklyn, and most indefatigably did they labor, one and all, to offer an exhibition of Works of Art which should be second to none ever seen before in this country. And they succeeded. It was the opinion of connoisseurs that the Art Gallery of the Brooklyn and Long Island Fair contained more works of *real merit* than any which had been offered to the public for many years. The most valuable picture in the collection was the original full-length portrait of Washington, by Stuart. This magnificent painting is the property of H. E. Pierrepont, Esq., of Brooklyn, and is valued at ten thousand dollars. Another painting by Stuart—Mrs. General Lee, was also exhibited. An examination of the catalogue, herewith presented, will convince the reader that the praise awarded to this collection is entirely merited.

CATALOGUE OF WORKS OF ART.

No.	Title.	Artist.	Owner.
1.	Washington,	Gilbert Stuart,	H. E. Pierrepont.
2.	Kentucky Home,	E. Johnson,	
3.	Passaic Falls,	L. R. Mignot,	R. Stuyvesant.
4.	Coast of Maine,	D. Huntington,	G. S. Stephenson.
5.	The Indolent Scholar,	Couture,	J. T. Sanford.
6.	Mrs. Lee,	Gilbert Stuart,	N. Luquer.

No.	Title.	Artist.	Owner.
7.	Landscape,	J. M. Hart,	Mrs. J. Ballard.
8.	Landscape,	J. F. Kensett,	John B. Prentiss.
9.	"Elaine,"	Geo. H. Hall,	G. G. White.
10	Calla,	J. Williamson,	H. Allen.
11.	The First Lesson of Charity,	D. Huntington,	G. B. Carhart.
12.	Lago di Garda,	Carmiencke,	Chas. Graff.
13.	Book Worm,	Spitzweg,	Le Grand Lockwood.
14.	Housatonic.	J. B. Bristol,	Waters.
15.	The Love Letter,		E. Dodge.
16.	Portrait,	H. Inman,	H. E. Pierrepont.
17.	On the Pemigewasset,	A. B. Durand,	G. S. Stephenson.
18.	The Love Test,	De Keyser,	J. T. Sanford.
19.	Summer Afternoon,	Geo. Inness,	H. W. Beecher.
20.	Flowers,	G. H. Hall,	J. C. Henshaw.
21.	Partridge and Young.	A. F. Tait,	J. B. Blossom.
22.	Washington's first interview with Mrs. Custis,	J. W. Ehninger,	W. Pate.
23.	Alps at Sunrise,	R. Gignoux,	A. A. Low.
24.	Game,	Adolph,	
25.	Lake George,	S. Coleman, Jr.,	J. T. Howard.
26.	The Confidante,	Wappers,	J. T. Sanford.
27.	On the Saco,	E. W. Hall,	Artist.
28.	Forbidden Fruit,	Patrois,	H. P. F. Odell.
29.	Landscape,	J. M. Hart,	J. B. Blossom.
30.	Maternal Love,	De Giorgi,	E. Dodge.
31.	Lace Work,	Giovanni Basti,	Wm. McLane.
32.	Valley in the Tyrol,	Ferrari,	"
33.	Calme Marine,		S. T. Eastman.
34.	"Done Gone,"	W. T. Davis,	S. Ward.
35.	Landscape,	S. T. Shaughnessy.	
36.	Sheep,	Robbe,	Cyrus Butler.
37.	Grapes.	J. F. Cropsey,	H. B. Husted.
38.	Light Triumphant,	Geo. Inness,	Mrs. E. T. H. Gibson.
39.	Moonlight,	J. A. Parker, Jr.,	Artist.
40.	First Snow,	R. Gignoux,	S. Hallett.
41.	Landscape and Sheep,	Koekkoek & Verboeckhoven,	J. T. Howard.
42.	Landscape and Cattle,	A. D. Shattuck.	
43.	Twin Elms,	L. R. Mignot,	G. G. White.
44.	View in Holland.	Springer,	W. McLane.
45.	Swan Inn,	W. Shayer,	S. B. Chittenden.
46.	Wood Scene.	W. H. Beard,	Artist.
47.	Columbus and the Cardinals,	T. H. Smith.	S. T. Eastman.
48.	Requiem of De Soto,	E. White,	Artist.
49.	Niagara—Winter,	R. Gignoux,	A. T. Stewart.
50.	Study from Nature,	J. F. Cropsey.	G. G. White.
51.	Landscape.	H. T. Boddington.	H. E. Pierrepont.
52.	Crown Inn.	W. Shayer,	A. A. Low.
53.	Summer,	Nicholson,	J. T. Howard.
54.	The Student's Departure,	Hasenclever,	J. T. Johnston.
55.	The Examination,	"	"
56.	The Return,	"	"
57.	Interior,	W. W. Whittredge.	H. L. Stewart.

No.	Title.	Artist.	Owner.
58.	Auction in the Studio,	Baumgartner,	J. T. Sanford.
59.	View on the Arno,	J. F. Cropsey,	W. I. Steele.
60.	Rocky Mountains,	A. Bierstadt,	S. B. Caldwell,
61.	Composition,	A. B. Durand.	A. A. Low,
62.	Pocahontas,	Muller,	O. O. White,
63.	Grapes,	Geo. H. Hall,	"
64.	Flowers,	R. M. Pratt,	Artist.
65.	Indolence,	L. Lang,	"
66.	Study,	J. F. Kensett,	"
67.	On the Passaic,	L. R. Mignot,	Cyrus Butler.
68.	A. Lincoln,	J. O. Jones,	N. Wiard,
69.	Col. Trumbull,	Trumbull,	D. T. Lanman.
70.	Mephistopheles,	W. J. Davis,	N. Wiard.
71.	Devotion,	T. Hicks,	Artist.
72.	Street Scene, Seville,	S. Colman, Jr.,	"
73.	The Meteor,	F. E. Church,	"
74.	Fisherman,	E. W. Warren,	"
75.	Fruit,	Mrs. Greatorex,	"
76.	View near Naples,	T. Cole,	John H. Prentiss.
77.	The Truant,	T. Le Clear,	Artist.
78.	Rocky Mountains,	A. Bierstadt,	
79.	The Mother,	R. W. Wier,	
80.	Fruit,	G. H. Hall,	J. C. Henshaw.
81.	The Duckling,	J. G. Brown,	Artist.
82.	Flowers,	W. T. Matthews,	"
83.	Fruit,	A. Fisher,	"
84.	Willows,	F. Bridges,	"
85.	Berdan Sharp-Shooter,	W. Homer,	"
86.	The Neglected Picture,	W. T. Davis,	N. Wiard.
87.	Currants,	Geo. H. Hall,	S. T. Eastman,
88.	Flowers,	W. T. Mathews,	Artist.
89.	"Beg,"	J. B. Whittaker,	Artist.
90.	Grapes,	Geo. H. Hall.	S. T. Eastman.
91.	Sweet Sixteen,	Geo. H. Baker,	R. Stuyvesant.
92.	Old Homestead,	J. L. Henry,	Artist.
93.	Bubble Blower,	Geo. C. Lambdin.	J. B. Murray.
94.	Coast of Sweden.	Carmiencke,	Artist.
95.	Little Knitter,	Geo C. Lambdin,	J. B. Murray.
96.	Winter,		H. W. Banks.
97.	Autumn Walk,	E. Benson,	Artist.
98.	Sunset,	Geo. Inness,	H. W. Banks.
99.	Study,	H. W. Robbins,	Artist.
100.	Twilight,	J. B. Bristol,	H. W. Banks.
101.	December Morning,	C. C. Griswold,	Artist.
102.	Hudson River,	S. T. Shaughnessey,	"
103.	Green Mountains,	J. D. Barrow,	"
104.	Leap Frog.		
105.	Album Girl,		
106.	De Witt Clinton,	H. Inman,	John H. Prentiss.
107.	Drawing,	R. W. Wier,	
108.	Crayon.		
109.	Crayon.		
110.	Captain Worden,	Mrs. Dame,	

No.	Title.	Artist.	Owner.
111.	Union Refugees,	J. Rogers,	
112.	Country Post Office.	"	
113.	Mail Day,		
114.	The Studio,	J. F. Weir,	Artist.
115.	Study,	J. F. Kensett,	"
116.	June,	J. W. Casilear,	Artist.
117.	"Comin' thro' the Rye,"	G. H. Boughton,	S. P. Avery.
118.	Wynkoop House,	J. McEntee,	"
119.	Near Genoa,	S. R. Gifford,	"
120.	Near Hurley,	W. Hart,	"
121.	Study,	W. T. Richards,	"
122.	What Have I Forgotten,	W. S. Mount,	"
123.	Westphalian Cottage,	W. Whittredge,	"
124.	Morning on the Mount,	R. W. Hubbard,	"
125.	Flowers,	Geo. C. Lambdin,	R. H. Manning.
126.	The Old Homestead,	G. H. Boughton,	"
127.	Mount Washington,	J. R. Gifford,	"
128.	Repose,	E. D. E. Greene,	"
129.	Autumn,	J. W. Casilear,	W. Hatfield.
130.	Indian Falls,	D. Johnson,	"
131.	Courage and Fear,	V. Nehlig,	"
132.	The Rye Path,	A. F. Bellows,	"
133.	Study,	W. T. Richards,	"
134.	"Can't See Me,"	S. J. Guy,	"
135.	First Day Out.	W. J. Hennessy,	"
136.	The Knight's Signature,	E. Vedder,	"
137.	Heldeburgh Mountains,	James Hart,	
138.	Summer Reverie.	P. P. Ryder,	Hatfield.
139.	Schoharie Kill,	S. R. Gifford,	Stephenson.
140.	Conway Valley,	S. Colman,	"
141.	Red, White and Blue,	W. Hart,	E. S. Mills.
142.	The Dell,	R. W. Hubbard,	"
143.	Fruit and Flowers,	W. Banta,	W. Banta.
144.	Little Cook,	E. Frère,	Healy.
145.	Calm.	De Haas,	J. H. Willets.
146.	Winter,	T. L. Smith,	T. L. Smith.
147.	Landscape,	De Peyster,	Artist.
148.	Sheep and Fowls,	Van Severendonck,	W. J. A. Fuller.
149.	Grand Canal,	Pritchet,	"
150.	Interior,	A. F. Tait,	
151.	Refractory Sitter,	S. J. Guy,	"
152.	Landscape.	Wissengardt,	"
153.	Apple Gathering,	Frauze,	"
154.	Old Tower Newport,	T. B. Thorpe,	"
155.	Roadside Inn,	W. Shayer,	"
156.	Landscape and Cattle,	"	"
157.	Fowls,	Van Limpertt,	"
158.	Still Bower,	Dommerhuysen,	"
159.	Niagara Falls,	T. B. Thorpe,	"
160.	View on the Thames—Hunting,	Williams,	"
161.	View on the Thames—Fishing,	"	"
162.	Landscape,	Miller,	C. H. Baxter.
163.	Crayon Study,	J. B. Whittaker,	Artist.

No.	Title.	Artist.	Owner.
164.	Crayon Study,	J. B. Whittaker,	Artist.
165.	Indian Corn,	J. Williamson,	S. T. Eastman.
166.	Twilight,	Geo. Inness,	H. W. Beecher.
167.	Albino Girl,	E. Johnson,	"
168.	Leap Frog,	F. O. C. Darley,	J. C. Henshaw.
169.	Medallion Portrait,	E. J. Kuntze,	Artist.
170.	Market Scene, Amsterdam,	Van Schendel,	Le Grand Lockwood.
171.	Old Dutch Porch,	J. P. Rossiter,	G. G. White.
172.	Hudson River,	J. F. Kensett,	R. L. Stuart.
173.	Scene in New Jersey,	J. F. Cropsey,	Artist.
174.	The Lovers,	F. A. Chapman,	W. H. Snyder.

STATUARY.

Of Statuary there was but a small collection, comprising The "Union Refugee," "Country Post-Office," and "Mail Day," by Rogers, a fine bust of Captain Worden, another of Rev. Dr. Cutler, another of President Lincoln, and a Pocahontas, by Mozier.

THE ART ASSOCIATION RECEPTION.

The Gallery of Paintings was opened to the public on Wednesday evening, March 17th, several days in advance of the opening of the Fair, a brilliant reception and Promenade Concert being given by the Committee in charge. The price of tickets was placed at one dollar, and it being the inauguration of the Fair proper, the opening of the first of the departments directly involved in the scope of the enterprise, it was looked forward to with considerable anxiety. This was to be, as it were, the feeling of the public pulse. It was to test whether the blood was creeping coldly and sluggishly, or leaping with generous ardor and excited anticipation. The success of the Reception resolved all doubts. Notwithstanding the high price of tickets, not much less than two thousand persons attended, the stream flowing uninterruptedly from seven o'clock to eleven. The Auditorium had been floored over level with the stage, in anticipation of the Fair, and a large space was thus afforded in the beautiful Academy for the promenaders, who moved to the bewitching strains of Dodworth's great band. It was a scene of rare loveliness. Youth and beauty, light and fragrance, the rich music of the band, and the sweeter melodies of laughing girls, the great Art Gallery flooded with a splendor which brought out the bright colors with which its walls were spread with almost startling vividness, and pervading all a sweet anticipatory sense of delights yet to come, of which this was but the faint foretaste—the sparkle of the foam of the rich wine yet hidden, and more than all the assurance which all those earnest workers now felt of the entire success of the great enterprise which had been their waking thought and nightly dream for so many laborious weeks—all these combined to make the Artist's Reception one of those rare events the remembrance of which, to all who participated will be "a joy forever."

THE ARTIST'S ALBUM.

One of the attractions of the Art Gallery was an Album of Sketches in Oil. This collection numbered one hundred and twenty pictures, by the following eminent artists:

Atwater, G. A. Baker, Brevoort, Cranch, Colman, Mrs. Edwards, Folconer, G. H. Hall, Hunt, Johnson, Kittell, Leutze, McEntee, McEwan, R. W. Miller, O'Brien, Parsons, Huggins, Warren, Waterman, Beckwith, Bellow, Miss Bridges, Carlin, Church, Callum, Durand, E. W. Hall, Wm. Hart, Hazeltine, Hicks, LaFarge, A. S. Miller, Ogilvie, Rondell, Ryder, Tait, White, Weir, C. Baker, W. H. Beard, J. H. Beard, Miss Beers, Craig, Cropsey, Greatorex, DeHaas, J. M. Hart, Lang, Loop, Mathews, A. J. Miller, Moran, Oertel, Robbins, Rossiter, Shattuck, Wimer, Barrow, Blauvelt, Casilear, Carter, Falconer, Gignoux, Griswold, Hennessy, Herrick, Hubbard, Lambdin, L. J. Miller, Mullen, Parker, Suydam, Sontag, Sommer, Wagner, Wood, Brandt, Bart, Boutelle, J. G. Brown, Brownell, Faschael, Gifford, Guy, Happel, Inman, Kensett, LeClear, Lossing, Owen, Parton, Smillie, Stone, Thorpe, Whittaker, Ward, Annable, Antwolle, Bellows, Benson, Florstadt, Bristol, H. K. Brown, Carmiencke, Darley, Daniels, Fish, Gray, Hill, Hooper, Huntington, Henry, Kessler, Lumley, Nichols, Nelson.

This superb collection of sketches was the fruit of a suggestion of Mr. R. Gignoux, the well-known Artist, of Brooklyn, and the project was early taken in hand by the Sub-Committee on Reception and Exhibition of Works of Art, greatly aided by Geo. S. Stephenson, Esq., who contributed an elegant carved walnut portfolio table for the reception of the sketches.

A circular to Artists was sent out as early as Jan. 18th, by the Committee on Reception and Exhibition of Works of Art, which said:

"As an effective means of aiding this cause, the Committee will form a collection of sketches; and a work from your hand is respectfully solicited. No uniformity either as to size or manner of execution is required, but we would suggest that they do not exceed 8x10 inches—an average of this would probably suit all conditions. They will be mounted with large margin, in separate and protective "passe-partouts," and will be contained in an elegant carved case and stand of black-walnut.

The FAIR will open on FEBRUARY 22d, but as it will take considerable time to mount them, the sketches should be sent (or notice when ready) at as early a day as possible to either of the Committee.

REGIS GIGNOUX, Chairman........................15 Tenth st., New York
R. W. HUBBARD,........................15 Tenth st., New York
JOHN WILLIAMSON,........................157 Montague st., Brooklyn.
N. B. KITTELL,........................804 Fifth av., New York.
J. A. PARKER, Jr.,........................157 Montague st., Brooklyn.
HENRY WARD BEECHER,........................69 Columbia st., Brooklyn.
SAMUEL P. AVERY, Secretary,........................108 Nassau st., New York."

How well this Committee performed their work is sufficiently attested by the results. The people of Brooklyn and Long Island owe a great debt of gratitude to the gentlemen concerned for their efforts in securing for the Fair this charming collection, which added so handsomely to the proceeds of the enterprise. To the artists who so generously contributed their works, they also owe their warmest appreciation and thanks.

About forty of these sketches were exhibited on the walls of the Art Gallery. The collection was disposed of in shares of ten dollars each, over five hundred being sold; the agreement among the shareholders being to meet after the Fair and dispose of the collection by a vote of the majority. This meeting was held in the Academy of Music on Thursday evening, March 17th. The pictures were divided into six collections of twenty each, and each was disposed of by lot, the box and stand making a seventh prize. The following were the fortunate drawers:

First—A, No. 196—H. G. Ward, 93 Wall street.

Second—B, No. 30—Mrs. C. A. Clark, South Brooklyn.

Third—C, No. 449—W. J. Steele, corner of Clinton and Gates avenue.

Fourth—D, No. 357—Thos. H. Sanford, 50 South street, New York.

Fifth—E, No. 467—L. Thompson, Baltimore.

Sixth—F, No. 386—Mrs. R. S. Bussing, 93 Montague street.

Seventh—(The case)—G, No. 391—Isaac Young, corner of Atlantic and Powers streets.

THE AMATEUR ARTISTS' ALBUM.

This collection of sketches, by Amateur Artists, was an exceedingly interesting and valuable contribution to the Fair. It numbered fifty-eight pictures, in oils, water-colors, and pencil, with one exquisite pen and ink sketch, by Professor Herzberg, of the Polytechnic Institute. The sketches were mostly by ladies and gentlemen of Brooklyn, although some came from New England, and one from New Jersey. One lady, seventy years of age, contributed some very pretty water-colors, which she painted expressly for the Album. They were studies from nature, and among the finest in the Album. There were also several exquisite heads, both in oil and water colors, all originals, by ladies of Brooklyn. There were also in the collection some beautiful autumn leaves, in water-colors. Mr. Hart, and Mr. Falconer, the eminent artists, each sent a sketch in oil, which were placed in the Amateur Album. Mrs. S. B. Chittenden, Chairman of the Ladies' Art Committee, conceived and carried out the happy idea of this Album. The sketches sent in she had mounted at Goupil's, who also made a very handsomely carved box-table, of black walnut, to contain the pictures. In addition to the sketches in the Album, Gignoux and Huntington each presented to Mrs. Chittenden, for the Fair, a painting in oil, which sold separately for $100 each.

The following are the names of the ladies and gentlemen who contributed to the Amateur Artists' Album, so far as they can be obtained;

Miss Kate Dana, Miss Ellen Ripley, by a Friend of Miss Dana, Mr. Jale, by a Friend of Mr. Jale, Mrs. Rossire, Miss Julia Reed, Mr. Max Sand, Mr. Charles Farley, Miss Lyman, Mrs. Newbold, Mrs. Dr. Littlejohn, Miss Dodge, Mrs. Beecher, Miss Beach, Professor Herzberg, Miss Ellen Robbins, Miss Helen Prentiss, Mr. Frank Vinton, Miss Kate Hillard, Miss Alice Cary, Miss Kate Ripley, Miss Mary Stranahan, Miss Kate Taylor, Miss A. W. Henshaw, Mrs. Perry, Mrs. Fowler, Miss Ward, Miss Cornelia Olcott, Mrs. Fox, Mr. Fay, by a a Friend of Miss Olcott, Miss Millard, Mr. Lodovici, Mr. McCallum, Miss Porter, Mr. Hart, Mr. Van Nostrand, Miss Van Nostrand, Miss Emma Wallace.

The Album was disposed of in shares, one hundred being sold at $5 each, thus realizing the handsome sum of $500. This Album was at first exhibited in the Art Gallery, but was afterwards removed to the Museum building. The final disposition took place on Monday evening, April 4th, in the Director's Room of the Academy. Fifty-eight sketches were by agreement divided into three lots, which were drawn for in the same manner as the Artists' Album. The first choice for eighteen pictures, and the handsome table was drawn by Mr. J. T. Howard. The second choice for twenty sketches was obtained by Mr. E. S. Mills, and the third and last lot by Mrs. J. C. Brevoort.

KNICKERBOCKER HALL.

THE History of Knickerbocker Hall, the refreshment department of the Fair, is a striking example of what energy and perseverance can do in the accomplishment of a task that might well be deemed an impossibility. The Committee charged with the duty of providing accommodations for the refreshment of the visitors, had they foreseen to what a gigantic scale the undertaking was to reach, might well have shrunk from the attempt. As it was, and not anticipating having to provide for a fourth part of the number they afterwards did successfully for two weeks, it is no impugnment of their courage or resolution to say that they approached their duty with many misgivings. It was reported, and with much truth, that the restaurants of most of the Fairs previously held had proved failures, and this was a fact not calculated to encourage them. But it is rarely that such a task has been entrusted to abler hands. The spirit of determination to conquer difficulties, and to win success at all hazards and cost, which was the ruling spirit of the whole Fair, nowhere was so necessary, or, fortunately, so fully developed and ardent as among the managers of the Refreshment Department, both ladies and gentlemen, and so it came to pass, that, having expected to feed a comparatively few persons every day, and finding instead that their doors were besieged by a voracious multitude, their determination rose with the occasion, and, after the guage of the work had been taken, which was done the very first day, no man went hungry from Knickerbocker Hall.

The Executive Committee were very naturally puzzled when they undertook to estimate the amount of room required for the Fair, as they did not know how many goods would be sent in, nor how large a concourse of people would need accommodation. A great diversity of views prevailed, some members of the Committee believing that the Academy of Music alone, would furnish accommodation sufficient for all the departments. Fortunately the majority of the Committee thought it would be better to err, if at all, on the safe side, and provide liberally. The result showed that this confidence in the large-heartedness of the people of Long Island was not over sanguine. The Committee seem to have calculated just right. There was room enough in all the departments, and it is not possible to see how any could have been accommodated in less space.

Knickerbocker Hall was one of the temporary buildings erected for the occasion. It was located on the lot adjoining the Academy of Music, on the West. The lot is the property of A. A. Low, Esq., Chairman of the General Committee, and was generously loaned for the use of the Fair. Ground was broken on Saturday, Jan. 23d, for a building 68 by 100 feet, and two stories in height. So vigorously was the work pushed, that, by the ensuing Saturday, the building was entirely enclosed. It was completed in ample time for the opening of the Fair on Feb. 22.

THE HALL WHEN COMPLETED.

The entrance to Knickerbocker Hall was from the lobby of the Academy of Music. At the door, gates were provided, opening in opposite directions, so as to keep the streams of ingress and egress divided. This ingenious arrangement prevented all confusion. Upon entering the door, the visitor found himself in a beautiful *salle a manger* fitted with tables, and all the appliances of a first-class dining-saloon.

The Restaurant was arranged as follows: On the right, on entering, was located the Confectionery Department, where waited a large number of beautiful girls, dressed in a uniform, of which the most striking feature was its patriotic trimming of red, white and blue. At this table every variety of sugar wares were to be found, and at very moderate prices. This source yielded an average of about $200 per day. In the centre of the room stood the cake tables, covered with productions of that description, which were perfect marvels of size and ornamentation. The central cake was adorned with a Temple of Liberty, in white sugar, not less than five feet high. In niches on the edges stood equestrian figures of Gens. Grant, McClellan, Fremont and Sigel. The likenesses were well preserved, and the action of the figures wonderfully striking and natural. The temple was surmounted by a figure of the Goddess of Liberty bearing the American flag. This gigantic cake was the most striking feature of the room, and arrested the attention of every visitor at once. It was made and presented to the Fair by Mr Robert G Anderson, of corner of Fulton and Clinton streets.

THE MAIZENA DEPARTMENT.

This interesting department occupied the north-western corner of the hall. It was under the personal supervision of Mr. W. H. Duryea, of the firm of Duryea & Co., 166 Fulton street, New York. This firm in the most generous manner furnished gratuitously all the Maizena required by the Fair, which, after the public became acquainted with the variety and delicacy of the dishes made from it, was a quantity something enormous. They also had the Maizena prepared, and furnished attendants without charge. Great as must have been the outlay of the Messrs. Duryea, in thus sustaining, at their own expense, a complete eating department of the Fair, it cannot but bring, as all good deeds do, its own reward, even in a pecuniary sense, for it introduced to wide public notice and created a taste for the delicious article which they prepare, which cannot fail to result in largely increased sales. Properly, Glen Cove should be credited with the above magnificent contribution of the Messrs. Duryea, as their Maizena mills are there located.

The western side of Knickerbocker Hall, as well as the gallery which ran around it on three sides, were occupied by the tables. Of these there were thirty on the lower floor, and forty-five in the gallery. On the southern side of the Hall were rooms for the accommodation of private parties, containing tables at which thirty could dine with comfort. Adjoining these were rooms for the carvers, and the cooking room of the Maizena department. At the left of the entrance lunch tables were kept constantly spread with choice viands, such as cold fowl, chicken and lobster-salads, tongue, ham, etc., at which persons could lunch without ordering from the bill of fare.

Having now given a general idea of the arrangement of the Restaurant, it is proper that the adornments of the Hall should be noted. The building being a temporary structure, of course great elaboration of ornamentation was required to cover its rude walls, and make it attractive. Never was there a greater triumph of the decorative art than was achieved in Knickerbocker Hall. It was a perfect miracle of transformation, and marvel of beauty. The walls were covered with evergreens, woven into stars, twined about the columns, festooned from the galleries, springing in arches to the very ceiling. In looking up at the mass of greenery which canopied the room, one might well imagine himself walking through the fragrant aisles of a forest of evergreens. Over the door on Montague street was a tasteful combination of flags, with evergreens. At the southern end of the building a fine portrait of Washington was hung, surrounded with flags and evergreens. The ground floor was encircled with arches, interspersed with shields, bearing the coats of arms of the States; these shields were also draped with flags. Indeed, a profusion of flags and patriotic emblems was everywhere. The walls were paneled with handsome mirrors. Over the cake table, in the centre of the room, was suspended a gigantic chandelier, burning two hundred lights. This was also elegantly draped with evergreens.

The Bill of Fare never lacked variety nor excellence. A member of the Committee furnished the following as an approximation to the amount of food consumed in a day: Besides Maizena, 100 turkeys and chickens, 100 grouse, quail, and ducks, 500 lbs. of beef, mutton and venison, 20 hams and tongues, 18,000 oysters, 15 lbs. trout, 20 lbs. smelts and other fish; cake, pies, 60 or 70 qts. jelly, 800 qts. ice cream, 250 gallons coffee and tea, 400 loaves bread, 3 bbls. crackers, 200 heads celery, 3 bbls. potatoes, besides sugar, butter, eggs, milk, flour, apples, oranges, pickles, preserves, etc. The articles of food contributed were enough to supply *seven-eighths of the demand.* If this is not weighty testimony to the rare generosity of the people of Long Island, we should like to know what would be.

The arrangement for receiving provisions was as follows: It was announced in the papers beforehand that on certain days the contributions of certain Churches would be received—six on each day, between the hours of eight and eleven. Between these hours the procession of messengers bearing meats, poultry, cakes, confectionery, jellies, pastry, vegetables, etc., etc., began, each article being duly credited as it was brought in. If there was a surplus of any sort of provisions, as there was sometimes of hams, tongues, and other things, the Committee would exchange them with dealers for other articles more needed. The following was the designated order for contributions from Churches:

MONDAY, 22d—Church of the Pilgrims, Church of the Messiah, South Second Methodist, E. D., New England Congregational, E. D., St. Mark's Church, E. D., Contributions by Mrs. J. Hall.

TUESDAY, 23d—Church of the Redeemer, York Street Methodist, First Place Methodist, Pacific Street Methodist, Second Presbyterian.

WEDNESDAY, 24TH—Second Unitarian, First Baptist, Church of the Saviour, Church on the Heights, First Presbyterian, Lee Avenue Reformed Dutch Church.

THURSDAY, 25TH—Pierrepont Street Baptist, St. Mary's Church, St. John's Church, Hanson Place Baptist, Universalist, E. D., Contributions by Mrs. W. H. Jenkins.

FRIDAY, 26TH—Christ Church; Holy Trinity, Grand Street Methodist, E. D., State Street Congregational, Centenary Methodist, Central Baptist.

SATURDAY, 27TH—Lafayette Avenue Presbyterian, South Congregational, South Fifth Street M. E., Reformed Dutch, E. D., Baptist, Greenpoint, Washington Street Methodist.

MONDAY, 29TH—Sands Street Methodist, First Presbyterian, E. D., Christ Church, E. D., Grace Church, Friends' Society, Central Presbyterian.

TUESDAY, March 1st—Plymouth Church, South Presbyterian, Harrison Street Dutch Church, St. Charles Borromeo, Elm Place Congregational, East Reformed Dutch Church.

WEDNESDAY, March 2d—Dutch Reformed (Joralemon street), Strong Place Baptist, Washington Avenue Baptist, Boerumville and Bushwick Avenue, First Baptist, E. D., First Street Methodist, St. Peter's Church.

THURSDAY, March 3d—Clinton Street Congregational, Westminster Church, North Dutch Church, Third Presbyterian, Moravian Church, Hanson Place Methodist.

Only a portion of the food consumed was provided through the Churches. The Gentlemen's Committee took upon themselves the furnishing of meats, oysters, fish, bread, crackers, vegetables, coffee, tea, and ice cream. The Ladies' Committee was responsible for turkeys and chickens, hams, tongues, pies, cake, jelly, fruit, etc. The sugar, butter, flour, milk, eggs, and numerous other articles which were used, were partly purchased and partly contributed.

The kitchen and store-rooms of Knickerbocker Hall were in the basement of the Academy of Music.

Five hundred persons could be comfortably accommodated at one time in Knickerbocker Hall.

The arrangements for receiving money were admirable. Mr. E. H. Close, the Cashier, of whose gentlemanly deportment and assiduous devotion to business there was but one opinion, was seated at a desk about in the centre of the room. Every four tables were presided over by a lady, who took up the checks furnished by the waiters, and received the money, paying it over at once to the Cashier. By this plan it is thought the losses from dishonesty were reduced to the smallest possible amount, and probably no such losses occurred.

Of the *corps* of colored waiters, and their accomplished and indefatigable *chef*, Charles Robinson, a word of warm commendation must be said. The waiters at first employed were mostly foreigners, but they were a failure. With them confusion and stupidity reigned supreme. With the advent of Robinson and his skilful compeers came order, neatness, civility, and promptitude. Never was the superiority of the black over the white as waiters more conclusively demonstrated than it was in the experience of Knickerbocker Hall.

The restaurant closed on Saturday night, March 5th, having netted to the Fair the splendid sum of *nearly twenty-four thousand dollars.*

For this result the public are greatly indebted to the able, judicious, and energetic management of Mr. E. J. Lowber, Chairman of the Gentlemen's, and Mrs. E. S. Mills, Chairman of the Ladies' Refreshment Committee. Honorable mention must likewise be made of Mr. William A. Husted, (Mr. Lowber's right hand man, and general purveyor of the Hall.) Mr. Rufus Crook, (whose experience as a restaurateur made his services of inestimable value, and who devoted his entire time to the work.) Mr. Robert G. Anderson, (a host in himself,) Mr. William S. Dunham, Chas. B. Loomis, and William S. Thompson. To Messrs. Robbins and Dorlan, for generous contributions of game and oysters, the warmest thanks of the community are due.

Of the ladies, in addition to Mrs. Mills, must be mentioned Mesdames A. B. Hall, Secretary and Treasurer, Emma Barnes, H. Waters, T. T. Buckley, H. Marchant, R. P. Buck, J. C. Hurlbut, F. H. Trowbridge, Geo. Thrall, H. W. Law, N. E. Smith, J. D. Cocks, F. E. Taylor, Joseph Greenwood, P. Waters, Mrs. Jenkins, Mrs. Beers, and Miss S. A. Russell.

For a detailed exhibit of the receipts of Knickerbocker Hall, acknowledgments to contributors, etc., see Appendix.

THE NEW ENGLAND KITCHEN.

IT was a most happy conception to reproduce at the Fair the old New England Kitchen, and faithfully was it carried out, to the unbounded mirth of the visitors, as well as to the great pecuniary profit of the Treasury. This was the *funny* feature of the Fair, and funny enough it was. The history of the New England Kitchen is as follows:

Early last fall a number of ladies of Brooklyn organized an association called the Sanitary Aid Society, the object being to work for the soldiers. At one of the meetings of this society, the subject of a Sanitary Fair was discussed. This was before any of the *great* Fairs had taken place.

It is singular to note that in several different quarters in Brooklyn this idea of a Grand Soldier's Fair was suggested before any steps of the kind had been taken elsewhere. When the ladies of the "Sanitary Aid" heard that a Fair had been resolved upon, they of course, abandoned their own project, and at once prepared to co-operate with the general movement. The plan of a New England Kitchen was broached, by Mrs. Ray Potter, President of the Sanitary Aid Society, and adopted with enthusiasm, and when the Committees of the Fair were appointed, a Special Committee was selected to take charge of the "New England Kitchen," comprising among its members the ladies and gentlemen who originated the plan. This committee took hold of the work *con amore*, their New England blood fired with the determination to make the

"Kitchen" a grand success, and to give to the particular project in hand a stamp of individuality and uniqueness which should render it at least as conspicuous as any department of the Fair.

The following extract from a Circular issued by the Committee, will explain the nature and scope of the project:

"The idea is to present a faithful picture of New England farm-house life of the last century. The grand old fire-place shall glow again—the spinning-wheel shall whirl as of old—the walls shall be garnished with the products of the forest and the field the quilting, the donation, and the wedding party shall assemble once more, while the apple-paring shall not be forgotten and the dinner-table, always set, shall be loaded with substantial New England cheer. We shall try to reproduce the manners, customs, dress, and if possible, the idiom of the time; in short, to illustrate the domestic life and habits of the people, to whose determined courage, sustained by their faith in God, we owe that government, so dear to every loyal heart. The period fixed upon is just prior to the throwing overboard of the tea in Boston Harbor."

It was originally contemplated to allow the projectors of the New England Kitchen a room in the rear of Knickerbocker Hall, 25x50 feet, which it was supposed would be ample for all its requirements. But this contracted space by no means accorded with the bold and sanguine views of the New Englanders, and they labored earnestly for the allotment of a larger space. It was finally agreed that, if the "Kitchen" Committee would guarantee a cash contribution of $1,200, to cover the additional expense, a larger building would be erected, giving them a space 40x100 feet. This amount was at once pledged, and the New England Kitchen was located under the same roof with the Hall of Manufactures, on the North side of Montague street, and opposite the Academy of Music. There was an entrance from Montague street, and also through the Hall of Manufactures, which communicated with the Grand Bazaar by the covered bridge heretofore mentioned. The main Kitchen, was 40x75 feet. The cooking-room, pantry, store-rooms and dressing-rooms occupied smaller apartments in the rear.

THE QUAINT FURNITURE AND APPOINTMENTS.

In this large room all the furniture and appointments were, as nearly as it was possible to have them, veritable antiques.

Long tables were laid in the centre of the room, for repasts in the New England style. The chairs on which the guests sat while eating, almost all had a history, and many of them were peculiarly interesting from their associations. One of these chairs was one hundred and fifty years old, and had been buried in the earth at the time of the Revolution to save it from the destroying hands of the enemy. Among the furniture in the kitchen was a table formerly belonging to Governor Bradford, a clock, whose face was smashed by a British bullet in the Revolution, and some oil paintings from the panels of the British frigate Guerriere, which Commodore Hull, in the Constitution, so gloriously captured. Many interesting trophies hung upon the walls, or were scattered about on the venerable tables. Among these was a rifle that belonged to Patrick Henry; several Bibles of the days of the Puritans; a canteen carried in the Revolutionary War; a file of the *Yankee* newspaper, published in Stonington, Ct., in 1826; an exact copy of the famous Newport *Mercury*, date 1760; the New England *Chronicle*, 1775 to 1778, containing an affidavit recounting the particulars of the Battle of Lexington; a piece of a bride's dress of a hundred years ago, and many other very interesting relics of "ye olden tyme."

On a platform in one corner were several ancient spinning-wheels, which had been exhumed from the rubbish of old family garrets, and here they hummed away as merrily as they were wont to do under the deft touches of the fingers that fed them with the snow white wool a century ago—fingers long since crumbled into dust.

The fire-place was, of course, an important feature of the Kitchen. It was of huge dimensions, and strictly after the old New England type. In its capacious mouth an ox might have been roasted with ease. From the traditional trammel, swung a gigantic pot, in which, from time to time, were cooked great messes of unctuous chowder, or steaming quantums of "mush." From the ovens at the side, emerged at stated periods spicy

Indian puddings smoking loaves of Boston brown bread, and famous dishes of pork-and-beans, crisped to delicious perfection.

The tables were covered with old-fashioned china, and the guests returned, under the rigid rule of the place, to the ante-silver-fork period, and had to content themselves with the two-tined steel. White sugar was religiously ignored, and "modern improvements" generally were at a discount. The idea was to live in the Past, and the Present was ignominiously banished. Many, before leaving the New England Kitchen, howsoever well satisfied with the new ways about us, were fain to conclude "the old is better." On the tables were bountiful supplies of toothsome viands—pork and beans, cider apple-sauce, Boston brown bread, pitchers of cider, pumpkin, mince, and apple pies, doughnuts, and all the savory and delicate wealth of the New England larder. The guests were waited upon by damsels with curious names and quaint attire. Just such New England girls as spread the cloths, and cut the loaves of a century ago, were the neat-handed waitresses of the New England Kitchen of the Brooklyn and Long Island Fair.

The venerable knitters in the corner, with their starched caps, and snowy kerchiefs crossed over the bosoms of their stuff gowns, the huge fire-place with its mighty logs, the dresser with its rows of shining pewter, the ever-ready churn, the tall clock sedately ticking in the corner, the ridge-poles strung with dried apples, pumpkins, glittering red peppers, seed-bags, and "yarbs" of healing virtues, the New England girls with their quaint costumes and uncouth speech—all made up a wonderfully striking scene, which, once behold, could not soon be forgotten. Now and then an Indian, hideous in horns and paint, would stalk solemnly through the crowd, and one could almost feel the scalp creep uneasily on his head, as he thought of those wild men of the forest, whose visits to the kitchens of our ancestors were not unfrequently the premonitions of the blazing home, and the midnight massacre.

A BEAUTIFUL WORK OF ART.

One of the most elegant ornaments of the Kitchen was an allegorical representation of the progress of our Republic, with a faithful portrait of President Lincoln in the centre, the whole being drawn with a pen and ink, by Mr. J. E. Payne, one of the Advisory Committee of the Kitchen. This elegant work of art was sold in one hundred shares of $5 each, and transmitted to Mr. Lincoln. Among the subscribers was Horace Greeley, who very much admired it during a visit to the Kitchen.

THE ENTERTAINMENTS IN THE KITCHEN.

When the New England Kitchen was opened, it was determined to give a series of entertainments in which should be reproduced some of the peculiar social customs of our ancestors. These were excellently arranged, and carried out in the following order:

THE OLD FOLKS' CONCERT.

This was presented simply to give an idea of the method of rendering the music of a century ago. The singers were in old-fashioned dress, and went through with a programme which included "The New Jerusalem," "Invitation," "Ode to Science," "Majesty," and other old fugue tunes, much to the edification and delight of the auditors. Two or three concerts were given on as many evenings.

THE DONATION VISIT

was held on Thursday evening, Feb. 25. The scenes of a giving visit to the Parson, in the olden time, being very humorously rendered.

THE QUILTING PARTY

was held on Saturday evening, Feb. 27, the "old folks" industriously stitching on the quilt during the afternoon, while the "young folks" were summoned in to close the evening with due festivity.

THE APPLE BEE

was given Wednesday evening, March 3d, and was one of the best of the series of entertainments given in the Kitchen.

Part of the Hutchinson family were present, and the company were treated to some excellent music. A fine personation of a lady of the olden time was given by a young lady of Brooklyn. In the course of the evening stories were narrated and riddles and conundrums propounded for the company to guess. The audience were treated to a plentiful supply of doughnuts, and the evening's entertainment was closed with the singing of the National Hymn.

THE WEDDING.

This was the grand crowning effort of the managers of the New England Kitchen to reproduce the manners and customs of the past age. It took place on Thursday evening, March 2, Rev. Jedediah Pounditext, (Rev. T. L. Cuyler) officiating in laced cocked hat and black knee-breeches. The bride and groom were Mr. and Mrs. David S. Holmes, of Williamsburgh. Refreshments were bountifully supplied to all present. One of the pleasing incidents of the occasion was the presentation of a mammoth frosted cake to the bride by the ladies of Knickerbocker Hall. The festivities of the evening were closed with dancing in which all joined merrily.

During the time the Kitchen was open, several interesting letters were received from distinguished persons, among whom were Vice-President Hamlin, Secretary Seward, and Edward Everett. The latter gave a graphic discription of the New England Kitchen in which he passed his boyhood.

A series of twelve stereoscopic pictures of scenes in the Kitchen, was taken by Mr. W. E. James, of 247 Fulton street.

The Kitchen was closed on Saturday night, March 5th, but the ladies of the Committee very generously re-opened it on Monday afternoon as an extemporized refreshment saloon, to supply the wants of the visitors to the Fair on Monday and Tuesday, Knickerbocker Hall having closed on Saturday.

The New England Kitchen was greatly cramped for room, and doubtless, had it had a space twice as large, it would have made a great deal more money. It was crowded constantly.

On the roll of honor for effective work in this department are Messrs. Goodrich, Coffin, Potter, Elwell, Murray, Kendall, Holmes; Mesdames, Swan, Cornell, W. B. Ackley, J. J. Couch, R. H. Manning, Plummer, Lambert, M. P. Mills, Wm. S. Murray, F. W. Leonard, Misses L. Rich, F. E. Cook, H. H. Daily, C. Dexter, Mrs. Peet, Manning, Misses Berry, Cook, Shepherd, Gault, Cochrane, Dix, the Misses Emerson, the Misses Watson, Mrs. Bicknell, Mrs. Brewster, Mrs. Stewart, Mrs. Moore, Mrs. Daily, Mrs. Holmes, Mrs. James.

A lady contributes to the Chicago *Journal* a very interesting account of the New England Kitchen, where she was one of the servers, which she closes as follows:

> In conclusion, I may say that I never enjoyed anything more than my five days work in the New England Kitchen. A more amiable, refined, sweet-tempered company of ladies never worked together, or in greater harmony. We felt mutual sorrow at parting, and bid each other good-bye, most affectionately, never expecting to meet again on earth. One was about to go to California, one to Chicago, one to Salem, Mass., one to West Pennsylvania, etc., etc. And so our little band broke up and scattered, and you would have thought, to have seen our parting, that we were friends of years' standing, and yet we parted under our assumed names, not knowing, except in a few instances, the real one. And very pleasant will it be for me, in after years, to hear myself addressed by my old name,
>
> EXPERIENCE.

THE HALL OF MANUFACTURES.

THE Hall of Manufactures was located, as we have observed, under the same roof with the New England Kitchen. It was a large frame apartment, 60x100, handsomely decorated with evergreens and flags, and filled with a very choice and valuable stock of goods.

On entering the Hall, through the covered bridge, from the Academy, the first object to be noticed on the right, was a soda-fountain erected by Mr. George Reynolds, of 260 Court street. Directly in front, and stretching the entire length of the Hall, was a table on which was exhibited every variety of housekeeping goods, of wood, tin, brittania, etc. On this table were also trunks, leather, rubber goods, a small steam engine, skates, guns and revolvers, and a host of other articles.

THE SEWING MACHINE DEPARTMENT was a very valuable one, nearly all the manufacturers of that now indispensable article having contributed to the Fair. The machines were arranged on a raised platform extending the entire length of the room, and their merry clatter made a pleasant variation from the incessant clamor of the crowd. There were other musical sounds in this Hall, Messrs. Mason & Hamlin having donated several of their parlor organs, which were never silent.

The "Burglar Alarm Telegraph," also kept up an unceasing silvery ding dong from its corner. There were two elegantly finished boats, several carriages, a large assortment of stoves, grates and heaters, any quantity of "hobby horses" and childrens' carriages, there were lamp and gas fixtures, chamber furniture, rustic seats, metallic coffins, paints, grindstones, agricultural implements, soap, hams, starch, flour, saddles, harness, hardware, stove blacking, marble-top washstands, an elegant pleasure boat from T. S. Dick, of Greenpoint, and another from H. T. Rigby, of East Warren street, there were machine-saws, casks and barrels, hay-press, cotton gin, fancy chairs, steam engine worth $700, from Hubbard & Whittaker, Union lamps, steam pumps, clothes mangles, and a thousand other useful and beautiful articles, all most tastefully and attractively arranged under the direction of Messrs. White & Nichols, of No. 208 Fulton street, who had general charge of this important room. The Grocery Department was under the skilful charge of Mr. Waring, of Fulton street. Two large Committees, one from the Eastern and one from the Western District, embracing many of our leading manufacturers and business men, had the collection of contributions for this Hall under their charge, and most effectively did they perform their duty. The names of these committees will be found in the Appendix. Too much praise cannot be given to Mr. White, cashier, ex-Alderman Jenkins, and W. W. Armfield, E. D., for their active efforts in this department.

SOME OF THE NOTABLE CONTRIBUTIONS.

The proprietors of the Universal Clothes-Wringer early made to the Fair the magnificent donation of five hundred of their excellent seven dollar machines. The agent of the Putnam Clothes-Wringer also contributed to the Fair as many of the machines as could be sold. These machines were deposited in Mechanics' Hall, where they could at any time be seen in practical operation. Another very useful article was Hawse's Patent Clothes-Dryer, which gave many of our housekeepers a "new wrinkle" in the clothes drying art, and which was only smoothed out by an incontinent purchase of the machine.

SOME OF THE FRUITS OF FREE-LABOR.

In this Hall were also exhibited a bale of cotton, made on the Sea Islands of South Carolina, by free labor, and contributed to the Fair at the solicitation of Albert G. Browne, Esq., supervising special agent of the Treasury Department at Beaufort, by E. S. Philbrick, Esq., agent of a New England planting company at Hilton Head. This cotton was fully equal to the best ever raised by slave labor, and was sold for $504, being rather more than its market value. There was another bale of free-labor cotton from New Orleans, together with a hogshead of sugar, and a barrel of molasses, all the gift of Hon. B. F. Flanders, supervising special agent of the Treasury Department; and also a hogshead of splendid free-labor sugar, sent by Messrs. Brott & Davis, of New Orleans, who, in transmitting it, wrote:

During the past year we have carried on thirteen plantations in the neighborhood of this city, and on all of them our laborers have either been employed at a fixed price for their services per month or by a proportion of the profits of the several crops; and now, in the closing of their accounts, we give ready testimony to the zeal, intelligence, and application of the negroes who have been in our employ, and the pecuniary success of the enterprise has been such as to amply justify us in leasing a larger number of plantations for the coming year.

It is also with us a matter of great interest that the Brooklyn Fair should, if possible, eclipse any of its predecessors for a similar purpose. Two of the partners of our house were for many years residents of the good "City of Churches," and though now citizens of the other extremity of the Union, have lost none of their interest in the concerns of their late home.

Wishing yourself and your associates in this benevolence the greatest success,

We remain yours, most respectfully, BROTT & DAVIS.

This sugar was sold readily for twenty cents per pound. It may well be believed that these tide-marks of the advancing wave of Freedom which is sweeping Slavery from this continent, were contemplated with at least as much interest and satisfaction as any other contributions to the Fair.

THE CINCINNATI BROOM.

In the centre of Mechanics' Hall was hung a mammoth broom, forwarded from Cincinnati to the Fair, with the following challenge to Brooklyn: "Sent by the Managers of the Cincinnati Fair, greeting: We have swept up $240,000;

Brooklyn, beat this if you can." To this, as soon as the magnificent result of our Fair began to loom up so that an approximate estimate could be made, some "sporting" member of the Committee on Manufactures appended the following addenda:

"Brooklyn *sees* the $240,000, and *goes* $150,000 *better*."

THE DEPOT OF THE WOMAN'S RELIEF ASSOCIATION.

The depot of the Woman's Relief Association, removed for the nonce from No. 6 Court street, was located in the Hall of Manufactures, where it occupied a snug corner, enclosed by a low railing. Here the processes of preparing and packing goods for the soldiers' and hospital use went forward unremittingly, cases containing some five thousand garments being on hand in the depot.

Thoughtful visitors to the Fair regarded this quiet spot with a rare and affectionate interest, for there was to be seen a glimpse of the inner life of this terrible struggle—the undercurrent, that, moved by the heavenly love and charity of woman, flows pure and strong and steady beneath the bloody, turbid tide of war. Here was to be seen the proof that the soldiers of the Republic are not alone the manly braves who bear up her glorious banner where blows fall thickly, and shrilly hum the bees of death, but that there are other soldiers working and fighting with woman's sublime constancy and faith, and a courage that endures when the hearts of strong men faint and fail—working with woman's weapons of purse, and needle, and encouragement and *prayer*, for the cause that is dearer than life. As the sweetest flowers of the forest, the early violets of Spring, nestle in the most secluded nooks, and are only traced by the incense they cannot conceal, so woman's part in this great struggle for nationality and freedom is performed out of sight, and is only known by the fruits it bears. It is not too much to say that, but for woman's hand, and woman's heart sustaining the national cause, that cause would ere this have sunk in gloom and blood.

With the women of our land so nearly a unit in patriotic devotion to that cause, it must surely prevail, and, by the grace of God helping us, it *shall* prevail. Already more than one noble woman has laid down her life from excessive labor in behalf of the Great Charity to which the Brooklyn and Long Fair ministered.* When the history of this War is written its most shining page will be that which records the faith, the courage, and the love of Woman, which fortified and blessed our Nation in its day of trial.

To the battle's bloodiest marge,
Where the foemen thickest charge,
And the flags of Freedom wave;
Where the cannon's crimson lips
Roar along the flaming ships,
Honor flies to crown the brave.

But the brightest crown she hath
Who, with woman's heavenly faith—
Girding weapon to his thigh—
Lest the holy cause should fail,
And her country's foes prevail,
Sends her dearest forth to die.

* Mrs. Caroline M. Kirkland, the favorite authoress, and Mrs. David Dudley Field, both lost their lives through excessive and exhausting labors for the New York Fair.

THE MUSEUM OF ARTS, RELICS AND CURIOSITIES.

THIS unique and interesting department of the Fair occupied the Taylor Mansion, on the corner of Montague and Clinton streets. Here were collected a vast number of relics of priceless value, which are cherished by their owners as more precious than rubies or diamonds, brought out to add to the attractions of this great effort in behalf of the National Charity, and most of which the public will probably never have another opportunity of seeing. Then there were the torn and battle-stained flags of many of our noble Union Regiments, side by side with numerous trophies wrested from Rebellion, on the historic fields, and in the glorious sea-fights of the war. China, India, Japan, and the Islands of the sea, also contributed of their rare and wonderful products to enrich and adorn this Grand Collection.

THE MUSEUM BUILDING.

On entering, on the left, the visitor found a small room where were collected a large number of paintings and other works of Art, contributed for sale. Some of these were of considerable merit. A catalogue will be found in the Appendix. Here, also, was exhibited the Album of Sketches by Amateur Artists, heretofore described.

In the main rooms, or parlors, on the first floor, was located the grand collection of Curiosities and Relics. To give an adequate idea of the wonders of this apartment, we must refer the reader to the catalogue in the Appendix. The unequaled collection of Washington relics, the mementoes of Chief Justice Jay, and the superb case of Mrs. St. John were constantly surrounded by eager, interested throngs.

On the same floor, on the other side of the hall, was the room devoted to the exhibition of Army trophies and mementoes. One of the most interesting features of this room was a collection of the various descriptions and sizes of shot and shell used by the Union and Rebel forces. The antique arms exhibited were also very curious. In this little apartment the visitor found himself face to face with grim-visaged War. But, after all, he only saw here a few waifs that had drifted out from the bloody turmoil in which our fathers, husbands, sons and brothers are surging, in this war for National life. It is one thing to contemplate with calmly curious gaze a few torn and scorched banners, and to handle a harmless fragment of shell which has once crashed through the side of a gunboat, but it is quite another to charge through the withering blaze of musketry that had to be faced by our gallant boys before they could call that miserable rag their own, or to hear the dreadful howl of the invisible shell as it comes, laden with death, to the crowded deck. There were lessons to be learned in that little room, and he was no true man whose prayers did not thence arise that God would, in His infinite mercy, bless and protect our gallant soldiers and sailors.

On the second floor, the three front rooms were fitted up as a Gallery of Engravings. The Sub-Committee on Engravings, consisting of Messrs. John M. Falconer, Chairman, Charles Congdon, Henry Ward Beecher, Charles Burt, S. P. Avery, and Chas. Parsons, determined that this department of the Fair should not be excelled in interest and beauty. An extract from their circular to Artists and Collectors, says:

"No public Exhibition of Engravings has ever taken place on this Continent, to our knowledge. Seeking to initiate such, we ask you to place at our disposal a part of the ample material that exists. We want, if possible, as Donations or on Loan, a full representation of the Chalcographic Art, from its most ancient date down to the latest discoveries and inventions of the day. It may be classified, viz:

Line, Mezzotint, Stipple, Mixed Engravings,
Etchings, Lithographs, Wood Engravings, Color Printings.

Also, Artistic Photographs, when choice and important in subject.

In every instance the Choicest Impressions are sought, and, if possible, framed under glass—failing these, prints from the portfolio will be acceptable. The greatest possible care will be taken of their surface and margins, in arranging and returning them when desired. Insurance will be effected when required."

The result was the finest collection of Engravings ever seen on this Continent. Rev. Henry Ward Beecher lent to the project his rare enthusiasm and electric force and spirit. He placed at the disposal of the Committee his own collection of choice proof Engravings—perhaps the finest in our city, and equaled by few elsewhere. Messrs. C. Burt, W. H. Swan, and J. M. Falconer, also contributed very largely to the collection, Mr. Swan contributing many of the best for sale. The variety, extent, and merit of this Gallery of Engravings can only be estimated by a study of the Catalogue which we reproduce in the Appendix.

A room next the Gallery of Engravings was occupied by a splendid collection of Eastern curiosities, Chinese and Japanese wares, etc. This room contained, of itself, material demanding a day's attentive examination and study.

In a small room on the same floor were some of Robert Fulton's models and drawings. These were exhibited by Chas. W. Copeland, Esq., the eminent civil engineer of this city. There was also in this room an elegant and complete working model of a pontoon train—wagons, boats, bridges, etc., constructed by the Engineer Corps of General Benham expressly for the Fair. This interesting and valuable model was purchased for presentation to the Brooklyn Polytechnic Institute.

On the second floor was also a room devoted to the sale of photographs, *cartes de visite*, moss, cone and leather work, seaweeds, collections of autumn leaves, and a large number of other articles which could not well be classified in any particular department of the Fair. Among the contributors to the large assortment of photographs—which comprised portraits of all our leading generals and public men, and copies of celebrated works of art—were Messrs. Sherman, Moran, and Brady. Mr. Sherman contributed superb colored imperial photographs of Rev. Drs. Storrs, Littlejohn, and Farley. Mr. Brady contributed large and elegant photographs of A. A. Low, Esq., and his Honor, Mayor A. M. Wood. All of the above photographers also gave a large number of orders for photographs to be sold to visiters to the Fair. The Brooklyn Institute contributed fifty photographic copies of "Brooklyn fifty years ago."

THE AUTOGRAPH ROOM.

Retired as was the modest room appropriated to the exhibition and sale of Autographs, and devoid as it was of any gaud or glitter to attract the crowd, it was speedily discovered by the thoughtful and appreciative, the antiquary and the student, that its narrow compass embraced a wealth which was, perhaps, paralleled by no apartment in the entire building.

Of Autograph Albums there were several conspicuous for tasteful and sumptuous binding, and more than one containing such autographic treasures as are rarely clasped between the covers of any single collection. Among the most noteworthy was an album contributed by Miss Mary C. Jarvis, containing patriotic sentiments and poems—many of them written expressly for the collection—from Bayard Taylor, Fitz-Greene Halleck, Rev. Dr. Muhlenberg, Geo. H. Boker, Ralph Waldo Emerson, Walter Channing, T. S. Arthur, Rev. A. Cleveland Cox, Hon. William H. Seward, J. Lothrop Motley, Charles Sumner, Major-General B. F. Butler, Major-General A. E. Burnside, Brigadier-General Anderson, Major-General Geo. B. McClellan, General O. M. Mitchell, Rear Admiral J. A. Dahlgren, Capt. John L. Worden, Edward Everett, Hon. John P. Kennedy, J. T. Headley, James Russell Lowell, William Cullen Bryant, Henry W. Longfellow, John G. Whittier, Henry T. Tuckerman, O. W. Holmes, John G. Saxe, Parke Godwin, George William Curtis, J. G. Holland, Donald G.

Mitchell, Nathaniel Hawthorne, James Parton, Regis Gignoux, Caroline Chesebro, Elizabeth T. Porter Beach, Mrs. L. H. Sigourney, "Fanny Fern," Mrs. Harriet Beecher Stowe, Dr. Hitchcock, F. D. Huntington, Horace Greeley, John Minor Botts, Rev. Dr. Farley, and others. Most of the contributions to the album were accompanied by private notes from those sending them, full of expressions of sympathy with and interest in the great object of the Fair.

It is a matter of regret that so few of the visitors to the Fair had an opportunity to examine this valuable album, as it was sold as soon as presented for exhibition, and removed at once. It brought two hundred dollars.

Miss Jarvis contributed another album scarcely second to the first in value, and, to many, of far greater interest. This contained autographic copies of the prayers composed for parochial use by the loyal Bishops of the Protestant Episcopal Church in the United States, touching the present grievous national crisis. This was sold for the sum of one hundred and fifty dollars. Mr. Geo. A. Jarvis contributed fifty lithographic copies of the prayers, which were readily sold at $3 each. Among Mr. Jarvis's contributions to this department was a letter of Benedict Arnold, and an autograph copy of Mr. Seward's famous despatch to Mr. Dayton upon the subject of French recognition of the Rebel Confederacy. Mr. George Jarvis, Sr., contributed an album containing autographic copies of the last Thanksgiving Proclamations of the loyal governors, the number being very nearly complete. Miss Kate Ripley presented a beautiful album, containing contributions from nearly all our best-known American poets, many of the pieces being composed for the book. This fine collection brought two hundred dollars. Miss Clara C. Harrison contributed an album, containing autographs of the statesmen of our country; and Mr. L. B. Wyman contributed a superbly bound album, containing autographs of a large number of public men, and all the members of the present Congress, which was sold for two hundred and fifty dollars.

Among the other autographs were letters from John Wesley, several of Washington, (one of which was to Franklin,) Walter Scott, Uncas, Israel Putnam, William Prince of Orange, Duke of Alva, Queen Elizabeth, and John Brown's last letter to his cousin, of which lithographed copies were for sale. Mr. J. Carson Brevoort exhibited a very interesting relic, being a letter of Hannah Arnold, mother of Benedict Arnold, to her son. Mr. William Kemble exhibited fac-simile copies of all the papers found upon Major Andre when captured by the American Scouts on the Hudson. Among other contributors to the Autographic Department were Messrs. Henry Ward Beecher, Ex-Governor John A. King, Theodore Dwight, Samuel Coleman, Gordon L. Ford, D. C. Kellogg, Governeur Morris, Mrs. J. R. St. John, Mrs. Annie Messenger and many more.

Among the ladies and gentlemen whose services were conspicuous in the collection, arrangement, exhibition, and sale of the articles in the Museum, were Mrs. S. B. Chittenden, Chairman of the Ladies, and Mr. E. S. Mills, Chairman of the Gentleman's Committees on Arts, Relics and Curiosities, Mrs. A. Henshaw, Mrs. Gordon L. Ford, Mrs. J. O. Low, Mrs. Chas. Congdon, Mrs. J. F. Howard, Mrs. Captain John L. Worden, Mrs. Captain Radford, Miss Cooper, Miss Rebecca Paulding, Mrs. William M. Richards, Miss Mary Stranahan, Mrs. A. C. Rossiere, Mrs. J. R. St. John, Mrs. Wm. St. John, Miss Sarah Luquear, Miss C. M. Olcott, Mrs. Henry A. Dike, Misses Eliza and Kate Ripley, Miss Kate Taylor, Miss Emma F. Wallace, Mrs. Edward Butler, and others. Messrs. J. M. Falconer and C. Burt hung the Engravings, and Mr. P. Ryder the Pictures in the sales room. Mr. Gordon L. Ford was of great service in the Autograph Room, and Messrs. John W. Frothingham, R. W. Hubbard and A. M. Muir, rendered valuable aid in many ways.

THE DRUM-BEAT.

THIS was the first attempt made at any of the Sanitary Fairs, to issue a daily newspaper. It is true, at some of the previous Fairs, Printing Presses were erected and in operation, from which daily bulletins were issued, but these were more for the purpose of showing the working of the press than with an idea of making a *bona fide* journal. In the Brooklyn and Long Island Fair a bolder project was conceived, being nothing less than the issue of a daily morning paper, with all its appointments complete. The following extract from the prospectus, issued by the Committee having the matter in charge, will show the design and scope of the proposed paper:

It will be under the editorial charge of REV. R. S. STORRS, JR., D. D., assisted by competent writers and reporters; and original contributions are already promised for its columns by eminent writers. In addition to articles original and selected, and a department of entertaining miscellany, it will contain a complete Directory to the Fair, and a daily report of the sales, incidents, and general chit-chat of the previous day.

The committee hope and believe that it will be a spirited and interesting paper, gladly welcomed and freely purchased by the patrons of the Fair, and distributed by them to their friends and correspondents in other parts of the country.

It will be printed on a sheet of eight pages of nearly the same size and general style with the pages of the "*Army and Navy Journal*," and sold for five cents per copy; and the committee hope for a daily circulation of eight to ten thousand copies. * * *

The committee are happy to say that such arrangements have been made for the publication of the paper, that *every dollar* received for advertisements will go directly, *without diminution*, into the Treasury of the Sanitary Commission.

Applications for advertisements may be made either at the office of the "Union," No. 10 Front street, Brooklyn, or of Messrs. Charlsley & Hatch, Bankers, No. 24 Wall street, N. Y.

S. B. CALDWELL, W. T. HATCH, J. M. VAN COTT,
CHAS. NORDHOFF, A. S. BARNES, *Committee*.

BROOKLYN, February, 1864.

The editorship of the paper was, as appears by the prospectus, offered to Rev. R. S. Storrs Jr., D. D. who generously undertook the onerous charge, associating with himself Mr. Francis Williams, City Editor of the New York *Evening Post*, who prepared for each day's issue a "Record of the Fair," written in the chaste and graphic style for which he is distinguished.

The first number of the *Drum-Beat* was issued on Monday morning, Feb. 22d, and the paper was issued daily thereafter, the last regular number appearing on Saturday morning, March 5th. A supplementary number was also issued on Friday, March 11. Each number contained twenty-four wide columns. The first page bore an appropriate vignette. The typographical appearance of the paper was universally commended.

Those who know anything of the difficulties which beset the establishment of a newspaper enterprise must concede that the *Drum-Beat*, considering especially the magnitude of the task undertaken, was most creditable to the industry and editorial ability of its distinguished conductor. Its columns were daily filled with interesting matter, nearly the whole of which was prepared for the paper. Among the contributors were some of the most eminent literary men of the country, although, unfortunately, some of the best things sent came too late for use. A regular and brilliant contributor to the paper was Captain R. W. Raymond, who wrote a series of articles over the signature "Augustus Watts," describing his "Experience of the Great Fair," which added not a little to the attractiveness and variety of the paper.

The principle adopted by the editor of the *Drum-Beat* in the conduct of the paper was to make it not merely an amusing trifle, to bring in by its sale a certain number of dollars to the Fair, and not even merely a compendium of choice literary reading to gratify the cultured taste. It was to make it, as far as possible, *an effective agent to keep alive, and augment the popular interest and the popular efforts in behalf of the Fair.* To this end its editorials and selected articles all tended, aiming to present the claims of our soldiers upon the sympathy and support of the nation in the strongest possible light. It was intended to be, and was, a vigorous and earnest *lay preacher* in behalf of the Sanitary Commission, and the great work in hand. None will deny that it did excellent service in this direction. The daily circulation averaged about six thousand copies.

Among the noticeable features of the *Drum-Beat* were its humorous illustrations, one or more appearing every day, generally of subjects *apropos* to the Fair. These were mainly from designs by some of our best comic artists, Messrs. McLenan, Bellew, Muller, and Beard; a number were from the pencil of a talented young lady, formerly a resident of this city.

The history of the *Drum-Beat* would be incomplete did we fail to notice the fact that the entire cost of the type-setting and printing was assumed by S. B. Chittenden, Esq., one of the members of the Executive Committee of the Fair.

We should also note that much of the success of the paper was due to the able management of its business department, by Messrs. Samuel B. Caldwell and W. T. Hatch, while the entire Committee, whose names are given above, were assiduous in their efforts to make it both a pecuniary success and an honor to the Fair.

THE CATTLE SHOW.

A cattle-show was not wanting to complete the interest of the Brooklyn and Long Island Fair. A splendid Durham Bull, presented by Elias Howe, Jr., occupied a comfortable stable near the New England Kitchen: he was sold by shares for $500. The pair of Steers promised by Mr. S. B. Chittenden were promptly forthcoming, and were sold at auction in front of the Academy on February 28th, for $295.

THE CALICO BALL.

IT was determined, as the Fair was drawing to a close, to terminate it with a grand "Calico Ball," the proceeds of which were to be appropriated to the Brooklyn Female Employment Society, to be disbursed for the benefit of the soldiers' families. Accordingly, on Tuesday evening, March 8th, a meeting of gentlemen was held in the Directors' Room of the Academy, to take the necessary steps for the Ball. After some discussion as to time, etc., the following resolution, offering by W. W. Goodrich, was unanimously adopted:

Resolved, That it is deemed advisable to have a Calico Ball, the same to be held on Friday evening of the present week, the proceeds of which shall be applied for the relief of the families of the soldiers of Brooklyn, and be paid into the hands of I. H. Frothingham, Esq., for that purpose.

The resolution was unanimously adopted.

It was then resolved that a Committee of one hundred should be appointed to carry out the object and purpose of the foregoing resolution.

Mr. McLean was unanimously selected as Chairman of the Committee.

The following Committees were subsequently chosen:

FLOOR COMMITTEE—Col. J. B. Woodward, Chairman. D. W. Van Ingen, W. L. Ogden, H. G. Cullen, Jr., W. R. Bunker, H. C. Ward, C. B. Hunter, W. C. Smith, S. P. Hurlbut, C. Hadden, Jr., Joseph O. Stury, W. A. McKee, C. P. Gulick, R. B. Woodward, F. A. Baldwin, Philip H. Briggs, A. H. Williams, James B. Bawbs, A. S. Gatche, Joseph Howard, Jr., H. D. Polhemus.

REFRESHMENT COMMITTEE—E. H. Stephenson, Chairman. Wm. H. Banker, B. F. Wyman, W. L. Ogden.

RECEPTION COMMITTEE—C. W. Blossom, Chairman. A. Mewer, A. McCue, Jos. B. Blossom, R. R. Lawrence, A. E. Sumner, J. L. B. Willard, Geo. D. Puffer, A. Degroman, Jr., W. W. Goodrich.

PRINTING COMMITTEE—S. G. Butler, Chairman. J. W. Cronson.

The ball was given with great *eclat* on Friday evening, March 11th. More than half the ladies wore in plain calico dresses. The music was furnished by Sanger's and Dodworth's Bands. The supper was served under the direction of Mr. Charles Varick, in Knickerbocker Hall, and it was the last of its glories. Henceforth it was

> "A banquet hall deserted,
> Its lights all fled, its garlands dead."

The Ball netted about two thousand dollars for the worthy object for which it was given. After the Ball, many of the ladies who were present sent their calico dresses to the Academy to be given to the soldiers' wives and daughters.

ACKNOWLEDGMENT TO THE PRESS.

IN CLOSING this History of the Brooklyn and Long Island Fair, it is but appropriate, as well as an act of simple justice to allude to the great services rendered the enterprise by the Public Press of the City, in both the Eastern and Western Districts, and throughout the Island. We express not only the feeling of the Executive Officers of the Fair, both Ladies and Gentlemen, but that of the entire community, when we recognize the fact that to the cordial support of the undertaking by the Press of the City and Island, during the preparatory steps, and the copious and graphic daily reports furnished by the city papers during the progress of the Fair, its great success was in a large measure due. While the press of the neighboring Metropolis—with a few honorable exceptions, of which should be particularly noted the *Evening Post*, which gave several very excellent notices of the Fair—to a large degree ignored our undertaking, the duty of awakening and keeping alive the popular enthusiasm devolved almost entirely upon the local Press, and most nobly and efficiently did they perform their work. In contrasting the results of the Great Metropolitan Fair just closed, with those of the effort of Brooklyn and Long Island, let it be remembered that, while the latter had the advantage of the support of the great Metropolitan Journals, which circulate all over the country, reaching even to lands beyond the sea, and thus interesting and impelling multitudes from abroad to contribute to its success, we were in a great measure cut off from these important aids. That a success so magnificent crowned our efforts, notwithstanding this drawback, is certainly a most significant tribute to the power and influence of our Press. Had we received the assistance that was reasonably expected from the Metropolitan papers, which are not wont to neglect events transpiring at their own doors of the magnitude and importance of the Brooklyn and Long Island Fair, it is highly probable the latter would have proved even a more formidable competitor than it did with the Metropolis and its numerous aids, for the honor of having produced the greatest of the Sanitary Fairs.

With a desire, therefore, for only that which is our rightful honor, it is but fair and just to claim for Brooklyn and Long Island, considering the amount of their population and the auxiliaries at command, that they have eclipsed all efforts yet made in aid of the United States Sanitary Commission.

IN CONCLUSION,

We felicitate our fellow citizens of Brooklyn and Long Island on the successful inauguration, progress, and results of our Great Sanitary Fair. Our preparations were made under the most auspicious circumstances, and with active and experienced agencies, to which we referred in the beginning, to form the germ of the thorough and efficient organization, under whose care it was conducted. The very heavens seemed to smile on us. At a season which with us is usually marked by severe cold, and often as severe storms, the large temporary buildings which were required in addition, to the Academy of Music and the Taylor Mansion, were erected almost to their completion under uniformly bright and genial skies, and not a casualty of any kind marred or saddened for a moment the progress of the work. The day of the opening was specially beautiful, rendering the military parade most agreeable to the men under arms, and to the throngs who beheld it. During the entire fortnight of the Fair, there was scarcely a day in which it was not pleasant to be abroad, and the same exemption from untoward accidents as attended these preparations continued to its close. Every individual among the multitudes who attended it seemed to regard it as a great Festival of Love, and to reciprocate the kindliest sympathies. When we speak of its results, we primarily refer to the Four Hundred Thousand Dollars it poured into the Treasury of the United States Sanitary Commission, for the care and relief of our sick and suffering soldiers. Thus viewed, they are goodly and grand. But the Island and its chief City will inevitably, unless grossly unfaithful to themselves, realize much more and greater. Brooklyn, especially, has seized and secured new vantage ground for future consideration and respect throughout the land, and for the truest greatness, attractiveness, and enjoyment within herself. She has nobly illustrated her resources. She has shown the taste, the wealth, the co-operative energy of her population. She has proved incontestibly the generous loyalty of her citizens. Now let her be faithful to the great trust, which, as an unavoidable inference, is in her hands. Whatever she needs in Institutions of Art, Learning or Charity, to make her, in a far higher sense than that of mere numbers, wealth, and growth, a great city, she shows to the world she has ability to possess. And if this Fair, in its great proportions and eminent success is appreciated by her citizens as it deserves, its future and best results will be found in the fresh and permanent impulse given to every wise purpose and plan for increasing the attractiveness of Brooklyn as a place of residence; paving in the best way, cleaning, and keeping clean the streets; improving and extending the Public Parks; perfecting the Civic and Sanitary Police; liberally fostering, and increasing the grades of the Public Schools, creating and sustaining a Great Public Library, and Schools and Galleries of Science and Art, and permanently endowing her admirable institutions of benevolence. The salubrity and loveliness of her superb territorial position will then be but the type of what should and may be hers—the proud pre-eminence of a model American and Republican city.

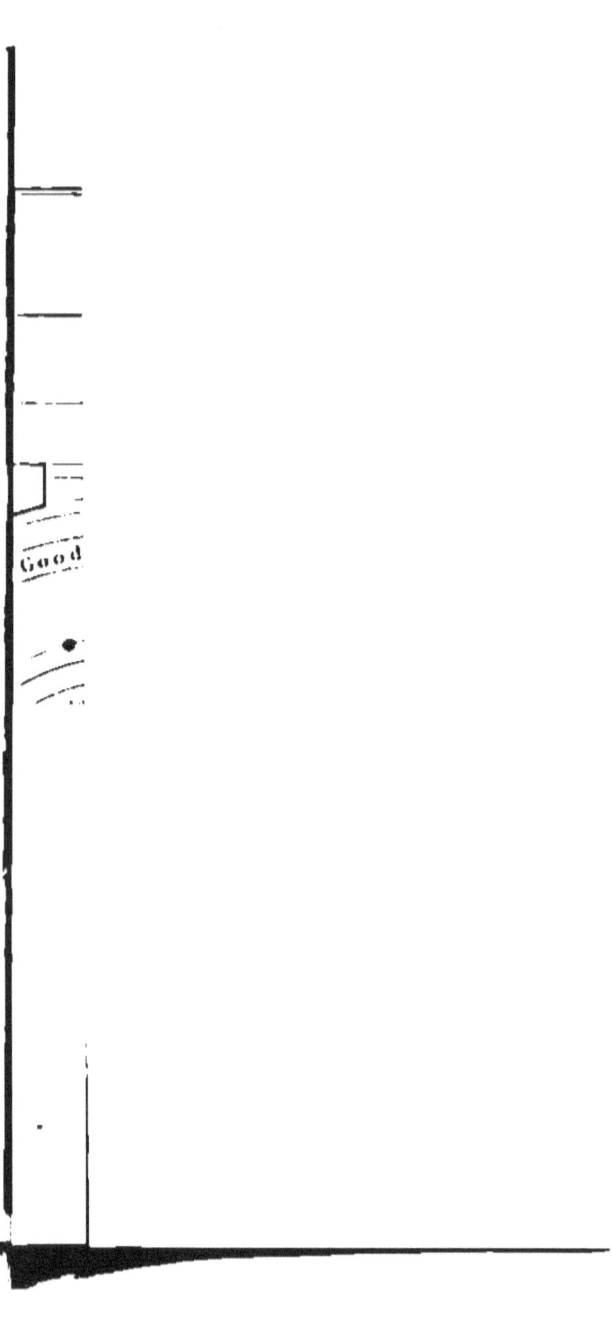
Good

APPENDIX.

APPENDIX.

Officers of the Brooklyn and Long Island Fair.

LADIES' GENERAL COMMITTEE,

WESTERN DISTRICT,

MRS. J. S. T. STRANAHAN, PRESIDENT.

CONGREGATIONAL CHURCHES.

Pilgrim Church.—Mrs. R. S. Storrs, R. P. Buck, James P. Dike, Camden Dike, James Humphrey, J. P. Robinson, Geo. Mygatt, Seymour Burrill, Ch. B. Caldwell, Cur Adams, John Bullard, Jr., W. T. Hatch, A. B. Hall, Sidney Green, E. E. James, Timo. D. Vail, A. F. Goodnow, J. H. Rodman, L. P. Kellogg, J. Balkley, Dwight Johnson, A. C. Brownell. Misses Emma Buck, Mary Hyde, Helen Phelps, Alice Gray, Mary James, Misses Green, Fannie Marsh, Laura P. Marsh, Emily Fish, Mary Sharpe, Josephine Mall.

Plymouth Church. Mrs. H. W. Beecher, R. R. Graves, Henry Dike, Henry Collins, Chas. Dennis, M. K. Moody, H. P. Ludlum, J. T. Howard, Robert R. Raymond, Charles F. Blake, G. W. Bergen, Aug. Storrs, A. H. Garland, G. G. Spencer, M. S. Beach, A. Fitzgerald, Chas. Parret, J. A. Newbold, D. S. Arnold, W. Wise, J. A. Ely, M. P. Brown, S. C. Fales, G. H. Livingston, John Bliss, Jr., L. Benedict, S. B. Benedict, J. Fanning, G. A. Bell, Daniels and daughters, E. E. Bowen, Jos. Howard, W. Gordon, J. B. Merwin, C. B. Camp, J. G. Voigt, Fuller, J. B. Murray, A. McCallum, S. Conant, Thos. Bird, D. Fanning, W. Kent, E. A. Tricady, R. Seagrave, H. E. Mathews, H. Morrill, Woodbridge, A. Graves. Misses A. Noble, Hinman, Duryea.

Clinton Avenue Church.—Mrs. A. S. Barnes, S. H. Brown, Henry Jones, Barnett, C. Knight, D. B. Dearborn, M. Packard, L. Andrews, Wm. Moses, Geo. S. Coe, C. P. Dixon, C. C. Woolworth, S. E. Warner, J. A. Dayton.

South Congregational Church.—Mrs. H. Heath, D. L. Barnes, J. L. Brownell, Jas. T. Bailey, J. B. Swift, Packer, J. Winston, A. Isaacs.

Central Congregational Church.—Mrs. J. C. French, H. J. Rice, H. M. Peckham, E. R. McIlvaine. Miss Carrie Pratt.

Tabernacle.—Mrs. William A. Bartlett, Samuel D. Crosby, Hy. Elliott, Miss Elizabeth Burke.

Church of the Saviour (Unitarian.)—Mrs. F. A. Farley, Ed. Anthony, W. S. Tisdale, A. M. White, J. E. Watkins, I. H. Frothingham, J. Atkins, O. W. Jennings, C. P. Sanger, S. H. Low, E. Blunt, S. W. Slocum, J. O. Low, H. B. Duryea, D. D. Badger, J. R. Jewett, T. Victor, Jas. Littlejohn, I. R. St. John, L. Bierwirth, Jas. W. Law, H. Trost, Hy. Poor, Hy. Kelley, George S. Cary, H. B. Duryea, Hy. Jessop, W. H. McCluney, C. F. Leavitt, Ann W. Cromwell, O. W. Baxter, H. E. Nesmith, William Lombard, A. D. Hall. Misses Kate Treadway, E. Victor, A. M. Farley, Allen B. Cary, E. Blunt, F. Boyd, J. Jessup.

Second Unitarian Church.—Mrs. H. H. Warden, D. Fairbanks, Wm. B. Kendall, John Norton, Jr., J. Hillard, H. H. Manning, P. Shaw, D. Brigham, Daniell, N. A Staples, Marcus, Greene, J. Maxwell, S. T. Clarke, E. Atkins, E. K. Whittlesey, W. Beare, F. Strong, Misses L. Arnold, Olcott.

Hon. Gibson, Swan, W. W. Rose, Beam, Cornell, Blackwell, Francis Knight, Halliday, Chas. Peters. Misses Sarah Boynton, Halsey, J. Beckmaster, J. M. Spear, Abbey, S. Thompson.

Westminster.—Mrs. Capen, Welch, Babcock, Rust, J. Edwards, Lawman, Jos. Radner, W. P. Dean, Lambert, H. S. Carpenter, W. A. Doubleday, J. Worth, Miss McMullen.

Greene Avenue.—Mrs. S. B. Brown, Anna Longson.

Reformed.—Mrs. A. McClellan, Madean.

DUTCH REFORMED CHURCHES.

First.—Mrs. Theodore Polhemus, John Herriman, Wm. Fowler, George W. Dow, Edward P. Beach, W. S. Herriman, A. D. Polhemus, Clerc, Waldron, H. Starr, J. W. Spader, Rockwell, Heddenburgh, Edward Newton, Lawrence, J. Adams, Lowber, James Morse, Warren Gray, Hart, E. H. Barker. Misses Suydam, Mary Moon.

Church on the Heights.—Mrs. Miller, Geo. S. Stephenson, Amos Robbins, Peter Duryea, James Myers, Schoonmaker, Orr, Lowe, Gregg, Hoyt, Taylor. Misses Smith, Mattocks, Clark, Louisa Van Ingen, Caroline Thurston.

Harrison Street.—Mrs. N. E. Smith, Akerman, Bal, Cromwell, L. Johnson, James A. Degraw. Misses Hotchkiss, Holmes.

North.—Mrs. Elmendorf, John P. Elwell, D. McDonald, Rd. Williams, Albert Brett, Higgins, Pierce, Imlay, Charters, Stone, Harrison. Misses Mary Williams, Carrie Evarts.

East.—Mrs. Wiggins, Gelhart, Dow. Misses Prior, Hopper.

South.—Mrs. T. S. Barholen, D. Bergen. Miss Mary Bergen.

METHODIST CHURCHES.

Sands Street.—Mrs. George Vining, Robt. Powell, Daniel Fairweather, Chas. Nordhoff, Abr. Inslee, Cutler. Miss Gascoigne.

Washington Street.—Mrs. Joseph Greenwood, Theo. Freeman, Chas. Voigt, T. D. Taylor, Burton, Jos. Spinney, Jere. Mundell, L. Beyninger, J. W. Gascoigne, A. M. Davis, Sawyer, Edward Rolph, Henderson. Misses Dodge, Seney.

Carlton Avenue.—Mrs. Pettit, Morrell, Lowber, Fisher, Mary Wilson, Hugh Miller.

First Place.—Mrs. Hunt, P. Waters, Carrie, Garrison, Robt. Crawford, Creamer. Miss Mary Barber.

Hanson Place.—Mrs. Woodruff, Hicks, Bailer, Bigby, Simonson, Coffin.

Fleet Street.—Mrs. R. Hatfield, Jas. H. Taft, Darley Randall, J. H. Richards.

Pacific Street.—Mrs. Smith Fancher, McKenney.

BAPTIST CHURCHES.

Strong Place.—Mrs. A. B. Capwell, M. Mills, W. A. Gellatly, Chapel, H. E. Sawyer, Chas. Whitney, H. Farrington, E. B. Litchfield, Jos. W. Vail, Jas. Taylor, P. Wyckoff, Barter, Townsend, J. E. Southworth, Wilson G. Hunt, Haywood, Thomas Hunt, Rollinson, Chadbourne, Crullos, Farren, Fred. Whitney, Lamson, Clark, Perry, L. B. Chase, Kelsey, P. W. Kenyon, M. Knight. Misses Addie Shotwell, Maggie Buckland.

Central.—Mrs. Gibbs, Fish, Clarkson, Young, Mason, Sarles, Amos Fish, T. T. Devan, Butler, Stille, Conant, Pollard, Bebee.

Pierrepont.—Mrs. Silas Ludlam, S. Gregory, Elijah Bliss, J. Plummer, P. A. Crocker. Miss E. Meacham.

First.—Mrs. W. Harding, J. V. Carpenter. Misses Fanny Raymond, S. Chestnutwood, S. Quereau.

Hanson Place.—Mrs. J. B. Bigelow, Joseph Mayer, Leonard W. Serrell, S. S. Guy. Miss Mary C. Rich.

Washington Avenue.—Mrs. H. Quereso, William Atkins, Catharine Corning, Thomas Vernon, L. Richardson.

Athenæum.—Mrs. J. S. Wheeler, James Borland, P. A. Hepburn, D. D. Baker, S. H. Marshall.

OTHER CHURCHES.

German Evangelical Church.—Mrs. H. Gerlichs, Thomas Achelis.

Moravian Church.—Mrs. E. Wilkins.

Friends' Society.—Mrs. A. W. Leggett, Susan Lukins, H. H. Underhill, Isaac Hall, Davis, C. Carpenter, Geo. Brown, John J. Merritt, Wm. Robbins, F. T. Carpenter, Henry Everett.

Roman Catholic Church—St. Charles Borromeo.—Mrs. Hy. J. Cullen, Peter Rice, Alex. McCue, John Greenwood, Wm. E. Robinson, Mad. D. St. Amant.

Jewish Synagogue.—Mrs. M. Baw.

MISCELLANEOUS.

Teachers.—Mrs. Chs. S. West, H. C. Osborn, A. W. Morehouse, J. H. Raymond, S. G. Taylor, Mad. Napoléon. Misses C. Parish, C. Harrison, Ranney, Hunter, M. E. Thalheimer, H. Graham, A. L. Jones.

Ericsson Aid Society.—Mrs. Alfred Lowber, R. Osborn, Vosburgh, Miller, Minne, Currie. Misses M. Lorch, Ella Vosburgh, Kate Osborn, E. Lowber.

Managers Chosen at Large (*W. D.*)—Mrs. R. Gignoux, J. C. Whitcomb, A. Crittenden, A. Belknap, A. M. Wood, Francis Vinton, L. Burnham, Gen'l. Crooke, L. Chapman, Col. Pratt, Col. Everdell, Elwell, Gen'l. Spinola, G. West, M. C. Dunkley, G. F. Dunning, Hy. Brookman, Talford, D. J. Lyons, Henry Sands, Geo. Hart, Durance, J. O. Voigt, C. F. Oliver, D. C. Middleton, Chs. Peters, W. H. Barber, Work, Henry Keler, John J. Morrow, Pope Catlin, L. D. Conklin, M. P. Brown, Chas. Woodbridge. Misses C. Prentice, Fanny C. West, Ayres Russell, Carrie Van Cott, Sarah Sims, Fanny Grey, F. Willing, J. Farrington, A. Totten.

EASTERN DISTRICT.

CHURCHES.

First Baptist.—Mrs. E. Robinson, W. W. Armfield, Thomas Wallace, O. M. Beach, S. W. Woolsey, E. A. Thurston, John D. Ross, Smith Place, Edwd. A. Jones, R. Trussell, W. S. Conant, Henry Dishrow, S. Kennedy, Wm. Braisted. Misses Anna M. Anderson, S. A. Anderson, J. Van Volkenburg.

New England Congregational.—Mrs. S. Ballard, R. Clark, A. L. Van Herrcom, Chs. Altman.

Lee Avenue Congregational.—Mrs. Theod. Bulkley, William Brush, Kneeland, F. Scholes, Wm. McFarland, F. Summers, S. Wyckoff. Miss S. Johnson.

Reformed Dutch.—Mrs. Charles De Bevoise, Henry Schenck, F. Schenck, Isaac De Bevoise, M. Kalbfleisch, Fred. Kalbfleisch, Miss Julia Merker.

Gothic Methodist Episcopal.—Mrs. Daniel Maujer, Chas. Maujer, Reading, Mather. Miss Mary Maujer.

Fourth Street Reformed Dutch.—Mrs. J. S. Morrell, E. Porter, Hy. Marsh, William Hanson, Wenham, J. A. Heath. Misses S. A. Hathorne, Charlotte Richards.

First Presbyterian.—Mrs. Samuel J. Starr, Chesebrough.

Christ Church, Episcopal.—Mrs. C. Y. Wemple, H. Barstow, Emily Egan. Misses M. B. Dominick, E. Ten Eyck.

St. Mark's, Episcopal.—Mrs. Joanna Barber, Abigail Jones, Catharine Thomas, Blake, Miss Harriet Jones.

St. Paul's, Episcopal.—Mrs. Robt. Fash, Robt. Rose, Dr. Franklin, Thos. Grover, W. Hale.

Second Universalist.—Mrs. P. Price, G. Ricard, N. Nisbwitz, J. F. Hicks.

Roman Catholic.—Mrs. J. Washington Hunt, William Lake, Jos. J. O'Donohue, John Loughran, Edw. Malone, Henry S. Hewson, M. Donovan, John McCoy, William Cleary. Misses Brush, Magrath, Willis.

Managers Chosen at Large (E. D.)—Mrs. William H. Jenkins, James Hall, Sylvester Beard, Dr. Wright, Peters, Prince, Jas. Gridley. Misses Julia Cooper, J. De Witt, Schroder, Seal.

LONG ISLAND TOWNS.

Greenpoint Baptist.—Mrs. Wm. Reid, Peter Boyce. Miss H. M. Sheldon.

Methodist Episcopal.—Mrs. A. M. Hallock, Rd. Thomas, Williamson, D. D. Boyce, John F. Smith, Dunn, Crane.

Universalist.—Mrs. H. J. Hill, Porter.

Flatbush.—Mrs. John Vanderbilt, John A. Lott, John Lefferts, J. V. D. Martense, John D. Prince, John M. Hood, Fox, Miss M. S. Schuyler.

Flatlands.—Mrs. John Hubbard, J. Doolittle. Miss Ann Lott.

Flatland Neck.—Mrs. Phebe Kouwenhoven.

Greenfield.—Mrs. Sarah J. Heath, Geo. M. Close, Henderson.

Gravesend.—Mrs. Jas. Cropsey, S. C. Gerretson, M. G. Hanson, Miss Eliza Lake.

Bay Ridge.—Mrs. J. O. Perry, C. Tracy, W. Sherman, Fletcher, J. Van Brunt. Miss M. Musgrave.

Fort Hamilton.—Mrs. Geo. Gelston, Miss Brown.

Glen Cove.—Mrs. John S. Valentine, Simmons. Misses Ella Valentine, Ella H. Coles, Emily Valentine, Mary Merritt.

Huntington.—Mrs. Smith Woodhull, C. D. Stuart, G. A. Scudder, H. B. Crozier, L. M. Thurston.

Smithtown.—Mrs. B. Anders Smith, J. Lawrence Smith, Geo. Harris.

Babylon.—Mrs. W. A. Cooper.

Southold.—Mrs. Col. Wickham, Wm. Y. Fithian, H. Jennings, R. T. Goldsmith. Miss Mattie Day Horton.

Bridgehampton.—Mrs. Chas. Hedges, Abr. Rose.

East Hampton.—Mrs. Dr. Huntington, Geo. Hand.

Patchogue.—Mrs. Hoover.

Setauket.—Mrs. Dr. Evans.

Jamaica.—Mrs. W. G. Cogswell, Wm. Story, John J. Armstrong, L. M. Jagger. Misses Phebe Hagner, Cornelia King.

Flushing.—Mrs. G. R. Hutchinson, Henry McFarland, M. Franklin, J. M. Lawrence, Walter Bowne, L. White, H. Leavitt, George Bradish, L. Carter, Thomas Willets, Robert Willets.

Astoria.—Mrs. Henry Smith. Miss Wyckoff.

Ravenswood.—Mrs. Samuel Brown, Miss Helen D. Nelson.

Yaphank.—Mrs. Wm. Sidney Smith.

New Utrecht.—Mrs. John Crane, Jere. Van Brunt, Jr.

Hempstead.—Mrs. Rushmore. Miss K. Riddell.

South Hempstead.—Mrs. Isaac H. Cocks.

Stony Brook.—Miss Nellie Oakes.

Oyster Bay.—Mrs. Fairchild, Commodore Baily, S. Townsend, Dr. Radcliff, Jas. Ludlum, Dr. Prior, Jas. Bartis, Butler Coles, Samuel Jones. Miss Susan Youngs.

Sag Harbor.—Mrs. Benj. Huntting, Nathan Howell.

Manhasset.—Mrs. Chas. W. Renkers.

Cold Spring.—Mrs. Edward Jones, Jas. Hewlett, Stewart, S. W. Jones.

Jericho.—Mrs. Daniel Underhill.

East Meriches.—Miss C. D. Topping.

GENTLEMEN'S GENERAL COMMITTEE.

A. A. LOW, PRESIDENT.

A

Hugh Allen, E. Atkins, Joshua Atkins, James F. Atkinson, W. W. Armfield, Frank W. Allen, J. P. Atkinson, George B. Archer, S. P. Avery, A. G. Allen, Cor Adams, J. C. Atwater, John H. Allen, D. S. Arnold, Edward Anthony, Thomas Achelis, R. G. Anderson, W. H. Arthur, Wm. Arthur, R. T. Anderson, R. L. Allen.

B

Hon. Silas J. Beach, Glen Cove; Charles J. Bulkley, Josiah O. Blossom, Charles W. Blossom, Jas. B. Blossom, J. Charles Berard, Charles E. Beebe, R. S. Bussing, Archibald Baxter, Hon. Conklin Brush, Arthur W. Benson, Nathaniel Briggs, Alex. H. Baylis, Samuel Booth, Thomas T. Buckley, Samuel E. Belcher, Hon. J. C. Brevoort, T. F. Bucklin, Jr., Silas G. Butler, Edwin Beers, John H. Boynton, Thomas Brooks, C. S. Brown, Bay Harbor; H. W. Beecher, L. S. Burnham, D. S. Barnes, R. C. Bach, John Ballard, C. H. Baxter, Charles N. Benedict, Roswell Brainard, C. J. Bergen, Hon. A. J. Bergen, J. S. Bailey, Alex. V. Blake, L. H. Brigham, Caleb Barstow, Charles Hart, W. H. Beard, Seymour Burrell, R. D. Barratt, Alfred S. Barnes, W. B. Barber, W. E. Bailey, Lucien Birdseye, H. L. Bartlett, M. D., J. C. Brevoort, R. H. Belknap, Chas. R. Bell, Norman S. Bentley, C. S. Baylis, Fritz Brose, J. B. Brush, J. K. Brick, Gustavus A. Brett, Geo. Baxter, Wm. Beard, J. Bullock, George A. Bell, S. M. Beard, J. H. Boynton, Wm. Burrell, Hiram Beaser, W. M. Brasher, Henry Brockman, Brinsmade, J. Charles Berard, John C. Beale, Leopold Bierwith, D. Bogart, Jr., Roslyn, Moses S. Beach, Henry W. Banks, Carlos Bardwell, Wm. Burdon, Wm. Burrell, J. N. Bennett, J. S. Barr, Birdseye Blakeman, R. S. Benedict, B. C. Baldwin, W. B. Batton, Jas. M. Bart, F. H. Bigelow, S. M. Beard, Henry W. Banks, D. D. Badger, J. S. Bance, Albert Bruen, A. H. Barnes, Samuel Booth, John Butler, C. E. Bertrand, Geo. C. Bennett, Tunis I. Bergen.

C

George S. Cary, Hon. John A. Cross, Peter C. Cornell, John D. Cocks, S. B. Chittenden, Charles Christmas, Stephen Crowell, Edmund W. Corlies, S. W. Cary, H. L. Cutter, George S. Coe, Wm. Churchill, Andrew M. Calamne, W. H. Cundit, S. B. Caldwell, Henry Collins, Lebbeus Chapman, H. B. Cromwell, Charles Congdon, Alfred H. Cox, Henry T. Cox, George Collins, Pickering Clark, F. A. Chapman, C. B. Caldwell, Wm. Colt, Daniel Chauncey, S. T. Clarke, A. Claflin, J. W. Camp, D. H. Conkling, John Cunningham, Edward Cary, R. P. Clark, Rufus Crook, Benjamin Carter, Samuel B. Caldwell, H. B. Claflin, John Crook, James A. Cannan, Samuel Coleman, H. Carmiencke, A. Chappel, C. B. Camp, J. K. Cecil, George Chappel, Patrick Cassidy, Thomas Carroll, W. Cahble, William Coles, William Couwenhoven, J. O. Currie, Col. William J. Cropsey, Isaac R. Cocks, Westbury; Gen. Phillip S. Crooke, Ferdinand A. Crocker.

D

M. F. H. De Haas, Edmund Driggs, William R. Doubleday, Cear Dunning, Charles Dennis, C. P. Dickinson, H. Dorr, H. H. Dickinson, E. W. Dunham, J. W. Degraaw, Charles Dimon, Thos. C. Durant, Jas. P. Dike, C. C. Dike, George W. Dow, Major Geo. H. B. Duryea, A. Dorlan, Courtland P. Dixon, Abel Denison, John H. Drake, R. W. De Lamater, W. S. Dunham, George Dickenson, R. F. Delano, William C. Dunton, C. Duffinger, George B. Douglas, John Doyle.

E

William Evans, H. M. Evans, S. J. Eastman, Wm. Everdell, Jr., Alex. W. Earle, B. Elliott, Daniel Embury, Prof. D. G. Eaton, C. L. Elliott, Henry Esler.

F

Frederick A. Farley, D. D., I. H. Frothingham, R. W. Fiske, Gordon L. Ford, James H. Frothingham, Charles S. Farley, S. H. Farnham, J. W. Frothingham, [illegible] Fenner, Geo. Field, Robert Ford, William C. Fowler, J. M. Falconer, Andrew Fitzgerald, Smith Faucher, D. K. Fenner, Thomas W. Fields, William A. Fowler, John S. Folk, J. M. Falconer, John Firth, John French, J. A. Fuller, David Fithian, Ed. R. Flanders, Chas. W. Fellows, Robert R. Fox.

G

Regis Gignoux, S. F. Goodridge, H. Graves, Walter S. Griffith, C. P. Gerrish, W. A. Gellatly, Hon. John Greenwood, E. F. Goodenow, Joseph W. Greene, E. T. H. Gibson, Warren D. Goodkin, James M. Griggs, Regis Gignoux, Sidney Greene, S. J. Gay, David A. Griggs, C. C. Greene, Peter W. Gallaudet, Samuel Godwin, Daniel Godwin, D. H. Gould, —— Geer, A. Greenleaf, Jr., James Gridley, W. D. Gookin.

H

A. Cooke Hull, M. D., Charles E. Hill, Hon. George Hall, S. L. Husted, James Hall, James How, G. S. Hutchinson, George T. Hunt, G. L. Haight, Hon. James Humphrey, John W. Hunter, John Halsey, W. H. Hazard, S. Emerson Howard, John B. Hutchinson, William Hannabs, W. S. Herriman, James D. Holcomb, Samuel Hutchinson, R. H. Hubbard, Theodore Hinsdale, John Harold, Hempstead; Joseph W. Harper, H. W. Herrick, Allen Harris, Williams Howland, Fisher Howe, Isaac Henderson, Thomas Hunt, James Hazlehurst, G. W. Hennings, William Hunter, Jr., F. Hinchman, Joseph Hazlehurst, John F. Harper, R. J. Hunter, Walter T. Hatch, Joseph L. Heath, W. Husted, H. W. Hennings, Gilbert Howell, A. P. Hayden, J. T. Howard, G. L. Harvey, F. Hathaway, Isaac Hyde, Jr., E. W. Hall, C. E. Hill, George T. Hope, Elias Howe, Jr., F. J. Hosford, T. K. Horton, Aaron Healey, William Higby, Norman Hubbard, James H. Hart, I. A. Havemeyer, George S. Harding, William Hager, R. H. Hand, W. R. Higgins, A. G. Hicks, G. W. Hubert, J. A. Heath, Harvey E. Hickes, Benj. J. Hitchings, J. Madison Huntting, East Hampton.

I

James M. Ives, Julius Ives, Jr., William M. Ingraham, Alvain Insley, Samuel Ingalls.

J

Dwight Johnson, George A. Jarvis, Charles Jones, H. P. Journeay, Henry Jones, W. H. Jenkins, H. Jackson, T. E. Jewell, J. Johnson.

K

Hon. John A. King, Nehemiah Knight, Hon. M. Kalbfleisch, John R. Kennaday, W. R. Kendall, Charles Kelsey, Henry A. Kent, George W. Kirtland, N. B. Kittell, Gamaliel King, M. S. Kerrigan, Thomas T. Knight, E. H. Kimball.

L

A. A. Low, Hon. John A. Lott, William C. Libby, Hon. Edward A. Lambert, Josiah O. Low, E. H. R. Lyman, Elias Lewis, Jr., Nicholas Luquer, Jr., John Lanman, Joseph Lord, R. H. Lowry, Louis Ludovici, R. B. Lawrence, Henry W. Low, Charles J. Lowrey, George D. Lincoln, Edward Lambert, E. J. Lowber, Frederick Lacey, Thomas Le Clear, J. P. Lord, T. L. Leitkins, Charles B. Loomis, B. Lowerie, W. B. Leonard, Nathan Lane, E. R. Litchfield, C. H. Lippitt, W. H. Lyon, F. H. Lummus, Walter Lockwood, D. Lansing Lambert, Elijah Lewis, John W. Lewis, John F. Loomis, A. Leininger, John Lefferts.

M

R. W. Meade, U. S. Navy, Hon. H. C. Murphy, C. A. Meigs, C. H. Meigs, Daniel Manjer, Thomas Messenger, Alexander McCue, William Marshall, C. T. Middlebrook, H. P. Morgan, J. T. Martin, Samuel McLean, Alexander McCollom, L. K. Miller, A. Montgomery, C. B. Marow, John D. McKenzie, James L. Morgan, R. H. Manning, E. S. Mills, Lewis Morris, Thomas Middleton, W. J. Miller, Philip Mayer, J. B. Murray, Henry Messenger, J. B. Merwin, Chaplin U. S. A.; Frank Moulton, A. K. Masters, Samuel M. Meeker, James McChesney, —— McGrath, Thomas H. Messenger, —— Marcus, —— Merriam, James Myers, W. D. Mangam, J. O. Moore, C. L. Mitchell, M. D.; J. L. Morgan, Edward B. Mead, John F. McCoy, George S. Moulton, Eli Mygatt, Jr., James O. Morse, William McEwan, T. F. Meyers, George Mygatt, Charles Morris, J. W. McNamee, John S. Masury, J. Morrison, James L. Moore, Joseph H. Mumby, J. H. McWilliams, W. D. Mangam, William Matthews, Robert Magan, Charles R. Miller, S. B. Meserean, Hempstead.

N

James R. Noyes, Curtis Noble, Henry E. Nesmith, John B. Norris, Willard M. Newell, J. O. Nodyne, J. Norton, Jr., George L. Nichols; William Nicoll, Huntington; Charles Nordhoff, Alexander D. Napier, Edward A. Nichols, Christian Neidig.

O

A. B. Orr, Robert C. Ogden, George M. Alcott, Hon. M. F. Odell, Jonathan Ogden, Samuel Osburn, Jacob Outwater, —— Oswald, Henry Oltman, Samuel Osborn, Jr., —— Ovington, Eugene O'Sullivan, F. S. Otis.

P

Henry E. Pierrepont, John H. Prentice, Hon. S. S. Powell, Henry R. Pierson, Theo. Polhemus, Jr., John F. Plummer, John F. Prager, E. D. Plimpton, George W. Parsons, William Peet, Charles Powers, W. W. Pell, Charles Parsons, William Pool, J. A. Perry, Alfred Porter, E. B. Place, E. A. Parker, Charles Perry, Col. Calvin E. Pratt, William M. Peck, J. Melville Prentice, Prof. Plimpton, W. H. Peck, J. L. Pyle, A. S. Perry, J. A. Parker, Jr., H. D. Polhemus, T. W. Prentice, Alex. P. Purves, James H. Prentice, Rd. Poillon, George S. Puffer, John Philips, O. W. Plympton, John D. Prince, C. S. Powell, Farmingdale.

Q

David S. Quimby.

R

Hon. James Rider, A. F. Roberts, R. W. Ropes, J. P. Robinson, Joseph Ripley, Lewis R. Reed, Jr., Amos Robbins, Thomas H. Rodman, George C. Ripley, W. M. Richards, Hon. George G. Reynolds, J. S. Rockwell, Peter Rier, Henry G. Reeve, Mattituck; Thomas Rome, Robert R. Raymond, Morris Reynolds, P. P. Ryder, George C. Robinson, J. H. Raymond, LL. D., Ripley Ropes, D. C. Robbins, A. Robbins, Enos Richardson, E. L. Roberts, —— Radford, U. S. N.; Wright Ramsden, George W. Robbins, Thomas Rowland, Henry C. Richardson, Joseph Reeves, John L. Ryder, Bernardus J. Ryder, Philip H. Reid, James Rider, Jamaica.

S

Hon. J. S. T. Stranahan, George S. Stephenson, Hon. J. C. Smith, Ambrose Snow, Charles J. Shepard, Hon. C. P. Smith, James D. Sparkman, Edmond Sanger, J. Milton Smith, Nathan Stephens, Lucius J. N. Stark, C. H. Stoddard, Henry Sheldon, Cornelius J. Sprague, Edward H. Stephenson, John Sneden, Sumner B. Stone, N. T. Sweezey, John J. Studwell, Henry Sawyer, Hon. Benjamin D. Silliman, W. P. Strickland, D. D., C. H. Sand, J. S. Shapter, J. E. Southworth, George E. Spencer, Charles Stanton, Fred. Sherwood, Samuel A. Sawyer, Sidney Sanderson, Benjamin F. Sherman, A. Smithers, Charles Starrs, W. H. Swan, —— Scranton, Frederick Schuler, J. N. Stearns, John Seymour, Thomas T. Sheffield, James M. Strail, Wm. C. Sheldon, Samuel H. Stewart,

U. B. Starr, — Sniffen, J. B. Spelman, John H. Stevens, Henry K. Sheldon, Henry Starr, R. S. Storrs, Jr., D. D.; Thomas Sullivan, A. E. Sumner, T. M. Spelman, Nathan Southwick, Alexander Studwell, J. C. Southwick, Bryant Stevens, James Seville, Jonathan Stewart, Robert R. Story, James Sharkey, John Shuster, Charles E. Smith, Hiram F. St. John, Watson Sandford, Geo. J. C. Smith.

T

Hon. James O. Tuthill, Riverhead, L. I.; Hon. W. M. Thomas, Richard S. Tucker, James Thorne, John F. Talmadge, M. D., George F. Thomas, C. A. Townsend, E. A. Tweedy, John N. Taylor, Frederick H. Trowbridge, George F. Thomas, Jr., W. S. Tisdale, C. J. Taylor, George Tucker, M. D. Thomas, R. H. Thompson, W. M. Tillman, C. B. Tatham, James H. Taylor, Alanson Trask, Benjamin Townsend, Samuel W. Truslow, William Tuttle, Alfred Thompson, Theodore Tilton, George H. Taylor, W. F. Trafton, W. M. Thomas, A. Thayer, S. W. Truslow, James A. Taylor, George Tucker.

V

Fritz W. Victor, A. V. B. Van Dyck, C. H. Victor, Newtown; Theodore F. Vail, Adrian Van Sinderen, J. P. Van Bergen, John James Van Nostrand, J. M. Van Colt, D. W. Van Ingen, I. Van Anden, Samuel Van Benschoten, Israel Victor, Theodore Victor, C. Van Dusen, Francis Vinton, D. D.; Benson Van Vliet, Samuel Vernon, A. M. Vail, O. J. Vining, Rev. Mr. Van Buren, A. H. W. Van Sicklen.

W

Hon. Alfred M. Wood, L. B. Wyman, Hon. William Wall, Alexander M. White, James M. Waterbury, James P. Wallace, James C. Wilson, Wilfred Wallace, J. L. B. Willard, W. H. Waring, George William Warren, A. C. Woodruff, Abm. Wyckoff, Isaac B. Wellington, Edward Whitehouse, W. W. Wicks, W. Wyckoff, D. Wadsworth, John Williamson, James O. Weld, Franklin Woodruff, John B. Wright, P. K. Weizel, J. H. Whittaker, C. D. Wood, D. D. Whiting, Professor R. C. West, John Winslow, Hon. Edward D. White, C. H. Williamson, O. L. Watrous, H. H. Warden, D. W. Wetmore, W. L. Wood, Joseph Wilde, A. D. Wheelock, Col. John B. Woodward, O. G. Walbridge, J. T. Whitehouse, Benjamin Wood, Jr., Caleb Smith Woodhull, David Wesson, Sidney Whittingham, John L. Worden, U. S. Navy; A. W. Warren, John O. Whitehouse, O. Whittlesey, A. D. Wheelock, H. H. Warden, James Wilcox, William Wise, Henry Waldron, G. M. Woodward, James K. Wheatley, J. S. Willard, D. S. Waring, Silvanus White, H. B. Whitty, Ashford Webb, J. B. Wickersham, George Wildey, Hiram M. Warren, Stedman Wright, Major G. C. Ward.

Y

J. T. Yeoman.

Z

J. L. Zabriskie, M. D.

GENERAL CIRCULAR

OF THE

BROOKLYN AND LONG ISLAND FAIR,

IN AID OF THE

United States Sanitary Commission.

In the terrible conflict now being waged for the preservation of our Government and Nationality, everything belonging to our personal, social, and political welfare is at stake, and the brave and gallant men in arms are perilling their lives, and giving up the comfort and joy of their homes, in our stead. They fight these hard battles for us. They endure these severe exposures for us. They are wasting away in the filth and starvation of Rebel prisons for us. And, when stricken down by the diseases of the camp, or wounded and maimed in the field, they have a right, sanctioned by every patriotic and humane consideration, to expect the Nation to come to their succor. The U. S. SANITARY COMMISSION, by its most disinterested and gratuitous labors, has proved itself the wise, prompt, faithful, reliable, and sufficient agent of the Nation in this regard; and, therefore, by a FAIR, to be opened on the birth-day of the Father of his Country, the 22d of February next, at the Brooklyn Academy of Music, we purpose and confidently expect to secure from the City, and the entire Island, a contribution of at least One Hundred and Fifty Thousand Dollars to its Treasury. The inspiring example of other Cities—Chicago, Boston, Cincinnati—should excite among us an honorable emulation. Let it be seen that in this great national crisis, we are at least as generous, self-sacrificing, and resolved, as the foremost of them. This enterprise has been undertaken at the instance of the Woman's Relief Association, and the War Fund Committee, of this City. As an earnest of the spirit which has prompted it and will carry it through, we point to the fact, that at a meeting of the General Committee, on the 19th ult., Twenty-five Thousand Five Hundred Dollars were subscribed on the spot; an amount already increased to Forty Thousand Dollars. As a further pledge that the enterprise shall not fail, we subjoin the names of those of either sex who have consented to share its Management; with those of the various sub-Committees, who are responsible for the complete working of the several departments of the FAIR. We appeal to our fellow-citizens and noble women here, and throughout the Island, and to those elsewhere who may fairly be expected to sympathize with us in our undertaking, to lend their aid by personal efforts, and by the largest contributions of Material and Money, of Agricultural Products, of the fruits of Manufacturing and Mechanical skill, of Works of Art; of anything and everything from their industry, ingenuity, or abundance, which may swell the grand result for which we look.

Further particulars in relation to the arrangements for the FAIR will be made known as early as possible, by Circulars from the several Special Committees, and by other documents from the Executive Committee; and a complete History of the FAIR, with the Contributions and Names of the Donors, will be published. A handsome Steel Engraved Certificate of Membership will be also given to every active contributor.

Meanwhile, any desired information in regard to the FAIR may be had of the Corresponding Secretary, either by personal application, at the Rooms of the War Fund Committee, 16 Court Street, daily, (Sundays excepted,) between the hours of 9 and 12, and 2 and 5; or, by mail to his address; or, for Ladies, at the Depot of the Woman's Relief Association, 30 Court Street.

FREDERICK A. FARLEY, D. D.,
Corresponding Secretary.

OFFICERS.

EXECUTIVE COMMITTEE

DWIGHT JOHNSON, Chairman.
FREDERICK A. FARLEY, D. D., Cor. Sec.
WALTER S. GRIFFITH, Rec. Sec.
JAMES H. FROTHINGHAM, Treas.
Mrs. J. S. T. STRANAHAN, Chairman.
Mrs. H. L. PACKER, Cor. Sec.
Miss KATE E. WATERBURY, Rec. Sec.
Mrs. G. B. ARCHER, Treas.

Hon. James S. T. Stranahan, Hon. Alfred M. Wood, Hon. John A. Lott, Samuel B. Caldwell, Ambrose Snow, Thomas T. Buckley, A. A. Low, Henry Sheldon, Chas. A. Meigs, William H. Jenkins, Joseph Wilde, H. B. Claflin, Elias Lewis, Jr., Hon. Edward A. Lambert, Ethelbert S. Mills, James D. Sparkman, Hon. John A. King, Arthur W. Benson, S. B. Chittenden, Henry E. Pierrepont, John D. McKenzie, Hon. James Humphrey, George S. Stephenson, Archibald Baxter, Joseph Ripley, Edward J. Lowber, Luther B. Wyman, W. W. Armfield, Peter Rice, Willard M. Newell, William Bardon, S. Emerson Howard.

Mrs. G. B. Archer, E. Anthony, H. W. Beecher, A. W. Benson, C. J. Bergen, R. C. Brainard, J. C. Brevoort, T. T. Buckley, W. I. Buddington, N. Burchard, A. Bradshaw, S. B. Caldwell, S. B. Chittenden, W. J. Cogswell, J. P. Duffin, J. W. Harper, A. Crittenden, Alfred M. Wood, L. Harrington, G. H. Huntsman, T. F. King, E. S. Mills, Morrell, W. W. Pell, H. E. Pierrepont, E. Shapter, H. Sheldon, J. C. Smith, J. D. Sparkman, G. S. Stephenson, J. S. Swan, A. Trask, J. Vanderbilt, H. Waters.

Finance and Donations.—John D. McKenzie, Chairman ; S. B. Chittenden, A. A. Low, Abm. B. Baylis, Peter C. Cornell, E. T. H. Gibson, Richard P. Buck, Charles E. Hill, Reuben W. Ropes, Rufus R. Graves, George B. Archer, James D. Sparkman, Charles A. Meigs, Theodore Polhemus, Jr., Josiah O. Low, R. W. DeLamater, E. W. Corlies, Charles W. Blossom, Joseph Ripley, Thomas Messenger.

Business Committee.—Mrs. E. Shapter, Chairman ; G. B. Archer, N. Burchard, W. I. Budington, A. W. Benson, C. J. Bergen, S. B. Chittenden, J. P. Duffin, T. F. King, E. S. Mills, A. M. Wood, G. S. Stephenson, A. Trask, H. Waters, N. Knight, H. Marchant, A. Crittenden.

Buildings and Decorations.—Arthur W. Benson, Chairman ; J. W. Degraw, John Bullard, Charles J. Lowry, William Burrell, James How, Corn. J. Bergen, E. L. Roberts, George F. Thomas, Thomas Messenger, William Hunter, Jr., Thomas Brooks, Joseph L. Heath, George A. Bell, William S. Herriman, Thomas Sullivan, Edwin Beers, J. A. Perry.

Mrs. T. F. King, Chairman ; A. W. Benson, H. Webster, J. Humphrey, H. R. Duryea, J. Bullard, H. B. Starr, Coe Adams, N. H. Kittell, W. S. Griffith, J. W. Gilbert, H. Laing, E. B. Litchfield, Misses Charlotte Coles, E. Hunter, Sarah Boynton, H. L. Waterbury, Phœbe Hagner.

Internal Arrangements and Reception of Goods.—George S. Stephenson, Chairman ; Alexander M. White, I. H. Frothingham, L. S. Burnham, R. H. Manning, George W. Hennings, John O. Morse, James Myers, Edward Anthony, George T. Hope, Samuel McLean, E. H. Stephenson, George C. Ripley, John L. Worden, Captain Radford, Theodore Hinsdale, William H. Swan, Charles B. Loomis, Hon. James H. Tuthill, Alexander McCue, George W. Dow, William Nicoll, Robert Ford, Hon. Elias J. Beach, Hon. James Rider.

Mrs. G. B. Archer, Chairman ; G. S. Stephenson, A. M. White, S. H. Low, J. P. Van Bergen, M. F. Odell, Miss C. Thurston, Mrs. S. McLean, J. Maxwell, D. Fairbanks, J. Eells, J. W. Emery, J. C. Atwater, C. B. Loomis, J. C. Smith, E. Shapter, J. D. Sparkman, N. Burchard, A. Bradshaw, J. S. Morrell, T. F. King, W. I. Budington, J. Vanderbilt, Miss Wyckoff, Mrs. Hensman, W. Cogswell.

Refreshments.—Edward J. Lowber, Chairman ; Rufus Crook, John Crook, D. H. Gould, A. Dowlan, Amos Robbins, William A. Husted, Isaac B. Wellington, Seymour L. Husted, Alfred Thompson, William S. Dunham, John B. Wright, A. E. Sumner, Robert O. Anderson, James A. Carman.

Mrs. E. S. Mills, Chairman ; A. R. Hall, Secretary and Treasurer ; H. Waters, T. T. Buckley, H. Marchant, H. P. Buck, A. W. Leggett, J. D. Hurlbut, W. C. Bowers, F. H. Trowbridge, Miss Russel, Mrs. C. Dinsmore, S. B. Gregory, H. Blanchard, G. Thrall, A. Burrowes, W. H. Marston, A. Wyckoff, E. Fish, Ralph, J. Redman, H. W. Law, C. W. Goddard, Wm. Lumby, L. Boyer, S. E. Smith, N. Putnam, John Greenwood, J. D. Cocks, E. Merrill, F. H. Taylor, J. Young, J. B. Hutchinson, D. Brigham, L. C. Andrus, W. H. Colton, S. S. Gray, H. Elliot, P. Waters, E. S. Simonson, Baxter, Cutter, Joseph Greenwood, R. Sharp, M. L. Hastings, R. W. W. Thorne, J. Myers, H. Tryon, J. P. Elwell, E. Beers, W. H. Beale. Eastern District.—Mrs. W. H. Jenkins, Chairman ; W. Sandford, J. Hall, S. Lounsberry, J. Loughlin, S. Jenny, R. Tompel, Ten Eyck, W. McFarland, P. Price, O. R. Brown, G. Taylor, W. H. Johnson, R. Dunn, Miss Mundy.

Arts, Relics and Curiosities.—E. S. Mills, Chairman ; Regis Gignoux, Charles Congdon, Gordon L. Ford, John Williamson, R. W. Hubbard, Charles Parsons, M. F. H. DeHaas, Samuel Coleman, Seymour J. Guy, Thomas Le Clear, W. H. Beard, S. P. Avery, P. P. Ryder, J. M. Falconer, I. A. Parker, Jr., J. Remsen Bennett, H. Carmiencke, N. R. Kittell, Chas. Hart, James H. Hewson, F. A. Chapman, John W. Frothingham, R. S. Storrs, Jr., D. D., H. W. Beecher, J. Carson Brevoort, T. L. Lothins, Alonzo Chappell, J. B. Whittaker, H. W. Herrick, A. W. Warren, William McEwan, E. W. Hall, C. L. Elliott.

Mrs. S. B. Chittenden, Chairman ; R. S. Storrs, Jr., H. E. Pierrepont, Regis Gignoux, J. C. Brevoort, E. H. Gibson, John T. Howard, G. L. Ford, A. N. Littlejohn, J. O. Low,

John Raymond, Charles Congdon, A. W. Benshaw, R. Vanderbilt, C. Rosier, J. H. Frothingham, Alexander McCallum, Helen Conant, W. H. Dudley, Francis Vinton, E. Van Nostrand, O. B. Stephenson, Thomas Messenger, Misses Rose Thomas, Alice B. Cary, Kate Ripley, Kate Treadway, Kate Taylor, Fay, M. H. Chittenden, Fannie Gray, M. Stranahan, Cornelia King, S. Loquer, C. M. Olcott, F. Bridges.

Music.—L. B. Wyman, Chairman; A. Cooke Hull, R. H. Raymond, A. V. Blake, C. A. Townsend, Willard M. Newell, George William Warren, William Pool, Edward Lambert, J. F. Talmage, P. K. Weisel, Ph. Mayer, Captain R. W. Meade, Pickering Clark, H. D. Polhemus, T. F. Meyers.

New England Kitchen.—Mrs. J. S. Swan, Chairman; W. W. Goodrich, R. W. Potter, S. J. Peet, L. W. Serrell, W. B. Ackley, M. C. Bicknell, M. Moore, A. F. Stewart, Ralph L. Cook, C. E. Adriance, Misses Mary L. Rich, Sarah Watson, Mary Shepard, A. F. Emerson, Mrs. A. M. Ewing, M. P. Mills, J. M. Carter, C. N. Kinney, W. S. Murray, J. J. Couch, R. H. Manning, Misses F. E. Cook, Josephine Gault, J. Dorlon, Mrs. George Farmer, Robert Foulds, Samuel McKay, A. H. Dailey, C. N. Flanders, A. S. Wheeler, Jared Brewster, J. W. Elwell, R. D. Benedict, Misses M. A. Berry, E. Wilder, A. Dudley.

Advisory Committee.—R. W. Potter, Chairman; James W. Elwell, Alva Oatman, Frederick Talbot, William J. Coffin, D. Tracy, A. H. Dailey, C. N. Flanders, R. H. Manning, William Peet, George W. Kendall, Elias Howe, Jr., Charles N. Kinney, Charles S. Messenger, B. F. Metcalf, J. S. Swan, C. S. Weatherbee, W. S. Murray, William W. Goodrich, A. P. Hawley, L. W. Serrell, Ralph L. Cook, Samuel Duncan, Luke T. Merrill, Robert Murray, Jr., George S. Woodman, J. E. Paine, Levi Wilder, D. B. Dearborn, C. P. Dixon, C. W. Dunlap, S. L. Parsons, J. B. Norris, J. J. Couch, C. H. Fellows.

Oration and Lectures.—H. E. Pierrepont, Chairman; James Humphrey, Benjamin D. Silliman, Judge Greenwood, R. W. Ropes, Edward Whitehouse, Rev. Francis Vinton, D.D.

Post Office and Newspapers.—Mrs. J. P. Duffin, Chairman; I. H. St. John, T. J. Conant, J. Humphrey, T. Hinsdale, J. M. Dimond, William Brooks, S. W. Putnam, Misses H. Gladwin, Brigham, Harrison, M. E. Thalheimer, A. L. Jones, Flushing; Kate Hillard, C. Van Cott, M. Stranahan, Mrs. George B. Lincoln, William E. Robinson, George A. Jarvis.

Benefits, Entertainments and Exhibitions.—Edward A. Lambert, Chairman; Edward Anthony, Charles H. Marvin, Isaac Henderson, John D. Cocks, J. B. Southworth, Professor Plimpton, Moses S. Beach, J. S. Burr, James Hall, Henry A. Kent, Benson Van Vliet, Livingston K. Miller, Theodore Tilton, Elias Howe, Jr., John W. Hunter, James P. Dike, E. D. Plimpton.

Mrs. E. Anthony, Chairman; H. Farnham, Miss Alice B. Cary, Mrs. J. P. Herriman, N. P. Waring, Howe Webster, S. E. Howard, Miss L. Oliver, Mrs. D. Fairbanks, Misses S. O. Anthony, A. E. Anthony, S. Farrington, Madame Napoleo, Mdlle. Millon, Miss S. Blunt, Mrs. McLean, Miss A. Cotton, Miss Marsh, Mrs. E. A. Lambert, Miss C. Coles, Mrs. D. J. Lyons, Hoyt, Miss M. Dunning, A. Hoppin, L. Tupper, M. Loquer, Mrs. W. M. St. John, A. S. Barnes, Misses Anna Totten, R. Norton.

Books, Publications and Printing.—Samuel B. Caldwell, Chairman; A. S. Barnes, J. H. Raymond, LL.D., George B. Lincoln, Adrian Van Sinderen, J. M. Van Cott, Bluheye Blakeman, John C. Beals, W. H. Arthur, John N. Taylor, George W. Parsons, W. T. Hatch, Charles Nordhoff, T. B. Messenger, D. Lansing Lambert, F. J. Hosford, J. R. Merwin, John F. Harper, W. W. Swayne, Melancthon Hunt, William Pate, C. C. Woolworth, Bradley R. Hard, George A. Olney, J. Sullivan Thorne, Thomas H. Messenger, Lucien Birdseye.

Mrs. W. I. Budington, Chairman; J. W. Harper, A. S. Barnes, C. Nordhoff, S. E. Warner, S. N. Cutter, W. W. Rose, Isaac Henderson, Miss Laura Marsh, Mrs. Daniel Fairweather, S. B. Caldwell, William Moses, E. A. Lambert, Miss Gascoigne, Mrs. Dwight Johnson, William Swayne, J. H. Richards, S. W. Sarles.

Seminaries and Schools.—Mrs. H. L. Packer, Chairman; C. J. Bergen, A. Crittenden, O. F. Dunning, M. E. Dunkley, William Brooks, Professor Eaton, H. C. Osborn, J. D.

McKenzie, L. Miller, D. M. Stone, C. R. West, J. H. Raymond, S. G. Taylor, Miss B. Gersham, Mrs. J. C. Whitcomb.

Dry Goods Merchants' Committee. Thomas T. Buckley, Chairman; H. B. Claflin, Nelson Knight, J. B. Hutchinson, W. C. Sheldon, R. J. Hunter, Samuel McLean, James S. Noyes, Henry Collins, Thomas Achelis, S. Hutchinson, W. R. Kendall, D. H. Conklin, James Hazlehurst, J. C. Atwater, T. W. Prentice, Alexander D. Napier, W. H. Lennard, Charles S. Baylis, H. P. Journeay, George Mygatt, J. L. B. Willard, H. P. Morgan, T. K. Horton, Samuel B. Stewart, Walter Lockwood, Elijah Lewis.

Fancy Goods.—S. E. Howard, Chairman; J. W. Greene, Henry Sanger, D. C. Robbins, J. S. Shapter, Charles Storrs, D. S. Arnold, W. H. Lyon, Abel Denniston, Alexander McCullum, J. Charles Berard, W. F. Trafton, James R. Taylor, G. H. Taylor, H. H. Dickinson, F. Hinchman, T. M. Spellman, A. P. Hayden, Enos Richardson, George S. Moulton, Carlos Bardwell, Benjamin Carter, Alexander P. Purves, Henry Elliott.

Mrs. H. Sheldon, Chairman; R. C. Brainard, S. Gracie, Bryan B. Smith, Hugh Allen, Misses Mary S. Griffith, Agnes Russell, Mrs. D. S. Mills, Henry Sanger, S. M. Beard, H. E. Hunter, J. S. Rockwell, Miss Mary C. Jarvis, Mrs. W. C. Sheldon, I. Badeau, Hermann Garlichs, B P. Lant, Miss E. L. Howe, Mrs. W. C. Perry, Alexander P. Purvis, T. Achelis, Miss Bertschinger, Mrs. R. Uckart, Misses Susan Nelson, F. C. West, J. Buckmaster Mary Miller, S. Johnson, H. and S. Duckwitz, C. Fellows, Madame St. Amant, Miss Maria Messenger, Mrs. W. Goddard, H. W. Beecher, W. H. Beare, Horace Warren, S. W. Truslow, William Raymond, Miss Harriet Tucker, Addie Wright, Mrs. Robinson, Misses F. Creagh, C. Bush, A. J. Derry, C. Richardson, Helen Usher, Amelia Boyd, Minnie Stanton.

Boots, Shoes, Leather, Hats, Caps and Clothing.—W. M. Newell, Chairman; Aaron Claflin, John T. Martin, Isaac Hyde, Jr., George Dickenson, James H. Prentice, Roswell S. Benedict, John Bullard, Edward A. Nichols, A. C. Baldwin, Nathan Southwick, John C. McCoy, S. B. Caldwell, Alexander Studwell, Jona. Ogden, Alanson Trask, Aaron Healy, C. B. Camp, W. B. Button, John O. Whitehouse, J. C. Southwick, Granville Whittlesey, William Higbie, James M. Burt, M. S. Kerrigan, James M. Griggs, A. D. Wheelock, John W. Lewis, F. H. Bigelow, John B. Woodward, William Evans.

Grocers and Hardware Merchants.—Henry Sheldon, Chairman; John J. Van Nostrand, H. H. Warden, Frederick Lacy, George A. Jarvis, Theodore Victor, S. M. Beard, Francis Hathaway, Charles R. Hill, Henry K. Sheldon, Solon F. Goodridge, James L. Morgan, Robert S. Bussing, J. S. Rockwell, Alexander M. Earle, O. L. Hoover, E. B. Place, James C. Wilson, William C. Fowler, Eugene O'Sullivan, Edward R. Mead, A. S. Perry, Henry W. Banks, Henry Starr, Edwin Atkins, Franklin H. Lummus.

Manufactures and Mechanic Arts.—Western District William Burdon, Chairman; B. F. Delano, Richard Phillips, Ship Builders; William Arthur, Henry Esler, Steam Engine Builders; Abram, Inslee, D. D. Badger, Founders; Jacob Outwater, David S. Quimby, Railing, Grates, and Fender Manufacturers; J. S. Bunce, Norman Hubbard, Boiler Makers; Charles Morris, John Firth, Piano Forte Makers; Robert Graves, C. Van Dusen, Wall Paper Manufacturers; H. Jackson, Albert Brown, Manufacturing Chemists; Elias Howe, Jr., James Willcox, Sewing Machine Manufacturers; Thomas Brooks, Bryant Stephens, Furniture Manufacturers; J. W. McNamee, George S. Puffer, Distillers; Saml. Vernon, William C. Danton, Paper Manufacturers; A. H. Barnes, Birdseye Blakeman, Publishers; William Wise, James H. Hart, Jewelers; Henry Waldron, John S. Masury, Paints and Color Manufacturers; James Hew, Fisher Howe, White Lead Manufacturers, W. M. Thomas, James Neville, Glass-ware Manufacturers; John French, Samuel Booth, Builders; John Butler, J. Morrison, Lamp and Chandelier Manufacturers; S. E. Cary, Jonathan Stewart, Upholsters; G. M. Woodward, James O. Morse, Iron Pipe Manufacturers, James K. Wheatley, T. A. Havemeyer, Sugar Refiners; T. E. Jewell, A. Greenleaf, Jr., Millers; J. S. Willard, Thomas T. Knight, Looking Glass and Frame Manufacturers; James L. Moore, Robert R. Story, Saddle and Harness Manufacturers; J. Johnson, J. A. Fuller, Brewers; Samuel Ingalls, George Chappel, Camphene Distillers; Thomas Rowe.

A. Thayer, Linseed Oil Manufacturers; James Sharkey, John Shuster, Marble Workers; S. D. Waring, George S. Harding, Coffee and Spice Grinders; B. T. Anderson, Joseph H. Mumby, Confectioners; A. M. Vail, Silvanus White, Skate Manufacturers; Patrick Cassidy, Iron Dealer; William Hager, Type Founder; Charles E. Smith, Umbrella Manufacturer; H. H. Hand, Trunk Manufacturer; Wright Ramsden, Plumber; G. F. [illegible], Stove Manufacturer; W. M. Brasher, Oil Cloth Manufacturer, George W. Robbins, Tin-ware Manufacturer; Charles B. Tatham, Lead-pipe Manufacturer; H. B. Whitty, Carriage Manufacturer; R. L. Allen, Agricultural Implement Manufacturer; Hiram F. St. John, Axe Manufacturer; F. S. Otis, Hoop-skirt Manufacturer; W. B. Higgins, Soap and Candle Manufacturer; Thomas Carroll, Tobacconist; David Fithian, Sash and Blind Manufacturer; John S. Loomis, Moulding Manufacturer; A. G. Hicks, Pencil Manufacturer; G. W. Hubert, Enamel-ware Manufacturer; J. H. McWilliams, Lock Manufacturer; John Phillips, Charles H. Baxter, Whiting Manufacturers; Richard H. Flanders, Oil Manufacturer; Julius Ives, Jr., Clothes Wringers.

Manufactures and Mechanic Arts. Eastern District—William H. Jenkins, Chairman, Samuel W. Traslow, Cordage; Thomas Rowland, Ship Builder, C. E. Bertrand, Sugar; William W. Armfield, Coal and Wood; James A. Taylor, Iron; Charles W. Fellows, Gas Fixtures, Henry C. Richardson, Hardware; Joseph L. Heath, Builder; Eckford Webb, Ship Builder; A. Leininger, Glass-ware, William Tuttle, Brass; J. B. Wickersham, Iron Rails; Watson Sandford, Stoves; James Hall, Iron; J. A. Heath, Cooper; Joseph Wilde, Coffee, George Wildey, Machinist; C. Dorflinger, Glass Manufacturer; W. Cabble, Wire-works; George C. Bennett, G. W. Plympton, Hiram M. Warren, Joseph Reeves, William Coles, Christian Neidig.

Manufactures.—Mrs. A. Truck, Chairman; Luke Barrington, Theodore Polhemus, Jr., John H. Prentice, Thomas Messenger, David Wesson, A. B. Baylis, Coe Adams, Joseph Ripley, W. J. Miller, J. P. Whitney, A. F. Hazen, J. Curtis, J. P. Wickham, C. Baylis, A. Cruikshanks, Nathan Beers, E. E. Estes, W. Spelman, D. Coven, E. A. Biden, Smith Fancher, A. Jewett, E. L. Bushnell, Peter Rice, L. B. Shaw, William Libby, C. H. Mills, Theodore Ovington, Miss Mary Connell, Mrs. F. H. Bigelow, N. Curtis, E. J. Hewlett, L. Burnham, Miss L. P. Brenchman, Mrs. Charles Marvin, L. Thomas, P. Wyckoff, B. H. Manning, Boyer.

Produce.—Arch. Baxter, Chairman; James P. Wallace, Samuel A. Sawyer, Smith J. Eastman, J. H. Holcomb, Curtis Noble, Seymour Burrell, George B. Douglas, Frederick Sherwood, Sidney Sanderson, Harvey E. Hicks, Alexander E. Orr, Smith Fancher, W. D. Mangam, James O. Weld, Hugh Allen, Stephen W. Cary, George Tucker, Coe Adams, Franklin Woodruff.

Kings County Town Contributions.—John Lefferts, Chairman; John D. Prince, Tunis I. Bergen, Dr. J. L. Zabriskie, Dr. H. L. Bartlett, Robert R. Fox, William Matthews, E. H. Kimball, John L. Ryder, Robert Magan, William Couwenhoven, Benjamin I. Hitchings, Bernardus I. Ryder, Charles R. Miller, Philip H. Reid, Rev. Mr. Van Buren, A. H. W. Van Sicklen, J. Ormiston Currie, Col. William I. Cropsey, Stedman Wright.

Flatbush. Mrs. J. Vanderbilt, Chairman; J. A. Lott, J. V. B. Martense, J. D. Prince, J. Lefferts, T. I. Bergen, Dr. Robinson, William Wall, J. M. Hood, W. Murphy, Miss M. S. Schuyler.

Windsor Terrace. Mrs. Hudson.

Flatlands. Mrs. A. Hubbard, E. K. Kimball, P. Couwenhoven, Doolittle, Miss Annie Lott.

Gravesend. Mrs. M. G. Hanson, S. Garretson, Misses E. Lake, J. Cropsey.

Fort Hamilton. Miss Brown.

Greenfield. Mrs. G. M. Close.

Bay Ridge.—Mrs. J. O. Perry, C. Tracy, J. Van Brunt, Fletcher, Miss M. Musgrave, Mrs. W. Sherman.

East New York. Mrs. C. R. Miller, P. H. Reed, A. H. W. Van Sicklen.

New Utrecht.—Mrs. J. Crane, J. Van Brunt, Jr.

Long Island Contributions.—Elias Lewis, Jr., Chairman; G. H. Vinton, Newtown; William Nicoll, Huntington; D. Bogart, Jr., Roslyn; Hon. Elias J. Beach, Glen Cove; Isaac H. Cocks, Westbury; S. B. Mersereau, Hempstead; James Rider, Jamaica; C. S. Powell, Farmingdale; John Harrold, Hempstead; Havens & Prince, Shelter Island; C. N. Brown, Sag Harbor; J. Madison Huntting, E. Hampton; H. G. Reeve, Mattituck, etc.; Goldsmith & Tuthill, Cutchogue; Hon. James H. Tuthill.

Chairmen of Ladies' Canvassing Committees.—Mrs. N. Burchard, W. W. Pell, H. Waters, A. Bradshaw, R. C. Benedict, J. D. Sparkman, Dr. Morrell.

Military, Fire Department, Police and Order.—Hon. J. S. T. Stranahan, Chairman; Gen. H. B. Duryea, Gen. Philip S. Crooke, Gen. J. C. Smith, Col. Calvin E. Pratt, Col. John B. Woodward, Hon. A. M. Wood, Major R. C. Ward, Major John S. Folk, Rufus R. Belknap, John Cunningham, John Doyle.

Auditing.—Ambrose Snow, Chairman; Hiram Bonner, Sidney Green, William Everdell, Jr., James Gridley, Daniel Godwin, John J. Studwell, W. D. Gookin, Ferdinand A. Crocker, Henry E. Rensmith, Charles Dimon.

THE CONTRIBUTORS TO THE FAIR.

The following list of contributors to the Fair are from the reports of the various Committees. They form as nearly a complete list of the contributions as it was possible under the circumstances to make—certainly as complete as the compilers of this History are able to give.

DONATIONS THROUGH THE COMMITTEE ON INTERNAL ARRANGEMENTS AND RECEPTION OF GOODS.

Miss Applegate and Bro., Prince st. $3 85
M. E. Abbott and F. A. Fenwick, 104 South Third st. 1 75
Wm. H. Arthur, 87 Nassau st. 102 70
Articles from a Lady 5 80
Mrs. Adolphus, 1 Cottage place, 8 85
Mrs. O. K. Barkley, 64 Carl st. 3 75
Mrs. Wm. Brine, 118 Montague st 6 00
Mrs. Bradshaw's canvassing ac'nt. 41 39
Mrs. Calvin Blanchard 6 00
John Butler, 118 Fulton st. 119 00
Edwin C. Burt, 57 Park Row 101 00
Bigelow & Co., 185 Fulton st. 75 50
Blind woman, 80 years of age 5 00
Bardet, Delaney, & Adamson, 67 Beekman st. 108 84
Brooklyn White Lead Co. 84 40
B. F. Babbitt & Co., 64 and 71 Washington st., N. Y. 250 00
F. W. Bassett & Co., Atlantic st. 80 00
Bethel Mission Sabbath School 104 85
Bramm & Bros., by Mrs. S. L. Brownell 88 00
Brooklyn Heights Seminary 278 36
Bert & Terhune 100 00
Miss Biggie, shoulder straps, &c. 19 60
Mrs. T. J. Bergen, boat and flag 30 00
Brooklyn Female Employm't Soc. 34 00
P. C. Barnum & Co., 124 Chatham street, N. Y. 16 00
Anthony Bussler 31 00
Barnstein & Bros. 33 98
Mrs. Brown and Mrs. Glover $1 50
Children's Society, Corning, N. Y. 41 91
A Lady in Canada (K. Nicholson). 14 85
J. & M. Christy, 240 Pearl st., N.Y. 80 86
J. C. Clark 5 00
Convent of the Visitation 108 10
Mrs. Carl, above 10 50
Mrs. Culbert, from manufacturers, 6 00
Church of the Restoration 720 58
Second Unitarian Church $1,444 47
do. by Mrs. H. M. Whiting 40 00—1,484 47
Central Baptist Church 783 61
Washington street M. E. Church 679 57
Fleet street M. E. Church 1,248 00
Westminster Church $765 37
By H. M. Smith 94 50— 766 87
Westminster Church Young Ladies' Society 388 79
By Mrs. J. Overacre 94 50— 435 80
South Fifth street M. E. Church 1,114 21
St. Peter's Episcopal Church 894 85
Elm Place Congregational Church 147 56
Third Universalist Society, Green Point 54 67
First Baptist Church, Green Point 278 85
Hanson Place M. E. Church 465 79
Hanson Place Baptist Church 404 78
York street M. E. Church 241 40
By Mrs. W. H. Beale 58 60— 300 00
Warren street Mission Church 307 78
First Ref'd Dutch Church 1,888 88

By Mrs. G. W. Dow..... [illegible] 10—[illegible]
Church on the Heights....2,[illegible] 42
By Mrs. Myers.......... 20 00
By Mrs. Robbins.. ...... [illegible]—1,610 67
First Presbyterian Church, E. D.. 175 37
Gothic M. E. Church.............. 150 10
Third Presbyterian Church....... 548 03
Athenæum Baptist Church........ 174 [illegible]
Strong Pl. Baptist Church.1,077 15
By Mrs. A. E. Piper .... 185 00—1,[illegible] 15
First Baptist Ch.Nassau st. 475 37
By Kemp, Day & Co.... 174 [illegible]— 549 67
Pierrepont street Baptist Church. 964 80
Thirty-one Families of First Presbyterian Church, Remsen st.... 748 [illegible]
Holy Trinity, Clinton st.......... 1,[illegible] 65
Bedford Avenue Baptist Church.. [illegible] 16
Ladies of St. Andrew's Church... 100 00
Sands street M. E. Church.1,[illegible] 84
By Mrs. Fairweather.... [illegible]—1,[illegible]
Christ's Church, South Brooklyn. [illegible]
St. Paul's Church............. ... [illegible] 10
St. Ann's Church, Washington st. 1,074 75
Washington Avenue Baptist Church . ... 1[illegible] 87
Do. from Tiffany & Co. by Mrs.W.H. Cotton. [illegible] 00— [illegible] 51
State street Congregational Ch. . [illegible]
Grace Church, Brooklyn Heights.. [illegible]
Church of the Saviour. .. 1,[illegible]
Do. by Mrs. J. H. Frothingham and Miss Carey.1,169 14—2,[illegible] 81
Franklin Avenue Presb. Church.. 1[illegible] 54
Second Presbyterian Church...... 1,1[illegible] 31
Pacific street M. E. Church........ [illegible]
South Presbyterian Church....... 1,[illegible]
Prot. Ref'd Dutch Ch. New Lotts. 75 34
Plymouth Church.........4,[illegible]
Do. from Beaufort, S.C. [illegible]
Do. Mrs.H.W.Beecher. 180 [illegible]
Do. from Mrs. Fuller.. 178 00
Do. from Ovington Bros 140 00—4,[illegible]
Lafayette Avenue Presb. Church.. 1,4[illegible] 47
First Presb. Church—additional.. 61 [illegible]
A few families in Middle Ref'd Dutch Church................... 404 [illegible]
East Reformed Dutch Church..... [illegible]
Central Cong. Church, Ormond pl. [illegible] 45
Carlton Avenue M. E. Church ... 16 00
Ref'd Dutch Ch., Clermont ave... [illegible]
Greenwood Baptist Church..... .. [illegible]
New England Cong. Church, E. D. 87 00
Pilgrim Church Inventory.4,379 80
Additional .... 35 00—4,414 80
Young Ladies' South Brooklyn Union League... .... $[illegible]
Rogers & Polk.................... [illegible] 70
Upholsterers in employ of Thos Brooks.... .... [illegible] 00
Miss M. Van Voorhis, Brooklyn.. 6 [illegible]
New York Rubber Co .... [illegible] 44
Miss Gertrude Halsey's school, No. 18 Concord st............ 7 40
Miss Hannah E. Wild, aged 13 yrs. 7 70
Mrs. Ormsby, Joralemon street... [illegible] 00
Mrs. Simonson, 196 Adelphi st. 10 00
Messrs. White & Nichols......... [illegible] 00
Mrs. Wells .... [illegible] 00
Miss Emily Everett............... [illegible]
Young Ladies of Mme Girard's school 143 77
Mrs. Samuel McLean from Mrs. Parish......................... 60 00
Mrs. Samuel McLean from Mrs. Downey .... [illegible]
H. A. White. 7 50
Susan Moore....................... 4 00
Jonathan Moore & Co............ 15 [illegible]
Mrs. Alexander McCue.......... [illegible]
Sidney pl. school, by Mrs. Fitch.. [illegible]
Mrs. Walling, one basket......... [illegible]
Mrs. Halsey .... [illegible]
S. J. Pardessus, 60 Liberty street, through Mrs. Trask.... .... [illegible]
Katy Graf, Shetland hood ...... 1 [illegible]
Rev. E. S. Staples, Brooklyn, E.D. [illegible]
C. Darling & Bro., [illegible] Fulton ave.. [illegible]
Miss Van Cleef, tidies............ [illegible]
Samuel McLean & Co. .... [illegible]
Mrs. Margaret Moore, above Harlem..................... .... 19 [illegible]
Miss Ellen A. Tappan. ...... [illegible]
Mrs. Isaac R. St. John.... .... 78 00
Mrs. Wilson....................... [illegible]
A Lady............................ 5 50
Ericsson Aid Soc. by Mrs. Lowber. 307 55
School of Protestant Orphan Asylum, Cumberland st............. [illegible] 00
J. L. Mott, Iron Works, N. Y..... [illegible]
David S. Quimby, cor. Henry and Poplar streets.... .... [illegible]
W. Jackson & Son, 346 Front st., N. Y........................... [illegible]
Sanford, Truslow & Co., [illegible] Water st., N.Y............ ... [illegible]
M.P.Levan, & Sanford Heaters, N.Y. [illegible]
C. F. Whitney, 20 Grindstones, do. 1[illegible] 00
Geo. F. Sutton, 77 Fulton st...... [illegible]

Picard & Hill, 185 Water st., N. Y.	$45 00
Misses Hattie and Louise Olay, Clermont ave.	5 00
Oakley & Keating, 73 South st., N. Y.	88 00
Mrs. J. P. Wickham, from R. C. Robbins	101 89
Mrs. T. N. Hickcox, 53 Park place.	4 80
C. H. Little & Co., 146 Atlantic st.	97 85
Chas. Jenkins, 23 Monroe place	18 00
Tuttle & Bailey, 74 Beekman st.	75 85
A. K. Larabee, N. Y.	60 00
T. Mansfield, 230 Water st.	20 00
C. J. Taylor, 89 Livingston st.	108 00
Devlin & Co., 459 & 461 B'way, N. Y.	201 00
Thos. M. Jenkins, Ryerson st.	45 00
Huntington & DuBois, 888 Fulton street	84 00
Philopatrian Society	456 19
Patent Package Co., Newark, N. J.	75 00
Steinway & Sons, 71 East 14th st.	385 00
C. Neidigr, 67 Bowery	108 60
Mrs. (Gamaliel) King, from a few of her friends	80 00
From a Lady, through Mrs. A. McCue	21 40
From members of Friends' Society, by Mrs. Jane Carpenter	580 07
Society of Friends, by Mrs. R. Underhill and Mrs. S. Lakins	948 60
Miller & Co., No. 9 Maiden Lane.	838 50
Hahn & Zippel, 29 Court st.	15 00
From the Sailors of the North Carolina, by Mrs. Capt. Meade	61 00
W. R. Tice, 6?? Fulton st., by Mrs. Trask	100 00
Mrs. Sherwell & Mrs. Draper, Great Barrington, Mass	65 60
Little Girl nine years old (Phebe Hamlin)	4 00
Mrs. Hook's School, through Mrs. Packer	31 80
Geo. Reynolds, 290 Court st.	87 00
Mrs. Chas. W. Spaulding	5 00
Miss St. John	18 00
St. Paul's Orphan Asylum	18 00
Lafayette Flint Glass Co.	81 00
Wheeler & Wilson Manuf'g Co.	393 00
E. Hadden, Remsen st.	70 10
F. O. Richardson, 107 John st.	68 50
P. Roulhans, by J. J. Vining	80 00
By D. S. Waring, Starch and B. Powder	70 00
A. Greenleaf, Jr., 18 Fulton ave.	141 00
J. Thompson, 2 caloric ext'r	10 00
Richardson, Boynton & Co., N. Y.	$75 00
Mrs. Jas. L. Moore	138 00
Union Sleigh Co., 88 Bergen st.	85 80
By Chas. Storrs	87 75
A. B. Sands & Co., 141 William st., N. Y.	108 00
Mrs. A. L. Mold, 181 Fulton st.	44 80
Stoddart & Morris	411 00
G. B. Owen, American Clock Co.	34 00
Mrs. Theo. Rogers, Remsen street, through Mrs. Henry Collins	40 00
Miss Garnett, embr.	8 60
C. J. Whitlock, Vase Lilies	35 00
Little Boy, Gold Pen, of his own make	8 00
Little Boy, Glass Case, of his own make	9 00
Samuel McLean, from W. B. Higgins & Co., Scotland	880 75
Samuel McLean, through Wm. B. Higgins and Mrs. McNee, of Paisley, Scotland	685 85
Mrs. H. E. Matthews	48 67
Young Ladies, Graduates and Scholars of the Farmington School, Farmington, Conn., and Graduates and Scholars of the Seminary on the Heights, Brooklyn	1,875 94
Anthony Bussler	61 00
Mrs. Capt. Foster, Shirt	2 00
Public School No. 8	20 50
Primary School No. 4, E.D., Teachers of	18 30
Public School No. 23	68 43
Public School No. 24	64 63
Public School No. 14	80 69
Public School No. 27—(This amount was raised by penny contributions, and the teachers sat up nights to make the articles)	104 10
Public School No. 15, Grammar Department	248 84
Public School No. 17	75 64
Public School No. 25	151 68
Public School No. 20	85 00
Public School No. 18, Primary Department	78 91
Public School No. 21	6 00
Public School No. 16, Girls' Grammar Department	44 12
Public School No. 11	119 88
Public School No. 15, Teachers and Pupils	104 68

Public School No. 16....	$[illegible] 64
Public School No. 8.....	[illegible]
Public School No. 15, 2d Class Girls	7 50
Public School No. 11, additional..	8 00
City School No. 17, from Mrs. Spice.	65 00
Mrs. Margaret E. Dodge (81 years of age,) 78 Middagh street, Patriot Bed-spread, purchased in $1 sales, and sent to the Paymaster	[illegible] 00
Rogers, Smith & Co..........	18 00
F. S. Woodward—Hair Restorer..	10 00
J. Darrington, 111 Atlantic st.....	143 35
Poppenhausen & Konig, by Mrs. W. J. A. Fuller....................	110 [illegible]
Public School No. 13, additional..	1 00
30 Parlor and Kitchen Holders....	1 60
Friends Society, additional, by Mrs. S. Lakens...............	87 00
East New York, through Mrs. Vanderbilt........................	60 00
Mrs. Waters, from Mrs. Honora Delmonico..................	65 00
Miss Orton, Court street	9 00
Ladies' Patriotic Union, South Brooklyn.......................	160 00
Soldiers' Aid Society, Norwich, Ct.	14 00
Chas. G. Smith, 136 Fulton st.....	[illegible] 00
Dr. Chas. H. Shepard, 63 Columbia st., Turkish Bath Tickets........	60 00
Mrs. Dell, 6 pair Slippers........	3 50
Mrs. Lord and Mrs. Messenger...	80 00
Schuyler, Hadley & Graham, by Mrs. Messenger..............	158 57
Bernstein Bros.................	[illegible]
Mrs. Brown and Mrs. Glover.....	1 [illegible]
C. W. Caldwell from Samuel Corn.	15 00
Do. B. Wolff & Co.....	15 00
Do. H. Rothstein......	15 00
Do. Roff & Hein......	15 00
Do. Rinaldo & Laskey.	15 00
Do. C. Frank's Sons...	15 00
Do. M. Mark's & Bro..	[illegible] 50
Do. Sprahon & Rahmer	15 00
Do. Isidor Bros........	15 00
Do. H. M. Silvermann.	15 00
Mrs. Wm. M. Haight, by H. P. Morgan............................	10 00
Fisher & Bro., McDougal st., N.Y.	60 00
Willard, Everett & Co., Boston, Mass..............................	30 00
Knigler & Glimmen, N. Y........	60 00
Three little Girls, through Miss Hiner...........................	6 25
Haggerty Bros., 8 and 10 Platt st..	1 65
Miss Walsh, of Yonkers...........	$[illegible] 00
Additional from Public School No. [illegible]....................	[illegible] 75
James Holdsworth..............	[illegible] 00
Miss Viola Smith.............	[illegible] 75
Mrs. B. Westlake...............	5 00
Grube & Metz, Music..........	18 50
Sanitary Commission, Washington, D. C., by Mrs. M. F. Odell	[illegible] 78
Young, Schultz & Co............	177 00
Lawrence, Griggs & Kingsbury, 47 Murray st., N. Y.............	100 00
Slarthar & Nichols, 65 Broadway.	800 00
Golding & Dunlop, 151 Broadway, by F. H. Bigelow..............	60 00
Sensstack & Rahmer, 141 Broadway, by F. H. Bigelow..........	64 00
Fleet street M. E. Ch., additional.	41 19
Mt. Prospect Industrial School...	[illegible] 67
Second Unitarian Soc., additional.	8 00
St. Ann's Church, additional....	3 00
Masters Hull and Mills..........	10 00
Third Presb. Church, additional..	17 58
Mrs. I. H. Frothingham, and Miss A. R. Carey, from their friends.	1,[illegible]
Mrs. Sanderson, Hammock	5 00
Mrs. C. B. Loomis, Fancy Goods..	[illegible] 00
Wm. J. Root, Lamp Shade......	4 00
J. Josef Stickler, No. 1 Lafayette Avenue, music...............	30 00
Public School No. [illegible], additional..	[illegible] 00
Prof. Pamalee, N. England Polka	15 00
Westminster Church, by Mrs. A. F. Hazen................................	1[illegible] 18
Mrs. Sargent, New Britain, Ct....	19 75
Packer Collegiate Institute, Collegiate Department....	111 [illegible]
Do. 1st Academic 1st Dept	1[illegible]
Do. 1st Academic 2d Dept.	[illegible]
Do. 1st Academic 3d Dept.	1[illegible]
Do. 2d Academic 1st Dept.	[illegible]
Do. 2d Academic 2d Dept.	[illegible]
Do. 2d Academic 3d Dept.	1[illegible]
Do. 2d Preparatory........	[illegible] 75
Do. 3d Preparatory........	1[illegible]
Pub. School No. 7, Primary Dept.	16 [illegible]
Do. No. 7, Female Dept..	87 [illegible]
Church on the Heights	40 00
Public School No. 11, additional..	4 78
Clinton Avenue Church..........	1,[illegible]
F. H. Amidon, 549 Broadway, by F. H. Frothingham	40 00
W. Wisdom, through T. Brooks..	10 00
South Cong. Church.....$1,[illegible]	

South Cong. Church, from South Orange Presbyterian Church, N. J. .... $94 13—	1,607 09
Mrs. Henry Sheldon, Chairman Fancy Goods Committee, from Miss F. Creagh	11 78
Do. from South Fifth street M. E. Church, additional	118 75
Second Presb. Church, additional.	10 00
Westminster Church, additional..	8 50
St. Ann's Church, additional.....	12 00
Plymouth Church, additional. ..	61 75
Sylvanus White, from A. Fuller & Co., Brattleboro,' Vt...........	25 00
Do. A Manufacturer.........	9 00
Do. S. & F. Boylston, N. Y..	60 00
Do. G. Lindemann & Co....	50 00
Do. H. Seymour, N. Y......	80 00
Do. J. C. Shaden...........	59 78
Do. Fred'k Stevens..........	30 89
Do. G. Gunther...	8 00
Do. R. Bellatby, N. Y.......	10 00
Do. Phillips & Manning.....	30 75
Do. W. A. Dodge...	49 00
Do. A Manufacturer........	5 00
Do. Meriden Cutlery Co....	20 00
Do. P. & F. Corbin, N. Y.	25 50
Do. Chas. Zinn & Co........	25 00
Do. Boyer, Smith & Co., N. H., Ct................ ..	18 00
Sylvanus White, from G. W. Koch..	15 00
Do. Musgrove & Young......	15 00
Do. Edward Behr............	30 00
Do. Atwater, Benham & Co..	100 00
Do. Wm. Belcher...	98 20
Do. E. P. Cooley, Manuf'er..	11 00
Do. S. Harrison & Son... ..	6 00
Do. Hills & Benton..........	9 75
D. S. Waring, from a Manuf'er...	30 00
Total..............	$[illegible]
St. Ann's Ch., additional, $300 00	
St. Ann's Ch., through Employment Society. 300 00	
St. Ann's Ch., proceeds of sales of French Dept....[illegible]	4,[illegible]
Tabernacle Baptist Church.......	91 74
Carlton Avenue M. E. Church.....	298 61
Mr. Palmer, Purser of the Steamship Sierra Nevada, "Everlasting" Plant............	100 00
Donations from several gentlemen in Toys and Dolls....	25 00
Ladies of Hempstead, additional.	41 10
Ladies of Merbine, additional....	35 [illegible]
Southampton, per B. H. Foster...	4 00
Huntington, per W. H. Nicoll.....	8 85
Port Jefferson....................	18 75

LONG ISLAND.

Articles from Astoria, Queens Co.	$308 12
E. F. Ketchum, Babylon........	4 00
Bay Ridge Association..	240 00
Ladies' Soldiers' Aid Society, Cove Oyster Bay...	274 09
C. Dorflinger & Co., Greenpoint.	570 80
East Hampton Soldiers' Aid Soc'y.	119 18
East Moriches, Miss R. A. Lewis.	2 00
Flatbush, town of, by Mrs. John Vanderbilt.......	1,697 11
Flatbush M. E. Church, by Mrs. John Vanderbilt...............	98 20
Flatbush, Windsor Terrace, by Mrs. John Vanderbilt...	64 52
Flatbush, St. Paul's Church, by	708 61
Flatbush, Ladies of..............	40 18
Flatlands, by Mrs. J. Vanderbilt..	252 62
Flushing, by Mrs. H. L. Packer..	6 47
Flushing, through L. B. Prince...	248 00
Flushing, Ladies of, through L. B. Prince........................	340 70
Flushing, by Robert Willetts.....	$20 00
Flushing, by Parsons & Co.......	10 00
Soldiers' Aid Society, Franklinville, L. I...	31 16
Farmingdale, L. I	4 00
Town of Gravesend...............	122 54
Ladies' Soldiers' Aid Society, Glen Cove..........	570 34
Ladies of Glen Cove.	8 00
Greenport, Chas. Bachman, by J. Howard..........	10 00
Town of Hempstead, by J. Harold.	67 [illegible]
Citizens of Huntington and Cold Spring.........................	75 80
Citizens of Huntington, by Mrs. Nichols....	6 00
Thos. Hallock, Mattituck, by J. Shirley........	4 74
Ladies of Jamaica....	278 08
Hon. John King, Jamaica.. .	30 00
Ladies' Aid Society, Jamaica ..	23 40

E. J. & J. W. Jerome, Mineola, Queens Co., by John Howard...	$7 00
Ladies of Queens Co.	14 [illegible]
A Lady from Shelter Island	4 00
Elias Lewis, Stuffed Owl, North Hempstead	25 00
Ladies of Huntington, by Mrs. Nichol..........................	25 [illegible]
Ladies, Sewing Aid Society, Melton Place by J. R. Rowland, Suffolk Co	[illegible]
Ladies of Riverhead, by Geo. Miller, Riverhead..........	6 00
New Utrecht, by Mrs. John Vanderbilt.......	184 51
Ladies of North Utrecht..........	108 47
A Lady of Newtown	6 00
Ladies of Newtown..............	490 61
Western District of North Hempstead, by C. W. Rogers...	4[illegible] 61
Women's Association of the Village of Oyster Bay............	[illegible] 40
Port Jefferson Invalid Soldiers' Relief Association.	191 87
Do. from James E. Bayliss..	[illegible] 00
Do. from Mrs. L. Stewart.........	15 00
A few Ladies of Ravenswood.....	67 25
Roslyn, Queens Co., L. I...........	59 16
Ladies of Rockaway.............	31 71
Ladies of Riverhead..............	[illegible]
Union Relief, Southold, L. I. ...	174 30
Soldiers' Aid Society of Queens Co., by Mrs. R. T. Kissam......	[illegible]
Sag Harbor, C. N. Brown	85 00
Ladies of Smithtown.........	$146 [illegible]
S. L. Thompson, Setauket........	14 30
Ladies of Southampton...........	53 [illegible]
Upper Aquebogue, by E. Lewis, Jr.	101 50
Wading River, Riverhead........	12 05
West Hampton or Beaver Dam...	14 [illegible]
Woodhaven, L. I., by Jno. Harold	5 [illegible]
Young Ladies of Peconic, Suffolk Co., by Miss Lizzie Goldsmith..	5 54
Jno. Hooper, Brooklyn, by Elias Lewis, Jr......................	25 [illegible]
Astoria, by a Young Lady, through Benjamin Blossom.............	25 00
Ladies of Hempstead, by E. R. Durkee	6 [illegible]
Mrs. W. Nichol, Huntington, L. I.	5 [illegible]
Women's Association of the village of Oyster Bay, additional..	134 [illegible]
Rev. J. S. Dobson, Moriches, L. I.	3 60
Havens & Prince, Shelter Island.	11 [illegible]
Young Ladies of Hempstead, by John Harold......	7 [illegible]
Ladies of Hempstead, by John Harold.......	7 [illegible]
Hallett Cornell, aged 94 years, Pudding Sticks................ ..	1 [illegible]
B. Skidmore, Amityville, L. I ...	80
N. F. Smith, Smithtown, L. I.....	1 00
Thos. S. Strong, Setauket, L. I...	[illegible] 50
Ladies of Bridgehampton, L. I....	[illegible] 00
Ladies of Flushing, by L. B. Prince	41 00
Total..............................	$[illegible] 97

GOODS RECEIVED WITHOUT INVOICE.

Two boxes goods from Fort Hamilton, through Mrs. Gelston.
J. H. & J. O. Cunningham & Co., 1 French Trunk, 1 Morocco Sac.
Pincushions from the country, through Mrs. Messenger.
Palmer & Co., Chocolate Cream Drops.
Mrs. Hill, Boonton, N. J., donation.
The Misses Martel, Greenwood, sundry articles.
Agnes Heath, 1 Pincushion.
Lewis Stocker, Music.
Strauss, Bianchi & Co., Artificial Flowers.
George A. Olney, 63 John street, lot of Goods.
Lot of Toys, etc., from Miss Sutton's private school.
Dried Fruit from Mrs. Goldsmith, Southold, L. I.
Seven Dolls, in mats and socks.
Little Charley Crowley, sundry articles.
Mrs. Parsons, sundry articles.
Mrs. J. Merill, Mats and Needle Case.

Mrs. L. A. Fuller, Grand avenue, Sea Moss.
Lehrecht & Orme, 3?8 Broadway, 8 Maps.
Sackett's Harbor, 1 box of Fancy Goods.

RECAPITULATION.

Ladies' Fancy Goods Committee	$18,945 78
Gentlemen's Fancy Goods Committee	4,801 98
Long Island	9,586 97
Various sources	78,[illegible] 67
Total	$108,[illegible] [illegible]

GEORGE G. STEPHENSON, Chairman Gentlemen's Committee.
MRS. GEORGE B. ARCHER, Chairman Ladies' Committee.

DONATIONS THROUGH THE LADIES FANCY GOODS COMMITTEE.

South Fifth st. M. E. Church, Rev. C. D. Foss	$1,[illegible] 98
Universalist Society, Rev. B. Peters, (E. D.)	454 08
Moravian Chapel, Jay st., near Myrtle avenue	108 80
The German Citizens	1,346 57
Poppenhausen & Koenig, per Mrs. T. Achelis	438 65
Unkart & Co., per Mrs. E. Unkart	184 30
The German Citizens, E. D.	857 19
Second Baptist Church, E. D., Rev. J. N. Tolm	63 50
First Baptist Church, E. D., Rev. S. Baker	1,419 65
Bushwick Neighborhood	875 80
First Reformed Dutch Church, E. D., Dr. Porter	848 08
New England Cong. Church, E. D., Rev. W. R. Tompkins	767 94
St. Paul's Church, E. D., Rev. J. W. Clarke	[illegible]
Lee Avenue Ref'd Dutch Church, Rev. J. McIlvaine	808 18
St. Mark's Church, E. D., Rev. S. Haskins	207 80
St. Peter's and St. Paul's Catholic Churches, E. D., Father Malone	884 00
First Presb. Church, Henry st., Rev. C. S. Robinson, additional	188 40
Third Presb. Church	80 00
A. T. Stewart & Co.	1,026 00
Mrs. Jas. Hall and daughter, E. D.	70 85
St. Mary's Church, Rev. D. M. Johnson, additional	30 00
St. Peter's Church, Rev. Dr. Paddock, additional	80 50
Brooklyn Y. M. Christian Asso.	$240 80
Through Mrs. Isaac Badeau and	
" Mrs. J. E. Ritchie	418 00
" Miss L. Agnes Russell	70 75
" Miss F. Creagh, additional, So. 5th M. E. Church, E. D.	97 73
" Miss Mary E. Jarvis	647 18
" Mrs. Henry Sanger	855 00
" Miss Maria Messenger	188 00
" Mrs. Horace M. Warren	180 95
" Mrs. W. C. Perry	43 75
" Mrs. W. H. Beare	85 30
" Mary S. Griffith	200 00
" Miss Amelia Beard, including a $5 gold piece, $17 96	116 67
" Miss Addie Wright	806 [illegible]
" Miss Susan Nelson	165 47
" Miss F. C. West	40 40
" Madame St. Amant	156 95
" Miss Harriet Tucker	480 41
" Miss Mary A. Taylor and St. John's Church	818 71
" Mrs. Hugh Allen	849 48
" Misses Duckwitz	207 85
" Mrs. R. J. Hunter	284 50
" Miss Minnie S. Stanton	193 75
" Miss Mary Miller	167 00
" Miss J. Buckmaster	49 78
" Mrs. J. S. Rockwell	865 05
" Mrs. B. F. Lunt	201 80
" Miss E. L. Howe	189 64
" Mrs. Bryan H. Smith	843 40
" Mrs. S. Gracie, and Grace Church, additional	173 01
" Mrs. A. P. Purves	151 50
" Miss A. J. Petry	84 30
" Mrs. Henry Sheldon	823 00

From Mrs. S. H. Garrison $50 00
" Miss Beal, E. D. 56 10
" Eagleton & Co., per Jas. C. Wilson 100 00
" Miss Caroline Northam 20 00
" Sundry Persons 18 00

CASH CONTRIBUTIONS.

Through 3d Presb. Church, Mrs. I. Budean 172 00
" Mrs. E. Unhart 180 50
" Mrs. W. C. Perry 10 00
" Mrs. Beare 9 00
" Mrs. Henry Sheldon 135 00
" Mrs. T. Arbelle 15 00
" Mrs. R. P. Laul 65 00
" Mrs. R. J. Hunter 210 00
" Mrs. H. Allen 6 00
" Mrs. Bryan H. Smith 148 00
" Mrs. A. P. Purves 5 00
" Mrs. T. W. Morrison, from St. Peter's Church 6 00
" Mrs. H. M. Warren, E. D. 41 00
" Mrs. C. W. Goddard and Mrs. D. S. Mills, from Bushwick Neighborhood 348 70

Through Mrs. S. Gracie from a few Ladies of Grace Church 650 00
" Madame St. Amant 135 00
" Mrs. Henry Sanger 60 00
" Mrs. Herm. Garlichs, from German Citizens 145 15
" Mrs. Schneider, E. D. 3 00
" Miss Mary E. Jarvis 25 00
" Miss Minnie S. Stanton 250 00
" Miss Addie Wright, E. D. 57 50
" Miss C. Bush, from St. Peter's and St. Paul's Catholic Church, E. D. 618 00
" Miss Mary S. Griffith 7 00
" Miss A. J. Berry, E. D. 11 00
" Miss Harriet Tucker 91 00
" Miss Mary Miller 10 00
" Miss J. Buckmaster 60 00
" Miss Amelia Beard, from Eli Beard, E. D., $100 .... 250 00
From Charles Wall, E. D. 250 00
" St. Mark's Church, E. D. 65 00
" Sundry Persons 6 80

Grand Total .... $[illegible]
Mrs. H. SHELDON, Chairman.

DONATIONS THROUGH THE GENTLEMEN'S FANCY GOODS COMMITTEE.

S. E. Howard	500 00	Geo. A. Clark & Bro.	100 00
Charles Storrs	500 00	Strassberger & Kuhn	100 00
Henry Sanger	500 00	Augustine Storrs	250 00
William H. Lyon	150 00	B. T. Pippey & Co.	100 00
James R. Taylor	500 00	P. T. Barnum	100 00
Abel Denison	250 00	A. P. Purves	100 00
J. W. Green	100 00	George Pearce & Co.	250 00
D. S. Arnold	250 00	Vyse & Sons	100 00
Charles Bardwell	100 00	Holmes, Booth & Haydens	100 00
Alex. McCallum	100 00	F. T. Mason	50 00
Carter, Stewart & Co.	200 00	Andrews, Giles & Co.	50 00
Enos Richardson	1,000 00	Wm. Topping	50 00
D. C. Robbins	250 00	J. S. Hollingshead	50 00
J. B. Spelman & Sons	200 00	Lawrence, Cohen & Co.	50 00
F. Hinchman	100 00	W. T. Peet	50 00
H. B. Dickinson	100 00	J. B. Cooper	50 00
Henry Elliott	200 00	A. Dougherty	50 00
C. F. A. Hendricks	100 00	Robbins, Calhoun & Co.	50 00
Mrs. Wm. H. Cary	200 00	J. M. Bradstreet & Son	50 00
Charles F. Blake	157 50	Seckel, Davis & Co.	50 00
Michael Snow	100 00	Benj. M. Smith	50 00
Joseph R. Brush	100 00	Scovill Manuf'g Co.	50 00
Geo. S. Cary	250 00	J. H. Dater	25 00
R. & G. Westlake	100 00	Joseph Gillott	25 00

Lawrence, Crofts & Co.	500 00
E. H. Arnold & Son	50 00
D. A. Taylor	25 00
D. B. Powell	25 00
E. Hodges	25 00
Sawyer & Judson	25 00
S. D. Rosenbaum	10 00
Milo A. Taylor	5 00
Anson, Herman & Co.	25 00
Cumings Menzing	25 00
J. Depriler	25 00
Bolles & Sufkes	25 00
John G. A. Vaught	25 00
Louis Strouffer	25 00
Burroughs, Allen & Co	25 00
Chas. E. Hale & Co.	25 00
A. J. Hull	25 00
Hayward & Briggs	25 00
A. Miller & Co	25 00
Williston, Knight & Co	25 00
S. F. Jenkins	25 00
R. O. Storrs	25 00
Lincoln, Tifft & Bacon	20 00
C. Hale	10 00
Hastings & Potter	10 00
Geo. P. Pithin	10 00
Andrew W. Gill	10 00
M. W. Robinson	10 00
Waterbury Hook & Eye Co	10 00
D. S. Hammond	10 00
Taylor, Richards & Co.	10 00
R. Fowd, Jr	10 00
H. H. Sparks	14 00
Thomas Yates	10 00
J. R. Hall	10 00
C. O. Storrs	10 00
D. Starr	5 00
J. Rosenthal & Co.	10 00
L. Saarbach & Co.	10 00
Holzinger & Bruckheimer	10 00
H. & N. Kayser	10 00
H. A. Tuttle	10 00
C. G. Sanford	10 00
L. Brandick	10 00
J. Stewart	10 00
Julius Wiele	10 00
W. A. Potter	10 00
Cash—J. W. P.	5 00
Grumbach & Marshall	5 00
Metz & Co.	5 00
H. B. Howell	5 00
Daniel Bickwell	5 00
John M. Wardwell	5 00
American Flask and Cap Co.	5 00
Barton, Alexander & Waller	25 00
C. F. Hanks	5 00
S. B. Church	5 00
Thomas Reynolds	5 00
Thomas P. Browse	5 00
Jared Pratt	5 00
Thomas Buckman	5 00
C. Waterman	5 00
J. C. Dickinson	5 00
C. S. Weatherby	5 00
J. L. Harlem	5 00
S. H. Jones	5 00
R. G. Dun	5 00
J. D. Wilcox	5 00
Washington Manuf'g Co.	5 00
D. T. Terry	5 00
D. B. Sanford	5 00
J. B. B.	5 00
119 Myrtle Avenue	5 00
Julius Flatto	5 00
Cash	5 00
Britton Brothers	150 00
S. H. & Co.	25 00
J. L. D	5 00
W. A. Wales	10 00
C. O. Morris	25 00
L. B. Binsse	25 00
F. T. Aatchman	50 00
John Bollecke	50 00
C. Peck	10 00
Louis Switzer	10 00
Ewald Caron	100 00
C. W. L. F. Morrow	25 00
J. Q. Preble	50 00
S. H. Emery	25 00
D. W. Robinson	10 00
Henry Baylis	10 00
John O'Hara	10 00
E. Fabrequette, Jr	10 00
J. Gernon	10 00
J. Fisher	5 00
Joseph McKee	1 00
M. Mullan	1 00
R. J. Clark	1 00
W. S. Liptrott	1 00
C. F. Van Blankensteyn	500 00
D. S. Barnes	100 00
Charles Payan & Co.	25 00
Robert Shaw	50 00
F. Jeffries	1 00
James Douglass	150 00
Sawyer & Judson	25 00
Williston, Knight & Co.	25 00
H. G. D. & T. M. Chace	25 00

W. S. Gove	735 00
Cash	5 00
Littlefield Bros	75 00
F. H. Congdon	65 00
Madison Mixter	15 00
B. Shaw	50 00
John McCracken	500 00
Nathaniel Hillyer	100 00
A. Brinkerhoff	15 00
Scranton & Co	1,850 00
Niederman & Shapter	180 00
Chas. F. Blake	91 50
A. Leesbeurgh & Van Aux	60 85
Keller & Lingg	44 75
R. T. Webster	65 00
Wallets—E. A. S	5 40
Geo. S. Moulton, Willimantic Linen Co	309 00
Comstock, Cheever & Co	697 65
Fletcher Bros. & Co	200 00
Hamil & Booth	100 00
James Barnett & Co	108 00
John Ryle	812 50
T. J. Vale	125 00
Johnson & Co	300 00
Johnson & Co	100 00
Jesse Oakley	300 75
J. R. Williams & Co	19 40
Linn Bros	75 25
Redfield, Rice & Co	78 00
Stafford Bros	75 95
Eberhard Faber	84 48
Novelty Rubber Co	50 00
T. R. Bynner	60 00
James D. Bard, Ag't	60 62
Kniffen Bros	55 00
A. Heuley & Co	97 50
Otto Kohlhage	28 50
Thaddeus Davids & Co	31 00
A. W. F. T. Peters	80 50
Wm. Kind	35 00
R. Esterbrook & Co	35 00
E. C. Pratt & Bro	28 00
Flagg & Briggs	15 49
Thomas Worsley	28 00
J. & A. Blumenthal	18 75
A. Jacoby	35 97
Melancthon M. Hurd	15 62
Dennison & Co	16 00
J. Bickendorfer	10 00
D. C. Silleck & Cox	20 80
R. Sondheim	10 75
Jacob March	5 80
C. B. Prime	5 80
J. F. Hopkinson	92 95
Nonotuck Silk Co	101 10
B. & S.	20 40
Meriden Britannia Co	160 58
D. C. Silleck & Cox	80 50
Bradley & Hubbard	94 48
R. Snyder	20 28
M. B. Davis	10 00
E. Schoonmaker	18 60
D. B. Judson	6 50
W. H. Van Wort	5 00
F. Donington	150 90
A. V. Blake	108 60
C. H. Coffin, large Shell Comb	
Pearce & Ruddock	15 50
N. F. Griswold	25 71
J. & W. H. Atwell	71 00
Geo. W. Stafford & Co	19 50
F. W. Robinson	25 50
American Pin Co. and North Stanley & Co	75 97
A. Picard	14 50
John C. Koch	89 00
Mrs. J. D. Wilcox and sister	8 12
Anson, Hermann & Co	11 69
L. Sarbach & Co	9 65
J. & L. Blumenthall	15 00
J. G. Wittie	10 00
Green & Daniels	151 50
Sidney Smith	15 40
Adolph Jacobi & Co	10 88
E. M. Bassett	80 00
Spiers & Champney	149 00
Alexander Nova	65 95
Sawyer & Judson	11 50
Fletcher Bros	978 11
Dennis Everett	87 16
Alexander King	67 95
Novelty Rubber Co	85 00
Armes & Bardwell	58 00
Hyman E. Hart	40 00
Glenn & Co	71 97
Jesse O. Keys	81 47
M. Cohn	70 00
O. G. Miller	30 00
J. Christadora	60 68
Benj. F. Badger	108 00
J. R. Torrey	9 00
A. G. Barry	34 00
A. Charvette	125 00
Patch & Smith	104 00
E. A. S.	2 00
Colgate & Co	49 50
American Whip Co	87 50

J. C. Welton............................ $10 00
E. Shepardson............................ [illegible]
G. G. Spellman............................ 43 [illegible]
Spencer Jaimeson & Co............................ [illegible]
A. B. Chapman............................ 5 00
B. F. Dabbitt............................ 218 00
Phalon & Son............................ 18 00
Mrs. Dale............................ 4 50
V. W. Parmelee............................ 50 00
Knives............................ $5 50
Steele & Co............................ 30 00
Samuel L. Stafford............................ 54 [illegible]

Total............................ $18,[illegible]
Congregation Beth Elohim............................ [illegible]

Grand total............................ $18,[illegible]

S. R. HOWARD, Chairman.

DONATIONS THROUGH THE COMMITTEE ON MANUFACTURES AND MECHANIC ARTS.

WESTERN DISTRICT.

Atlantic Steam Engine Works............................ $100 00
Engineering Dept. of the same............................ 55 [illegible]
Iron Founding do............................ 80 87
Boiler Making do............................ 94 75
Wm. Arthur............................ 100 00
Wm. Arthur, Jr............................ 10 00
Alex. Arthur............................ 5 00
Robert Bowie............................ 5 00
Henry Smith............................ 5 00
Arch. Lamson............................ 5 00
James Wilcox............................ 2,000 00
Richard Poillon............................ [illegible] 00
Charles Morris............................ 450 00
J. Morrison............................ 910 00
T. Rowe............................ 100 00
J. Johnston............................ 50 00
Union White Lead Co............................ 940 00
S. Stevens............................ 200 00
E. R. Rand............................ [illegible] 00
J. K. Wheatly............................ [illegible] 00
A. Bruen............................ 50 00
D. S. Hines............................ [illegible] 00
W. W. Hume............................ 600 00
Thos. Brooke, additional............................ 50 00
J. L. Moore, do............................ 41 00
H. Jackson, do............................ [illegible] 00
D. S. Warlow, do............................ 15 00
Dewhurst & Emerson............................ 150 00
Nelson & Aldrich............................ [illegible] 00
T. J. Leary............................ 5 00
W. L. Bender............................ 10 00
James Gallagher............................ 5 00
G. M. Woodward, Steam Pump............................ [illegible] 00
George Shelton............................ 5 00
P. H. S............................ 5 00
Conover & Wusly, one grate............................
Hubbard, Ways & Whittaker, proprietors of Bardon Iron Works, one steamer engine............................ [illegible] 00
Workmen of Bordon Iron Works............................ [illegible] 80
James Holdane............................ 5 00
Davidson & Dickerson............................ $[illegible] 00
Howard & Fuller............................ 50 00
Employes of the same, as follows:
- Joseph Peet............................ 2 00
- John Dyer............................ 2 00
- Patrick O'Keefe............................ 1 00
- John Miller............................ 1 00
- Wm. O'Brien............................ 1 00
- Edward Gormly............................ 1 00
- Thomas Corr............................ 1 00
- J. Bresnahan............................ 1 00
- John Clifford............................ 1 00
- Cornelius O'Donnell............................ 1 00
- John Gallagher............................ 1 00
- James Woods............................ 1 00
- Richard Main............................ 1 00

Wm. Gilchrist, with M. Vassar & Co............................ 65 00
From Messrs. Husted & Carll:
- 1 Medallion Carpet............................ 150 00
- 1 Large Mosaic Rug............................ 80 00
- 2 Dog Mats, $3............................ 6 00
- 8 Velvet Mats, $2 50............................ 20 00
- 16 Yards Drugget, $2............................ [illegible]
- 12 Yds Cocoa Matting, $1 25............................ 15 00
- 6 Axminster Hassocks, $4............................ 24 00
- 12 Cornices, $4............................ 48 00
- 8 Pair Shades, $12............................ 96 00
- 1 Emb'd Piano Cover............................ 35 00
- 2 Mosaic Pictures............................ 85 00

From Foundry & Machine Works of Abraham Inslee............................ [illegible] 11
The hands of this establishment have contributed one day's pay each............................
The hands of A. Campbell's Printing Press Manufactory, 28 Water st., have contributed............................ 10 55
Arthur Rumrill & Co., N. Y.—Gold and Coral Chatelaine, $20; two Chatelaine Pins, $30............................ 50 00

J. Sturn, N. Y.—Morocco and Velvet Jewel Box	$15 00
Ball, Barnard & Rogers—Set of Jet and Gold Bracelets, Pin, Ear-rings, and Necklace, in Morocco Case	185 00
Hiram Young, N. Y.—Silver-plated Tea Set	45 00
Geo. C. White, N. Y.—Silver-plated Tea Set	65 00
L. & Mathey, N. Y.—One Silver Hunting Case detached lever, No. 18,084	80 00
J. G. Gerrich, N. Y. and Brooklyn	15 00
Jas. McMurray, Brooklyn	10 00
Edwd White, Brooklyn	4 00
E. A. Harrison, Brooklyn	10 00
Robert Hall, N. Y. and Brooklyn	10 00
Rockenbaum, Cole & Hall, N. Y.	10 00
Thos. Johnson, Brooklyn	4 00
Leonard Decker, N. Y. and Bklyn.	8 00
J. R. Lipsker, Brooklyn	5 00
Blunt & Lawrence, N. Y.	10 00
A. T. Hanks, Brooklyn	5 00
Three combination castor and Fruit Stands	31 00
Gold and Pearl Mounting to Jewelry	40 00
E. V. Haughwout & Co., 488, 490, and 492 Broadway, N. Y.—20 doz. Cups and Saucers	40 00
M. Gould & Sons, 188 William st., N. Y., 1½ doz. Rods, at $30	45 00
Miller & Co., 9 Maiden Lane—1 Sword, Sash, and Belt, complete, $125; 1 case Shoulder-straps, all grades, $227,50	352 50
W. B. Kendall, 51 Chambers st., N. Y.—2 Turkey Rugs, at $12, $24; 6 Turkey Mats, at $6, $36	60 00
Hastings & Wood, 51 Chambers st., N. Y.—41 yds. Colored Matting, at 10s	58 35
Thos. K. Purdy, Fulton and Nassau st., N. Y.—8 pair Window Shades	48 00
Starr Arms Co.—1 Carbine Case and 100 Cartridges, $40; 2 Revolvers, Case, and 100 Cartridges, $35 75; 1 Revolver, Case, and 100 Cartridges, $24 75	100 50
Campbell & Hardick Bros.—No. 1 Steam Pump	140 00
Abraham Campbell	10 00
From Machinists in Establishm't.	$18 84
Thos. Hind	1 00
Frederick F. Hassam, of Boston, 1 pair of Patent Skates	25 00
John Shuster	250 00
James Sharkey	250 00
Fails & Co.	50 00
J. Ouchterlony & Co.	25 00
John Wilson	10 00
Cash	20 00
Mr. Rucher, 6 Rocking-horses, $60; Fancy Goods, $32	92 00
J. G. Reither	25 00
C. Darring & Bro., 1 Chess Table	10 00
J. S. Owen	10 00
Miller & Wilson, N. Y.	25 00
Ingersoll, Watson & Co., N. Y., 1 Table and 9 Chairs	25 00
G. C. Lester	5 00
J. H. Lester	5 00
A. & A. S. Thorp, N. Y.	25 00
J. Sank	1 00
J. Mattern	2 00
A. Reeder	5 00
G. Rollen	2 00
R. Stephens, 1 Rosewood Table, $35; 1 doz. Chairs, $18	53 00
J. Fryer, 8 Walnut Brackets	8 00
R. J. Lockwood, 1 Turkish Chair	25 00
Through D. S. Hines—W. W. Howe	100 00
Henry Esler & Co.	50 00
Employes of Henry Esler & Co.	41 67
Employes of Hydraulic Works	159 52
Jos. Goldmark, 175,000 Percussion Caps, wholesale cash value	140 00
Henry Esler & Co., 1 working model Steam Engine	100 00
Additional contributions through Wm. Wise—N. Y. Vulcanite Jewelry Company, Invoice Vulcanite Jewelry	80 00
Augustus Bergstein, N. Y., fine Gold Eagle and Enamel Brooch and Earrings	80 00
Through John W. Massey—Henry Waldron	100 00
Reynolds, Pratt & Co.	100 00
Robert Colgate & Co.	100 00
Massey & Wheaton	100 00
Mineral and Manufacturing Co.	20 00
Baldwin & James	5 00
Through James H. Hart—Messrs. Mahie, Todd & Co.	25 00
P. M. F. & Co.	20 00

C. H. & Co.	$20 00
Joseph Scott	15 00
C. S. Ford	10 00
S. E. Seymour	10 00
Messrs. A. C. & Co.	10 00
Buckingham, Cole & Hall	10 00
Wm. Rahl	10 00
John A. Riley	10 00
B. & G. S.	10 00
R. & B.	10 00
F. W. Taylor	5 00
W. & H.	5 00
E. Humbert	5 00
H. C. & Co.	5 00
S. B.	5 00
Cash	3 00
L. Cobb	1 00
S. T. Dearby	10 00
F. & Co.	3 00
C. M. & Co.	5 00
W. S. Billcocks	5 00
A. R. & Co.	10 00
Contributions in goods—Messrs. Spooner & Welch	20 00
A. & H. Griffith	28 00
James H. Hart & Co., per bill	150 00
Robert Knight & Son donate one group classical Figures, $25; 1 Picture of Evangeline, $6 50; 1 Picture of Faith, $6 50	38 00
Sherk & Brothers donate 1 Oil Painting by Carmiencke	25 00
Noel, Saorell & Antoine donate 6 Convex Looking-glasses each $7 50	45 00
Weston, Covel & Sherwood donate 6 circle Frames for above glasses (value $2 50 each) $15; 1 Cushion Stand, $5	20 00
Samuel Walters donate 1 Oil Painting by Cass	50 00
Mrs. Hosicke donates 1 Picture of Humboldt in his study	15 00
Arthur Waller, 1 Cushion Stand	5 00
Cash	3 00
From South Brooklyn Steam Engine and Boiler Works, D. McLeod, Proprietor and workmen	254 00
James Binns	25 00
Cash	25 00
Through D. Fithian, from Messrs. Kenyon & Newton	40 00
Do. Kirk & Clark	10 00
Do. Prentice & White	4 00

Through D. Fithian: Clark & Blerds	$12 00
From D. P. Gardiner	8 00
From J. Lucas	10 00
From Litchfield & Ketcham	5 00
From D. Fithian & Lobser	25 00
Through G. J. Vining from Messrs. Tuttle & Bailey	50 00
Do. Bruce & Cook	50 00
Do. Phelps, Dodge & Co.	50 00
From Waterbury Brass Agency	10 00
P. Rollhaus	50 00
Dickerson, Reed & Co.	10 00
Dayton & Carter	25 00
E. Ketcham & Co.	147 73
Vining & Powell	200 00
E. Tompkins	50 00
S. J. Pardessus	50 00
John August	50 00
From the Starr Arms Co., 267 Broadway, N. Y., articles valued	150 50
F. W. Gulteau, goods	22 00
Brewster Rose	25 00
Collections by Geo. S. Puffer, of Distillers' Committee of Manufactures and Mechanic Arts, etc.: Dodge & Olcott	100 00
Anonymous, through Brooklyn Post Office to Bach & Co.	14 00
Wm. N. Puffer	10 00
Eugene Blordet	5 00
John P. Puffer	5 00
M. McKinney	5 00
Geo. S. Puffer	105 00
Collections by John Butler, of Manufactures and Mechanic Arts Committee, in sums varying from 1 to 25 dollars	201 25
Additional subscriptions through the Brooklyn Navy Yard: H. Y. Mason, Floating Dry Dock Co.	100 00
R. Buckman & Co., ship-builders	50 00
Ship-carpenters' Dpt., Navy Yard	17 50
Ordnance Dpt., do., Machinists	16 75
John Duval, for Brooklyn Brass and Copper Co.	450 00
Wilmot & Kissam, Manuf'g Co.	100 00
Smith & Jewell	200 00
C. H. Jewett, 1,000 lbs. Wh. Lead	100 00
Lesley & Elliot, goods	80 00
S. P. Chapin, Sewing Machine	65 00
J. & E. Stevens, Cromwell, Ct., Iron Toys	40 00
E. Ketcham & Co., goods	147 79
Through the Manuf'g Committee	

of the Western District: E. Mitchell & Co., 8 tons coal......	$30 00
John Muchmore, 8 tons coal......	30 00
Joshua Rodgers & Son, 8 tons coal.	80 00
T. D. Hudson, 6 tons coal.........	60 00
C. D. Willets, 8 tons coal........	20 00
Edmund Kirby, 8 tons coal........	80 00
Clarendon & Davidson, 2 tons coal.	20 00
Hendrickson & Fleet, 2 tons coal.	20 00
J. M. Larrabee, 2 tons coal.......	20 00
Geo. H. Thurston, 2 tons coal.....	20 00
W. D. Hazard, 1 ton coal.........	10 00
Marston & Power, 1 ton coal......	10 00
H. G. Powers, 1 ton coal..........	10 00
E. D. A. Smith, 2 loads wood.....	8 00
Wm. Pierson, 1 do.	4 00
De Baun & Bros., 1 do.	4 00
M. T. Kelly, 1 do.	4 00
C. & W. Taylor, 1 do.	4 00
G. H. Powers, 1 do.	4 00
Wm. B. Walters, 1 do.	4 00
Daniel Smith, 1 do.	4 00
Kelly & Willard, 1 do.	4 00
Donations received through the Ladies Manufacturing Committee: From W. W. Swayne.....	30 00
Mr. Tice, Plated-ware......... ...	100 00
Mr. Christman, Watch-stand......	8 50
Through Miss M. Cornell: White & Nichols, 1 Bracket	5 00
Knight & Son, 1 Bracket	3 00
J. Worthington, Perfumery........	4 50
Geo. Close, Perfumery...	4 50
Thomas Brooks, Table............	15 00
E. Werner, piece of Furniture, 25; 8 Breastpins, 15................	40 00
Gale & Son, plated Sugar Dish....	18 00
Through Mrs. L. Thomas.........	50 00
Through Mrs. N. Beers: Timothy Cornwell.........................	25 00
Cash..........................	7 00
Philip Weck, 25 Kegs	6 25
N. L. Beers, 8 Heaters	30 00
Through Mrs. S. Fancher.........	50 00
Cash	1 06
Miss J. Lawrence	5 00
Through Mrs. Joseph Ripley: J. R. Park, Flowers....	
Through Mrs. D. Carno: George W. Hill........................	10 00
Edmund Hill	19 50
Thomas Slater....	10 00
John Fraser, 10 doz. Doyleys	30 00
A Friend, 54 yards Linen	27 00

Mr. Harrison, 1 Goblet.......	$25 00
Through Mrs. J. F. Wickham: D. C. Robbins, Toilet Articles.......	60 00
Through Mrs. L. S. Burnham: S. J. Parkeman, Glass Shades.....	50 00
C. H. Little & Co., Feather-dusters, etc	17 87
John Craig, 1 Trunk....	20 00
Mrs. L. S. Burnham...............	50 00
A. F. Kindberg..........	25 00
C. W. Little & Co........	25 00
Thos. Prescott......................	5 00
Mrs. Molineux.....................	5 00
A School in Fort Greene Place....	4 50
Mr. Rogers.........................	1 00
Mrs. Foster	3 00
Bertha Shellard...........	25
Leslie Molineux	25
Ella Foster........	75
Fancy Articles from Mrs. L. S. Burnham and others....	80 25
Through Mrs. Theo. Ovington: Ovington & Bros., Crockery, etc.	100 00
Mrs. Andrews, Wrappers, etc... ...	17 40
Through Mrs. J. L. Brownell: Brennan & Bros., 400 fine Cigars, and 1 dozen Foil, retail..........	61 50
J. H. Colton, Atlas, etc..........	14 00
Merwin & Bray, 1 pair Revolvers..	100 00
Through Mrs. W. J. Miller: Mr. Zogbaum, Musical Instruments.	165 00
Mrs. Zogbaum, Fancy Work: Mrs. Von Moire, Painting; Mrs. Kahl, Fancy Work...........	3 00
John McCafferty............	1 00
Mr. W. J. Miller, Silver Plated-ware...................	150 00
Mrs. Bassett, Slippers........	5 00
Through Mrs. J. F. Whitney: Mrs. J. F. Shortland.................	25 00
Mr. C. B. Douglass.......	5 00
Mr. R. G. Ware..........	5 00
Through Mrs. P. Wyckoff: cash, 8; Phantom Bouquet, 20; Cake, 5; Fancy Articles, 5 50; Tobacco; 1 doz. boxes Perfumery, 12; H. P. Sandford, Slipper-boxes, 5.	58 00
Through Mrs. L. B. Shaw...... ...	27 50
Henry Owen.......	10 00
Mrs. A. F. Roberts...............	10 00
E. A. Kent.......................	5 00
G. W. Martin...	5 00
S. Fitzharris..............	2 00
John Phillips	5 00

H. Boyd $1 00
A. T. Baldwin 5 00
T. L. Mason 25 00
D. S. Voorhees 10 00
Mrs. C. D. Lewis 1 00
W. P. Sweet 5 00
S. H. Scott 2 00
—— Darden 1 00
Mrs. D. S. Waugh 2 00
J. O. O. 5 00
Mrs. W. M. Price 5 00
Mrs. S. Sahuny 5 00
C. B. Lockwood 5 00
W. S. Wallace 10 00
Geo. W. Morrison 5 00
Anonymous 5 00
David Haviland 5 00
B. Stevens 1 00
Mrs. T. Shortland 5 00
P. Dollard 5 00
Mrs. W. Everetts 1 00
S. W. Thompson 20 00
H. S. Johnson 5 00
J. H. Gresham 1 00
Geo. Reeveland 1 00
T. R. Major 5 00
H. Tompkins 1 00
J. H. Jones 1 00
J. M. Keller 2 00
H. McClair 2 00
Andrew James 1 00
C. Hesson 1 00
W. T. Smith 1 00
Wm. Morrell 50
Mrs. A. F. McDonald half dozen Shaving Tidies and 6 Emerys; B. & N. Schmitz, 1 Bracket ....
Through Mrs. F. H. Bigelow: Mr. F. H. Bigelow 25 00
Through Mrs. E. A. Bidae; C. P. Buckingham, Central Elevator 100 00
E. A. Biden 20 00
J. Barry 1 00
Cash 1 00
A. Kurth, Table-cover 10 00
E. Bidee, 1 doz. small Flags 5 00

Through Mrs. A. Cruikshank; J. Terril, Infant Shoes, 6; L. Doscher, 1 doz. bottles Extracts, 3; G. Williams, Fancy Articles, 4.25, $1[illegible] 25
Through Mrs. Luke Harrington; From B. G. Wilder & Luke Harrington, Salamander House Safe, [illegible] 00
Through Mrs. Peter Rice: A Painting 300 00
Peter Rice 200 00
W. D. C. Biggs 2 00
Cash 2 00
D. Thomas 1 00
E. Kirby 10 00
Z. Pearsall 10 00
G. T. Neale 25 00
N. Hough 10 00
R. Talmage 5 00
C. W. Spencer 25 00
N. H. Wolfe, & Co., 2 bbls. Flour; J. M. Fiske & Co., 2 do.; Wheeler & Fellman, 1 do.; J. J. Marvin, 5 do.; J. S. Winslow, 1 do.; Ferguson, 1 do.; E. R. Lorimer, 1 do.; J. Lathrop, 2 do.; Plombier & Co., 5 do.; Wheaver & Briggs, 2 do.; Holt & Co., 2 do.; C. McAuley, 1 do.; S. Buckley, 1 do.; L. Roberts, 5 do.; L. M. Hoffman, 2 do.; R. Robson, 2 do.; H. T., 2 do., Hecker & Bro., 5 do., and 2 bags Farina; A. Baxter, 25 bbls. Flour; J. Worth, 5 do.; Jessie Hoyt, 2 do.; Darling, Allerton & Moore, 5 do.; J. Wilmot & Co., 2 do.; W. C. Whitlock, 5 do.; J. Yomans, Jr., 7 do.; Saxe & Co., 5 do.; F. A. Esty, 1 do.; Isaac Reide, 5 do.; E. Titus, 1 bbl. of Crackers; E. Treadwell, do.; E. W. Colman, 5 bbls. Flour ....
O. Tate .... [illegible]

Total amount $20,047 54

WM. BURDON, Chairman.

MANUFACTURES AND MECHANIC ARTS.

EASTERN DISTRICT.

	Medal.	Cash.		Medal.	Cash.
Wm. B. Jenkins		$100 00	F. Kalbfleisch		$100 00
L. F. Hawes		250 00	C. W. Cooper		100 00
Reeve & Company Sewing Machines	$250 00		Wm. Cooper		250 00
			James Hall		50 00

	Mdse.	Cash.
N. Whyroff		$100 00
John Beach		50 00
W. B. Allen		50 00
J. W. Bulkley		25 00
Chas. J. Debevoise		25 00
Peter Whyroff		10 00
H. V. Schenck		25 00
Franklin S. Schenck		10 00
George Wildey		
John Dolan		30 00
Gold & Garrison		50 00
F. B. Polley		10 00
J. R. Walker		5 00
J. L. Heath		
H. B. Scholes		250 00
Benjamin Welis		100 00
Isaac Gerry		100 00
James B. Collins		50 00
Porter Fitch		50 00
J. R. Hutchinson		50 00
Chas. Phiser		25 00
A. H. Badger		50 00
O. M. Beach		50 00
Grover C. Furman		25 00
James Gridley		50 00
D. L. Young		50 00
John J. L. Hallenbeck		25 00
R. S. Weed		25 00
W. H. Sandford		25 00
P. Sheldon		25 00
George R. Kreuger		25 00
H. F. Burroughs		25 00
W. H. Hoyt		25 00
H. M. Warren		25 00
Frank F. Leighton		10 00
David H. Gildersleeve		10 00
Wm. H. H. Smith		10 00
Richard James		10 00
Dewitt & Nephews		10 00
Thomas Bonner		5 00
Charles R. Bostwick		5 00
John Cameron		5 00
Leonard Tilton		5 00
Leoni Cromwell		5 00
Jas. H. Taylor 5 boxes, best family Soap, and 8 doz. Yeast Powders	37 00	
Thos. Sherrill, 3 doz. Sheep Linings	84 00	
A. Stainger, Thill & Co.	133 18	
A. Selberg		15 00
Ebbinghouse & Co.		5 00
Employees Stainger, Thill & Co.		4 41

	Mdse.	Cash.
Lafayette Glass Works, Glassware	41 00	
Hugo Walter, Glassware	67 50	
C. H. Fellows, Gas-fixtures	200 00	
Robert Thomas, Window-screens	80 00	
Vanwyck & Brinkerhoff, Fancy Goods	18 00	
Smith & Swap		2 00
Mr. Sandford, Sanford, Truslow & Co., Stoves	310 00	
Employees of do.		100 00
Richardson & Boynton, Range	75 00	
T. Merrifield, Stove	30 00	
J. L. Mott, Iron Works, Merchandise	40 00	
Tuttle & Bailey, Registers	20 00	
A. Hampton, 1 Grate, and 1 fire-place Heater	35 00	
Wm. Jackson & Son, 1 fire-place Heater	50 00	
Wm. P. Lowe, 3 Sandford Heaters	48 00	
Perkins & Hill, Cabinet	45 00	
Ralph Pomeroy & Co.	20 00	
Josiah Heath & Co., Cooperage	30 00	
Employees of do.		20 50
Jas. W. Flynn, Cooperage	58 00	
Ira Ford, Cooperage	18 00	
John Thompson, caloric Foot-warmers	10 00	
H. Smith		10 00
Mr. Solon, Tool-chest	10 00	
F. S.		10 00
Samuel Wendell		5 00
John Gallagher		5 00
Wmsb'g P. O., E. M. F.		25 00
Charles Harper		5 00
Christian Neidig		100 00
Christian Neidig, Table	5 00	
William Taylor & Son		100 00
W. W. Dean		5 00
Henry C. Richardson		100 00
Morrell & Tiebout		50 00
C. Dubois		20 00
C. Baston, Tin-ware	20 00	
John M. Murray, Wire Goods	5 00	
C. Merrill & Co., 2 Drills	24 00	
H. C. Richardson's employees		13 00
F. F. Rowland		200 00

	Mdse.	Cash.		Mdse.	Cash.
Ariel Patterson..		200 00	Fairbanks & Co., Scales...	85 00	
W. Secor		50 00	F. Nishwitz, Mowing Machine	115 00	
Conklin Brainard..........		15 00			
William Marlow..........		10 00	Henry Waterman, Saws..	54 00	
H. E. Talmadge...........		20 00	C. Dorflinger & Co........	870 00	
Wm. Perrine..............		250 00	Greenpoint Sugar House..		140 00
Cash........		100 00	Greenpoint Oil Co.........		35 50
Cash........		75 00	Employees of Dun & Co..		95 94
A. Harman & Sons........		250 00	H. E. Williams............		25 00
William Wall, Jr.........		200 00	C. E. Bertrand & Co......		100 00
Samuel Truslow..........		250 00	Julius Schwab............	31 50	
J. H. Adams & Coombs...		100 00	Joseph Wilde, Coffee.....	100 00	
Chas. H. Jewett, half ton White Lead............	140 00		F. G. Richardson	80 00	
Wm. W. Raymond & Co., Metallic Burial Cases...	190 00		Total	$3,810 68	5,003 87

WM. H. JENKINS, Chairman.

DONATIONS THROUGH THE DRY GOODS COMMITTEE.

CASH CONTRIBUTIONS.

H. B. Claflin........................	$1,000 00	Anthony & Hall....................	$100 00
Nehemiah Knight................	500 00	Woodward, Lawrence & Co.......	100 00
Collins, Plummer & Co...........	500 00	Dommock & Moore...............	100 00
S. McLean..........................	500 00	Hunt, Tillinghast & Co...........	100 00
Chas. S. Baylis....................	500 00	Sprague, Cooper & Colburn.......	100 00
Hoyt, Sprague & Co	300 00	Rice, Chase & Co.................	100 00
W. H. Mellen.......................	250 00	F. Newman........................	100 00
Jas S. Noyes.......................	250 00	Carhart, Bacon, Greene & Co......	100 00
Griffith, Prentice & McComb	250 00	Pastor, Hardt & Lindgens........	100 00
S. Hutchinson	250 00	Slade & Colby	100 00
R. R. Perry	250 00	Ezra W. Frost.....................	100 00
W. C. Langley......................	250 00	Howell & King	100 00
H. W. T. Mali & Co.............	250 00	Recar & Co.........................	100 00
Tefts, Griswold & Kellogg..	250 00	Wm. Lottimer & Co	100 00
J. B. Hutchinson..............	250 00	Wm. B. Leonard...................	100 00
Lord & Taylor............	250 00	B. H. Hutton.	100 00
Hazlehurst & Smith	250 00	Chapman & Co......................	100 00
T. T. Buckley......................	250 00	M. E. Lord.........................	100 00
D. H. Conkling	200 00	Bowers, Beekman, B. Jr. & Co...	100 00
F. Skinner & Co.............	200 00	Arnold, Constable & Co	100 00
Low, Harriman, Durfee & Co	200 00	E. S. Jaffray & Co	100 00
N. P. Miller...........	200 00	W. Forman Hunt.................	100 00
Garnor & Co....	200 00	Walter Lockwood.........	100 00
F. Butterfield & Co..............	200 00	George Wyggatt	100 00
Horton & Sons......................	200 00	Thomas & Co......................	100 00
W. C. Sheldon......................	200 00	Chas. Welling & Co...............	100 00
Brumley & Kellogg............. .	200 00	Stanfield, Wentworth & Co.......	100 00
G. M. Richardson & Co..........	200 00	Wicks, Smith & Co........	100 00
Jonathan Earle........	150 00	E. R. Mudge, Sawyer & Co........	100 00
E. S. Eames........................	100 00	Wm. Brand & Co..................	100 00
Henry Stone..............	100 00	W. H. Lee & Co....................	100 00
Knower & Platte..................	100 00	E. W. Bancroft............	50 00
J. & H. Auchincloss......... ...	100 00	Streeter, Paxton & Potter........	50 00

Van Wyck, Townsend & Co.	$100 00
S. e. Tiffany	50 00
Parker, Walker & Co.	50 00
Turnbull, Slade & Co.	50 00
J. L. B. Willard	50 00
Andrew & Bowers	50 00
Fisher, Donnelly & Co.	50 00
Lindsley, Chittick & Co.	50 00
Thos. Slocom	50 00
Wm. Watson & Co.	50 00
Linder & Kingsley	50 00
David Lamb	50 00
Boreham, Allien & Diggleman	50 00
Robert Simpson	50 00
Edward Fuller	50 00
Faulkner, Kimball & Co.	50 00
Denny & Jones	50 00
Gideon Pott	50 00
H. Hearnquin & Co.	50 00
Foster Swan	50 00
A. T. Montael	50 00
H. & A. Sturtsbury	50 00
Chas. Heiners & Co.	50 00
Becher & Co.	50 00
Jenkins & Huntington	50 00
Stone, Bliss, Fay & Allen	50 00
Forstman & Co.	50 00
Girard, Barbey & Co.	50 00
A. Lawson & Harriman	50 00
Noell & Oelbermann	50 00
John E. Seward	50 00
H. Becker & Co.	50 00
Geo. Bogge	50 00
Hardt & Co.	50 00
John Slade & Co.	50 00
Haviland, Lindsley & Co.	50 00
W. B. Johnson	50 00
J. B. Hyde	25 00
D. O. Spencer	25 00
J. Sys & Co.	25 00
Crook & Scott	25 00
Bulkley & Co.	25 00
H. A. Schnabel	25 00
Dale Bros.	25 00
W. H. Backus	25 00
Brand, Ellon & Co.	25 00
Wm. Granby	25 00
Adam Craig	25 00
A. Baker	25 00
Ogden & Hewitt	25 00
Jos. N. Ely	25 00
Peter Donald	25 00
Cash	25 00

D. O. Campbell	$25 00
Booth & Tuttle	25 00
John D. Lewis & Co.	25 00
Halbrook, Hoyt & Co.	25 00
C. H. Lippitt	25 00
C. D. Spencer	25 00
Jordan, Marsh & Co.	25 00
Fairchild & Fanshaw	25 00
Garrett & Clark	25 00
Kessler & Co.	25 00
Jas. F. White & Co.	25 00
Bailey & Southard	25 00
Wm. Brummer & Co.	25 00
Dale Bros. & Co.	25 00
A. Rusch & Co.	25 00
Butler, Cecil & Rawson	25 00
Campbell, Magie & Co.	25 00
Haggerty & Co.	25 00
D. F. Schwank	25 00
Woodbridge & Morris	25 00
Marshall Oliver	25 00
Humphrey & Dempster	20 00
A Lady, per T. Aebilie	20 00
"R." & Co.	15 00
Adolph Lippman	15 00
Hill & Chapman	15 00
T. Pettit	10 00
Mr. Millwater	10 00
Jas. Ward	10 00
Paul Walter	10 00
Harman Dale	5 00
Ph. Dickerson	5 00
G. B. Smith	5 00
Peter Delano	5 00
W. H. Barr	5 00
Chas. Rhode	3 00
E. Kahn	3 00
A. B. Smith	3 00
W. Bower	2 00
Strauss & Co.	2 00
D. S. Fogerty	2 00
Jas. McInerney	2 00
J. McGill	2 00
S. More	1 00
K. Lewis	1 00
G. Baer	1 00
R. M. Brown	1 00
R. Clarke	1 00
A. Johnson	1 00
Cash	1 00
Total money subscriptions	$15,494 52

CONTRIBUTIONS OF DRY GOODS.

Low, Harriman, Darling & Co....	$550 00	G. M. Richmond & Co............	$105 00
Walcott & Campbell	550 00	Garner & Co......................	100 00
S. McLean	480 00	Becar & Co	125 00
Stewart & Co, Brooklyn..........	335 00	Lador Bros. & Co.................	100 00
Lathrop, Luddington & Co........	275 00	Edward Armstrong.................	100 00
W. H. Chapman & T. P. Chapman.	275 00	Buckley, Sheldon & Co...........	100 00
J. M. Dunbar	275 00	Huntington & Dubois	96 00
A. A. Low & Bros................	250 00	H. Knight........................	69 00
Geo. Bliss & Co..........	200 00	J. W. Dummell	50 00
T. Victor & Achilles............	213 25	A. Roesler.............	40 00
E. Lewis........	185 00	R. J. Hunter.....................	40 00
W. & J. Sloan & Co..............	185 00	Hubbard & Northup................	34 00
Butler, Cecil & Rawson..........	125 00	Angell & Co......................	17 00
E. & J. Myggatt.................	135 00	R. Stimmons.....................	16 00
Wm. B. Kendall..................	135 00		
Wm. Rogers......................	185 00	Total Dry Goods...	$5,274 75
Wm. H. Smith....................	104 50		

FOREIGN CONTRIBUTIONS THROUGH THE ABOVE COMMITTEE.

From Bradford, England.

Thornton, Homans & Co..........	$1,400 00	Geo. Mason, Esq................	$110 00
A. & S. Henry & Co	920 00	Mrs. Thos. McClune......... ...	75 00
Schwann, Kell & Co.............	400 00	Mrs. Homan.................	60 00
Titus, Salt & Sons.............	300 00	Miss Homan................	25 00
N. S. Langee & Co..............	325 00	Mrs. Hodson....................	25 00
Jas. Drummond, Esq.............	140 00		
Mrs. Wm. Peel, and Miss Peel....	180 00	Total from Bradford, England.....	$4,280 00

From Manchester, England.

A. & S. Henry & Co......	$375 00	McHaughton & Tom..............	$35 00
Chamberlin, Heard & Downer.	225 00	Wm. Faulkner..................	35 00
Thornton & Co....	100 00	Hargreaves, Reid & Co..........	25 00
Mrs. H. Thornton, Sr.	100 00	Omerod, Jervis & Thompson....	25 00
H. W. Steinthal, Esq..........	100 00	Christopher Wood, Esq.........	25 00
H. C. Bowker, Esq..............	100 00	Jas. Barker, Esq......	25 00
Stewart Zigomala, Esq.	100 00	Royce, Smith & Co......	25 00
Thos. Johnson, Esq..	75 00	R. Whitworth & Brother.....	20 00
Jas. Baillie, Esq.................	75 00	Christopher Wood & Co.........	17 00
Kay, Richardson & Co....	50 00	Butterworth & Brooks...........	13 00
Elkanah, Armitage & Co........	50 00	Thos. Hoyle & Sons.............	15 00
Robert Barbour & Bro.........	45 00	Bradshaw, Hammond & Co.......	11 00
Thos. Sykes & Bro.............	45 00	Bamly & Craven.................	7 00
Thos. Brown, Esq	40 00	G. & R. Halt......................	6 00
H. Harriott..	40 00		
Tootal, Broadhurst & Lee....	40 00	Total from Manchester, England..	$1,753 00
Tom Stanert, Esq...	50 00		

From Glasgow and Paisley, Scotland, through W. B. Higgins and Thos. McNair, Esqs.

W. B. Higgins & Co... ..	$440 00	McArthur & Finlay..............	
M. Whitehill & Co.... ...		Campbell & Balloch, and others whose names were not furnished to the Committee...........	810 00
Forbes & Co....			
Morgan & Co.			
Greenlees & Co..			
Easton & McColman		Total from Glasgow, etc..........	$1,250 00
Gray, Butler & Co...			

From Huddersfield.

Subsequently received from A. & S. Henry & Co. .... $[illegible] 00

Donation from Paris.

Emile Granier 50 00

RECAPITULATION.

Foreign contributions .... 7,[illegible] 00
Domestic contributions 8,774 75
Cash .... 86,384 [illegible]
Total .... $[illegible] 04

THOS. T. BUCKLEY, Chairman.

DONATIONS THROUGH THE COMMITTEE ON REFRESHMENTS.

THROUGH THE CHURCHES OF REFRESHMENTS AND MONEY BY LADIES' COMMITTEE.

	Refreshments.	Cash.		Refreshments.	Cash.
Strong Pl. Baptist Church	$[illegible] 16	$18 00	South Congregational	$100 00	$[illegible] 00
First Ref. Dutch Church	397 93	190 00	Pacific st. M. E. Church	30 00	
Holy Trinity	[illegible]	51 00	Plymouth Church	[illegible] 00	77 00
Church of the Pilgrims	217 [illegible]	9 00	Second Unitarian	63 90	97 00
Society of Friends	49 53	49 50	Clinton Ave. Congrega'l	119 77	8 00
First Presb., Henry st.	104 10	13 00	Hanson Pl. Baptist	11 71	1 00
South Presbyterian	168 81	3 00	Elm Pl. Congregational	17 00	86 50
Christ Church	[illegible] 00	55 00	Hanson Pl. M. E. Church	48 [illegible]	45 00
Church of the Saviour	184 [illegible]	65 00	First st. M. E. Church	[illegible] 16	105 50
Lafayette Ave. Presb.	175 18	94 00	Sands st. M. E. Church	91 [illegible]	19 60
Pierrepont st. Baptist	111 [illegible]	9 00	Washington st. M. E. Ch.	60 [illegible]	38 00
Church of the Restoration		133 00	St. Mary's Church	50 80	43 50
Church of the Messiah	68 00		Moravian Church	7 [illegible]	37 00
St. Peter's Church	[illegible]	107 00	R. D. Ch. on the Heights	[illegible]	14 00
Central Presbyterian	65 68	45 00	Grace Church	34 30	[illegible]
St. Ann's	[illegible] 50	130 00	St. John's Church	6 60	35 95
Central Baptist	45 [illegible]	63 00	Centenary M. E. Church	53 81	18 00
First Baptist	840 81	56 50	North Dutch Church	56 11	
Third Presbyterian	70 63	33 00	York st. M. E. Church		73 45
Westminster	84 78	11 00	St. Charles Borromeo	81 [illegible]	65 00
Washington Ave. Baptist	14 65	8 00	Bushwick and Bowling-		
East Ref. Dutch	34 65	6 00	ville	66 75	
State st. Congregational	80 46	15 00	Loyal families Sec'd Pres-		
Middle R. Dutch Church	116 67	357 00	byterian, Bremen st.	47 50	
First Pl. M. E. Church	97 [illegible]	69 00	Paid by parties unknown		10 55
Church of the Redeemer	4 68		Bay Ridge Episcopal Ch.	21 50	
Second Presbyterian	[illegible] 91	98 00	St. Luke's	8 50	

EASTERN DISTRICT CHURCHES AND OTHER SOURCES.

	Refreshments.	Cash.		Refreshments.	Cash.
South Fifth st. M. E. Ch.	$1[illegible]	$41 00	Grand st. M. E. Church	$[illegible]	$15 00
Reformed Dutch	74 00	4 00	South Second M. E. Ch.		14 00
St. Peter's and St. Paul's	7 63	25 00	St. Mark's	35 [illegible]	6 [illegible]
New England Congrega'l	62 65	29 50	Contributions from Green-		
First Baptist	78 [illegible]	10 00	point	118 [illegible]	[illegible]
Christ	74 50	48 00	Contribut's through Mrs.		
Lee Avenue Ref. Dutch	97 40	10 30	W. H. Jenkins	[illegible]	13 [illegible]
Universalist	177 30	60 50	Contribut's through Mrs.		
First Presbyterian	67 83	17 00	J. Hall	139 [illegible]	8 00

DONATIONS FROM OTHER SOURCES IN REFRESHMENTS.

Primary Depart't Public School No. 11—Cakes	$17 00
Confect'y—J. & M. Christy, N. Y.	20 00
Box of Rabbit's Medicinal Yeast	7 50
C. E. Anderson, No. 55 Myrtle avenue—Cake	50 00
M. Shaw, N. Y.—Two Statuettes in sugar of Washington	8 00
L. Siegel, No. 180 Pearl st., N. Y.—Pies and Cake	10 00
Thompson & Weller—Two stands of French Mottoes	80 00
Mrs. Stuart, Gramercy Park, N. Y.—Cake	36 00
Flatbush contributions	18 00
Gravesend contributions	5 00
Maillard, N. Y.—Candy	23 40
Mrs. C. W. Copeland—Cake with ship	75 00
Henry's Restaurant—Crullers	20 00
Setauket, L. I.—Dried Currants and Apples	6 00
Mr. Corey, farmer, to D. Welsmore—Poultry and Vegetables	$48 00
Mundell, Myrtle avenue—Pickled Oysters	12 50
Miscellaneous contributions from individuals	135 81
Four thousand paper bags—G. Michler	20 00
Total	$582 81
Total value in refreshments collected in Churches	4,207 94
Total value in refreshments collected in Eastern District	1,163 10
Total in refreshments	$5,814 [illegible]
Total cash collected in Churches	$4,694 25
Total cash collected in E. D.	871 90
Total in cash	$5,[illegible] 15

MONEY DONATIONS THROUGH GENTLEMEN'S REFRESHMENT COMMITTEE.

South Second st. M. E. Church, Rev. J. W. Horne, Pastor	$1,000 00
A. G. Jerome	100 00
S. B. Chittenden, 1 pair Oxen	225 00
Lowber, Asiresne & Co	500 00
H. A. Raw	10 00
Cuthbert & Cunningham	225 00
Thomas B. Kerr	75 00
Thos. Rodgers	100 00
Mrs. Geo. W. Brown	100 00
Sundry donations, 5 dollars each	175 00
B. Samuels	25 00
H. H. Dickinson, Soda-water	700 00
D. G. Farrell, Soda-water	$700 00
Chas. Trott	75 00
Mrs. J. H. Frost	150 00
E. S. Higgins & Co	25 00
J. Diamond & Co	20 00
Seymour L. Husted	1,000 00
Amos Robbins	500 00
Isaac R. Wellington	500 00
Wm. B. Hunter	100 00
Charles J. Buckley	100 00
Unknown	100 00
Total	$5,789 00

MERCHANDISE DONATIONS THROUGH GENTLEMEN'S REFRESHMENT COMMITTEE.

I. Van Anden	$16 00
Isaac W. Rushmore	21 40
L. R. Crandell	5 00
W. H. Richards	9 00
A. H. Campbell	5 00
C. A. Turner	11 00
C. M. Hemstead	9 00
John C. Williams	9 00
Jacob Dolmer	5 75
H. W. Hawkhurst	5 00
L. D. Brokaw	12 00
F. T. Weldon	15 00
Ellsworth Bond	8 00
A. W. Monsfort	5 00
Wm. Frost	$4 00
Messrs. Kipps	11 00
Mrs. M. P. Beach	25 00
Chas. E. Bohne	110 25
Geo. F. Nesbit & Co.	45 00
A. Bartis	20 00
Thompson & Lyon	[illegible]
D. Titus	[illegible] 00
J. M. Fuller	17 75
H. B. Coon	6 00
Wm. Barker & Co	25 61
T. Clarke & Co.	10 00
John Savery & Sons	10 00
E. R. Durkee & Co	23 00

Name	Amount	Name	Amount
Galloway & Sons	65 00	Phillip H. Grogan	$55 00
Rufus Crook	50 00	H. Mayer	22 00
M. Muir	1 25	W. H. Van Name	11 40
Hass & Zipfel	15 00	White & Fraser	11 00
Martin Fullerton	15 00	S. D. Barnes & Co.	11 00
Edward Harvey	200 00	J. & G. Thompson	11 00
Joseph Wild	25 00	C. Van Name	11 00
J. F. Mason	15 00	B. & W. Decker	11 00
Geo. Wilson	10 00	J. J. Houseman	11 00
Clarence Hedge	2 50	E. C. Burbank	11 00
C. W. Schwensch	12 00	G. D. Post & Co.	11 00
J. H. McAuley	10 00	Alex. Frazer	11 00
N. Cooper	5 00	Wm. Phillips	8 00
Joseph Hegeman	16 50	Charles Mott	5 00
J. B. Sutton	10 00	Delmar	5 00
John B. Wright & T. R. Woolsey	50 00	D. W. Whitmore	2 50
Clarke Jervis	10 00	Grocers' and Hardware Committee	90 25
J. Dawson	10 00	Knickerbocker Ice Company	45 00
W. H. Schwarzwaelder	25 00	J. Sprott	11 00
Peter B. Anderson	20 00	T. Sweeney	10 25
R. E. Sinclair	23 16	J. H. Mumby	1 00
Union White Lead Manuf'g Co.	5 00	F. B. Kirby	10 00
B. F. Corlies & Macy	5 00	C. E. Anderson	41 00
R. Stratton	100 00	Robert O. Anderson	204 00
First Baptist Church, through Mr. Sweeny	101 00	Mrs. Robert O. Anderson	50 00
Mansell & Thompson	140 00	D. H. Gould	110 65
P. Rollhaus	5 00	John E. List	11 00
W. Hutcheson	200 00	G. P. Wright & Co.	11 00
W. M. Rodgers & Co.	150 00	J. E. Merrill & Co.	11 00
Thompson & Weller	200 00	Henry Miller	11 00
J. E. Dobson	10 00	Andy Bedell	11 00
From Southampton	6 00	W. H. Christie	22 00
Van Ostrand & Wright	5 00	Wm. Jackson	15 00
B. McManus	15 00	Paul Mead	25 00
Second Unitarian Society, through Mrs. Arnold	7 00	J. F. Brown	10 00
		Clark & Hemslon	25 00
		Geo. Barton	25 00
Mrs. Curtis	2 00	—— Wildorf, Baker	10 00
J. H. Crook	100 00	G. M. Thompson	5 00
Shelter Island	6 00	E. R. Gillespie	10 00
Weeks & Co.	7 50	Alfred Thompson	7 50
Duryea's Maizena	1,000 50	Noble & Douglass	25 00
A. & P. Dorlon	125 00	Goff & Smith	11 00
Dorlon & Shaffer	50 00	Clarke, Clapp & Co.	25 00
J. C. & D. D. Whitney	7 00	T. Porter	17 40
Ovington Bros.	207 75	A. W. Leggett	17 50
From Chicago	65 15	W. A. Keeler	25 00
Beard & Hayward	15 00	Cartwright, Harrison & C.	20 00
J. W. Schoonmaker	10 00	Valentine & Bergen	20 00
Young, Davidson & King	5 00	Horace Gray	45 10
J. E. Colyer	15 00	J. F. Seymour & Co.	50 00
Frank Miller	17 50	Tallman, Dufcane & Co.	21 50
W. S. Dunham	11 50	Brown, Case & Banks	23 00
Miss Hirschman	15 00	Gordon, Fellows & McMillan	48 00

A. Mumford	$15 00
J. Q. Adams & Co	88 00
Jas. Borland & Son	30 00
A. M. Terry	50 00
R. P. Getty & Son	48 00
Rowe & Bonvie	50 00
I. E. & R. H. Place	31 00
Kent & Co	30 00
Stanton, Sheldon & Co	80 40
S. A. Tucker	107 00
B. T. Babbitt	7 80
—— Burrows	15 40
Haywood & Co., Buffalo	10 30
H. A. Graff	13 00
D. S. Quimby	60 00
Dominick Colgan	19 00
James Carman	33 85
Edward Conway	3 40
—— Hanson	3 40
Geo. Applegate	4 75
Geo. Kinkle	9 50
Wm. Young	3 40
W. S. Lister	8 80
L. Marsteller	9 80
Jos. Lockitt & Co	581 40
Wm. Byrnes	19 00
J. E. Lockwood	7 50
W. Roth	6 50
—— Keator	5 80
Thomas Elton	4 30
Vandel Stewart	8 40
Philip Airts	1 40
J. S. Stryker	$8 00
John Bayber	3 40
H. Cummings	30 00
Thomas Prescott	5 00
J. Weeks	7 50
J. Wall	3 00
D. T. Conklin	10 00
P. Hanley	18 60
J. Lyons	5 00
J. Dempsey	8 00
A. T. & J. O. Oswald	35 00
C. Simmons	14 00
C. Sniffin	18 00
John Wilson	10 00
Produce Committee's lottery	250 00
Total	$8,736 19

Total donations in cash	$59,650 25	
Total donations in merchandise	12,759 44	
		$72,409 69
Gross receipts		$81,438 18

DISBURSEMENTS.

Paid Treasurer	$68,590 00	
Meals furnished to sundry committees	1,000 00	
Paid sundry bills	7,671 19	
Paid labor, etc.	3,777 85	
		$81,450 18

E. J. LOWBER, Chairman.

DONATIONS THROUGH THE GROCERS' AND HARDWARE COMMITTEE.

Henry Sheldon	$1,000 00
Thomas Hunt	1,000 00
Thos. C. Durant	1,000 00
Henry K. Sheldon	500 00
S. M. Beard	500 00
Jas. C. Wilson	500 00
John J. Van Nostrand	500 00
Hon. Wm. Wall	500 00
Edward B. Mead	500 00
Henry A. Kent	500 00
R. Valentine and G. W. Bergen	500 00
J. S. Rockwell	500 00
Theodore Victor	250 00
George F. Duckwitz	250 00
Fred'k W. Victor	250 00
Charles H. Victor	250 00
E. B. Place	250 00
H. H. Warden	250 00
Francis Hathaway	$250 00
Eugene O'Sullivan	250 00
Charles E. Hill	250 00
S. P. Goodridge	250 00
A. M. Earle	250 00
Thomas Achelis	250 00
F. H. Lummus	250 00
H. W. Sage	250 00
Jas. L. Morgan	250 00
Edwin Atkins	250 00
Joshua Atkins	250 00
Fred'k Lacey	250 00
Wm. A. Fowler	250 00
N. K. James	250 00
Sturges, Bennet & Co	250 00
Samuel Smith	250 00
J. M. Nichols	250 00
R. A. Packer	250 00

George L. Brewer	$250 00	Jesse S. Carman	$50 00
E. B. Litchfield	250 00	Ed. L. Kalbfleisch	50 00
David Moffat	200 00	H. T. Crosby	50 00
S. N. Osborne	200 00	Cash—Sundry Persons	100 00
Henry W. Banks	200 00	Lewis Morris	50 00
George A. Jarvis	200 00	Theodore Reimers	50 00
James L. Truslow	200 00	Francis S. Morgan	50 00
Packard & James	200 00	J. & D. [illegible]	50 00
Sheffield & Co.	200 00	W. M. Cummings	50 00
Bentley & Burton	200 00	Fowler & Ward	100 00
W. Bailey, Lang & Co.	150 00	N. C. Beard	50 00
Charles McDougall	100 00	Herman Stutzer	50 00
A. V. Blake	100 00	Danl. Talmage & Co.	50 00
A. F. Goodnow	100 00	Edward Perkins	50 00
Müller & Kruger	100 00	E. S. Weichmann	50 00
H. W. Gray	100 00	O. A. Voight	50 00
S. Livingston	100 00	H. S. Barger	50 00
David H. James	100 00	P. W.	50 00
J. M. Goetchius	100 00	George Tapscott & Co.	30 00
William Leighton	100 00	Curtiss Ackerly	25 00
H. B. Wardell	100 00	George F. Bechtel	25 00
R. A. Wardell	100 00	A. Reamers	25 00
George P. Payson	100 00	J. L. Hathaway	25 00
W. C. Fowler	100 00	P. West, Jr.	25 00
W. Davis	100 00	J. C. & D. D. Whitney	25 00
John Scrymser	100 00	Geo. W. Rockwell	25 00
Wm. A. Brown	100 00	D. H. Way	25 00
Aug. Nourbohn	100 00	Capt. Geo. A. Potter	25 00
George G. Spencer	100 00	Weismer, Ackermann & Co.	25 00
S. T. Caswell	100 00	Ado Birgham	25 00
John C. Beatty	100 00	Funck, Meincke & Wendt	15 00
Robert W. Beatty	100 00	Geo. J. Kraft	25 00
Thomas Faye	100 00	Henry Ahern	25 00
Martin & Ritchie	100 00	J. Bruner	25 00
George L. Nichols	100 00	Hagemeyer & Brun	25 00
David Woods	100 00	George Husher	25 00
Joseph S. Case	100 00	A. P. Plant	25 00
R. W. Russell	100 00	Mr. Ely	20 00
B. H. Howell	100 00	A. Battles	20 00
Warner Greave	100 00	J. Q.	10 00
Joy, Corning & Co.	116 00	C. Grew	10 00
E. Pavenstedt & Co.	100 00	Fred'k Heyne	10 00
T. B. Bunting & Co.	100 00	R. C. Winterhoff	10 00
John B. Bogert	100 00	Edward T. Young	10 00
McCombie & Childs, proceeds of 10 bbls. *Flour*	110 00	J. A. Servers	5 00
Dean Sage	75 00	Mrs. Kempf	5 00

EXTRA SUBSCRIPTIONS FOR BENEFIT OF FAIR, PAID TO THE FEMALE EMPLOYMENT SOCIETY THROUGH GROCERS' AND HARDWARE COMMITTEE.

We, the undersigned, subscribe the sums set opposite our names for the manufacture of flannel garments by the Female Employment Society of Brooklyn, for the comfort of our soldiers, under the auspices of the *United States Sanitary Commission*:

Messrs. Stanton, Sheldon & Co.	$175 00	Messrs. Sherman, Tallmadge & Co.	$100 00
" Hamilton & Crooke	100 00	" Wylie & Knevals	100 00

Messrs. E. rie & Co $100 00
John W. Hall & Co........ 95 00
Mr. Rob't O. Edwards 65 00

Total $350 00
Total cash collections........ $1,451 00
Amount of merchandise donated, viz.: By R. R. Mead and others, Hardware $189 47
By A. Swain, 7 bbls. Cranberries.. 108 00
By F. H. Lummus, 8 Cotton Gins.. 194 00
By Bassett & Marr, Scales, etc.... 118 00
By Parker & Whipple, silver Table-bells........ $18 25
By Putnam Manuf'g Co., Clothes-Wringers........ 278 00
By Thos. W. Griffen & Co., 8 bbls. Flour........ 48 00
By Jones, Boyd & Co., Pittsburg, 1 box Casteel........ 54 68

$1,014 68

Grand total $2,465 68

HENRY SHELDON, Chairman.

DONATIONS THROUGH THE COMMITTEE ON BOOKS, PUBLICATIONS AND PRINTING.

D Appleton & Co., N. Y., Books, etc........ $1,000 00
Hosford & Ketcham, N. Y., Stationery........ 300 00
Horace Waters, N. Y., Music........ 300 00
Barnes & Burr, N. Y., Books........ 275 00
Wm. Pate, N. Y., Engravings........ 210 00
Harper & Bros., N. Y., Books........ 250 00
Ivison, Phinney, Blakeman & Co., N. Y., Books........ 186 75
Jno. C. Beale, N. Y., Stationery.. 186 80
G. & C. Merriam, Springfield, Mass., Books........ 168 60
Owens & Ajax, N. Y., Books........ 150 00
John H. Williams, N. Y., Engravings........ 114 50
Bradie & Co., N. Y., Books........ 108 80
Geo. A. Jarvis, Brooklyn, Books.. 185 00
G. P. Putnam, N. Y., Books........ 108 00
Chas. Scribner, N. Y., Books........ 100 00
Geo. W. Carleton, N. Y., Books... 100 00
Mason Bros., N. Y., Books........ 101 78
Ames & Barnes, N. Y., Stationery. 100 00
E. Smith, Lee, Mass., Books........ 60 00
M. E. Church, First street, Brooklyn, Books........ 80 00
Dick & Fitzgerald, N. Y., Books.. 70 00
W. J. Pooley, N. Y., Engravings... 61 40
Jno. D. Chase, Brooklyn, Stereoscope........ 80 00
Robt. Carter & Bros., N. Y., Books. 65 00
Geo. W. Childs, Phila., Books.... 59 00
Geo. A. Olney, N. Y., Photograph Album........ 50 00
Berlin & Jones, N. Y., Books........ 50 41
Stearns & Beale, N. Y., Stationery. 50 00
J. H. Stearns, N. Y., Stationery.. 50 00
Schermerhorn, Bancroft & Co., N. Y., Books........ 48 00
Roberts & Bro., Boston, Books... $47 35
J. G. Gregory, N. Y., Books........ 40 00
W. J. Martin, N. Y., Books........ 40 00
T. Nelson & Sons, N. Y., Books... 38 35
Henry Chadwick, Books, Brooklyn *Eagle* 37 50
"Green Point" Books........ 38 00
Althof, Bergmann & Co., N. Y., Sundries........ 30 00
Collins & Bros., N. Y., Sundries.. 30 00
J. L. Blamire, N. Y., Sundries.... 30 00
A. Wallack, N. Y., Sundries........ 35 00
Geo. R. Cholwell, N. Y., Sundries. 30 00
F. W. Tappan, N. Y., Sundries.... 37 50
Jno. Foley, N. Y., Gold Pens..... 34 00
Jas. Summerfield, N. Y., Sundries. 35 00
Rev. S. H. Canfield, D.D., Brooklyn, Books........ 29 40
S. Raynor, N. Y., Sundries........ 25 00
A. King, N. Y., Sundries........ 25 00
J. Miller, N. Y., Books........ 25 00
Eyre & Spottiswoode, N. Y., Books. 35 00
Ward Dickson, N. Y., Books........ 25 00
R. B. Dovell & Son, N. Y., Books. 25 00
Werner & Huber, N. Y., Books... 20 00
McLoughlin Bros., N. Y., Books... 20 00
Wm. Wilstead, N. Y., Books........ 20 00
Board of Publication Ref. Dutch Church, N. Y., Books........ 20 70
Sawyer & Thompson, Brooklyn, 25 00
C. A. Bunnet, N. Y., Books........ 25 00
D. B. Brooks & Brothers, Salem, Mass., Books........ 25 00
J. P. Bramhall, N. Y., Books........ 24 50
P. A. Brady, N. Y., Books........ 18 75
"A Friend," Books........ 14 50
D. S. Holmes, Brooklyn, E. D., Books........ 19 50
Brewer & Tileston, Boston, Mass. 10 00

Ten Volumes Bryant's Poems, from Author, with autograph...	$30 00
Mrs. Sigourney, Books..........	4 00
M. Colton, N. Y., Books.........	15 00
F. S. Copley, N. Y., Sundries.....	10 00
McFeeters & Co., N. Y., Sundries.	10 00
G. Hayward, Brooklyn, Sundries..	16 50
B. R. Hard, N. Y., Stationery...	18 50
H. A. Reilly, N. Y., Sundries.....	10 75
M. Mikendorf, N. Y., Sundries....	10 00
"Williamsburg," Sundries.......	9 00
Kate McClellan, Brooklyn, Sundries....................	15 00
Eastern District, Sundries.......	7 00
Sadlier & Co., N. Y., Sundries....	9 00
John Pate, N. Y., Sundries.......	5 00
J. Rosenthal, N. Y., Sundries.....	19 50
R. C. Hastings, N. Y., Sundries...	5 00
Sundry anonymous donations.....	63 75
H. Noble, N. Y., Sundries........	5 00
Total donation of goods..........	$3,753 75

CASH DONATIONS.

W. W. Swayne, by Mrs. Swayne..	$100 00
J. J. Parcell, do. do.......	100 00
A. Mason, by Mrs. Swayne......	$25 00
B. & P. Lawrence, do. do.......	20 00
J. & A. Blumenthal, do.......	15 00
C. R. Sheehan, do. do.......	10 00
G. Swift, do. do.......	10 00
J. Wilson, do. do.......	5 00
T. B. O'Connor, do. do.......	5 00
B. Hook, do. do.......	50
I. Henderson, by Mrs. Henderson.	100 00
Charles F. Miller....	25 00
M. Weir..........................	10 00
D. B. Moses........	5 00
C. Depew.........................	25 00
S. C. F. Odell, by C. Nordhoff....	100 00
Mrs. Cutter......................	25 00
R. Vandervoort	20 00
C. F. Reubrichs..................	100 00
Corlies & Macy, by J. C. Beale....	25 00
W. A. Speight & Co...............	25 00
H. Rambridge.................	25 00
R. Caldwell, Palisbury, N. Y....	10 00
Campbell, Hall & Co..............	250 00
W. & C. K. Herrick, Books, etc. .	200 00
Total amount of goods and cash...$[illegible]	[illegible]

THOS. H. MESSENGER, Chairman.

DONATIONS THROUGH THE COMMITTEE ON BUILDINGS AND DECORATIONS.

Wm. Spence, 10 days	$25 00
John Wilson, 20 days............	50 00
Richard Whipple, 20 days.	50 00
J. H. Scribner, 20 days..	50 00
Tappan Reeve, 20 days..	50 00
Thos. Conway, 5 days......	12 50
Jesse Folk, 20 days.......	60 00
C. L. Dennington, 20 days.........	50 00
W. H. Noe, 5 days	15 00
Robert White, 20 days....... ...	50 00
W. H. Hazard, 20 days...	50 00
D. S. Voorhees, 20 days...	50 00
Abraham Purdy, 5 days..	12 50
G. Scott, Jr., 10 days...	25 00
H. Werner, 5 days.	12 50
P. F. O'Brien, 20 days.....	50 00
M. J. Murphy, 5 days............	12 50
S. & W. C. Smith, 13 days	32 50
Joseph Platt, 20 days............	50 00
Wright & Brooks, 20 days...... ...	50 00
Surdicor & Lee, 6 days...	15 00
J. S. Raymond, 20 days...........	50 00
Joseph Kirby, 10 days............	25 00
Abram Mance, 10 days......	25 00
H. A. Phillips, 10 days.	25 00
E. & J. Wheadon, 7 days..........	$10 50
James Locke......................	25 00
Thomas Sullivan..................	50 00
H. N. Conklin, Son & Beers, Lumber..............................	500 00
Crow & Austin, Lumber..........	100 00
Johnson & Spader, do............	100 00
Sage & Co., do......... ...	200 00
H. Thomas & Co., do............	100 00
Watson & Pittenger, do	250 00
J. W. Hallingsea & Co., Lumber..	50 00
Westlake & McKee, do...	100 00
H. W. Adams, do....	200 00
—— Duty, do....	50 00
White & Nichols, 7 kegs Nails...	45 00
Young & Barnett, 5 do	20 00
Whitmore & Bro., 5 do.......	20 00
Thos. B. Smith & Co., 5 do........	30 00
J. D. Willis, 4 do...	24 00
John Bruce, 2 do........	12 00
Phelps & Graham, 2 do........	12 00
James C. Brower, 2 do........	12 00
J. J. Phillips, 1 do........	6 00
Joseph H. Howard, cash.........	25 00
Spencer & Martin, Lime and Brick	25 00

T. B. Jackson, 26 days..............	$40 00	Martin & Canda, Lime and Brick	$50 00
W. Martin, 6 days....................	15 00	Kenyon & Newton, Sashes.......	10 00
Osborn & Fish, sash..............	20 00	David Fithian, do........	15 00
D. J. Lucas, Sashes................	18 00	Cornelius Sprague.............	10 00
Clark & Bierds, do................	20 00	Wm. M. Newell..................	5 00
Kirk & Clark, Doors..............	19 00	A. Buckmaster..................	5 00
David P. Gardiner, Sashes........	6 00	Henry Sheldon....................	15 00
Litchfield & Ketcham, do	10 00	Dwight Johnson..................	5 00
Prentice & White, do.......	5 00	W. L. Dunham....................	10 00
James Whelan, Stairs.............	40 00	Fisher Howe.......................	25 00
R. W. Hopes..........................	10 00	T. Polhemus, Jr...................	20 00
E. D. Plympton.....................	25 00	Wm. S. Herriman..............	30 00

The Committee are indebted to many others for important services, and to the following persons for the use of lots: Mrs. Harriet L. Packer, Sylvester Hoadlow, Esq., Allen Dodworth, Esq., A. A. Low, Esq. F. J. Nodine, Esq., for use of stable. Gamaliel King, Esq., Daniel L. Northop, Esq., Peter G. Taylor, Esq., Wm. A. Fowler, Esq., Water Commissioners, for use of large hydrant. John Cunningham, Esq., Chief Engineer of the Brooklyn Fire Department, for use fire apparatus for the protection of the buildings. Leonard Cooper, Esq., for personal services. Mr. George Gamjee for several loads of evergreens. Brooklyn Fire Department for use of their decorations. Wm. Ayman & Co., loan of bunting and flags. Thomas Brooks, for the loan of flags. Husted & Carll, and Mr. A. S. Fuller, for loan of various decorations. Stewart & Co., for loan of decorations and labor. Stephen Kidder, for loan of mirrors. W. Payne, for loan of decorations and personal services. Admiral Paulding and St Nicholas Society, for loan of flags.

REPORT OF THE SUB-COMMITTEE ON DECORATIONS.

The following is an abstract of the report of the Sub-Committee on Decorations, of which Mr. J. H. Degraw was the efficient chairman:

As the Advisory Committee provided no department for Horticulture, no arrangements were made to make a large display, and in many instances merchandise of various kinds were sold on different tables with flowers. If it had not been for this circumstance, there can be no doubt but the Treasurer would have received from this source considerably over three thousand dollars. Your Committee feel that they cannot close their report without directing your attention to a number of Gentlemen who most liberally contributed to the furnishing of the decorations. We leave the Committee from the Brooklyn Horticultural Society to report the contributions to the Horticultural table. The Horticultural Society rendered the Committee most valuable service. The evergreens were mostly from Greenwood, amounting to a large number of double-team loads; they were all furnished by Mr. George Gamjee, without any expense to the Committee. Your Committee view that he should be presented with a special notice of our appreciation of his patriotism and benevolence. The Committee were also much indebted to the Brooklyn Fire Department for generous loan of all their anniversary decorations. We acknowledge with pleasure the loan of all the bunting for decorating the Auditorium, from Messrs. William Ayman & Co.; also the loan of near fifty flags from Thomas Brooks, Esq. We feel under many obligations to Messrs. Carl & Husted for the loan of various articles suited for decorating, as well as for their personal services, and furnishing a number of men in their employ, on all occasions when they were required. The Committee with pleasure acknowledge the services of Mr. Stephen Kidder, in furnishing all the looking-glasses for Knickerbocker Hall; also of N. Waring, Esq., for the loan of flags; also to Stuart & Co., in furnishing men from their establishment on various occasions; also the Commandant of the Brooklyn Navy Yard, for a large supply of flags; also to the St. Nicholas Society for the loan of their large flag; also to a number of Gentlemen, of whom the Committee did not obtain their names, who furnished flags and other decorations; also to A. S. Fuller for a large quantity of horticultural decorations from New Jersey, furnished at his own expense; also to Mr. Weir, for his constant attention to the requirements of the Committee during the Fair.

The following is the account of the Horticultural Table.

Total receipts..............		$2,900 15	Sub'ns paid by Mrs. King..	$100 00
Total disbursements.....$1,290 65			Contributions from Decorating Committee to pay unpaid bills, due by the Horticultural table	[illegible]
Account from Jane E. Degrauw	150 00	1,440 65		
Nett result of table................		[illegible]		
Cont'b from Jane E. Degrauw....		150 00	Total	[illegible]

The Building and Decorating Committee gratefully acknowledge the following contributions, for the aid and display of the Horticultural Tables:

Miss Jane E. Degrauw, a very elegant basket of wax flowers.

Mrs. Packer, for a constant supply of boquets and baskets of flowers.

Mrs. Fisher Howe, for a collection of plants, and a constant supply of boquets.

Mrs. J. S. T. Stranahan, for contributions of boquets on several occasions.

Mrs. Humphreys, for a large basket of flowers.

Mrs. James Weir, of Bay Ridge, for several baskets of flowers, most beautifully arranged, and presented at various times.

A. A. Low, Esq., for a number of fine baskets of flowers at various times.

Mr. Wm. Collopy, for a very elegant large size basket of flowers.

Isaac Buchanan, Seventeenth street, New York, for a large collection of his choice varieties of petunia seeds.

Mr. James Parks, for plants, seeds, and boquets, on several occasions.

James Mellin, for baskets of fine flowers.

Thomas Cavannah, for a very beautiful ornamented design.

Mr. Edward Simpson, for a very elegant basket of flowers on the opening evening.

John A. King, Esq., of Jamaica, for a fine collection of cut flowers.

William Davidson, for plants and cut flowers.

Messrs. Dallasdowse and Zeller, of Flatbush, for a collection of plants.

William Schrymageur, of Greenwood, for a collection of plants.

Messrs. Parsons, of Flushing, for flowers and evergreens.

Dr. Grant, for a large number of grape vines, including his new seedling "Iona."

Mr. Clarke, of New York, for two fine baskets of flowers.

John N. Laughl, for a box of very handsome cut camelias.

Miss Lockwood, for two handsome standard orange trees.

AREA (IN SQUARE FEET) OF FLOOR SPACE PROVIDED.

Academy of Music—First floor, Auditorium	7,030		
" " First floor, stage portion	3,040	10,070	
" " Second floor, Auditorium	3,040		
" " Picture Gallery	3,060	6,100	
" " First floor, lobbies	8,500		
" " Second floor, lobbies	1,230	9,730	
Total in Academy of Music			25,900
Restaurant adjoining the Academy of Music, and connected therewith, a temporary structure—Main floor	6,300		
Galleries	2,800		
Total in Restaurant			9,100
New England Kitchen, opposite the Academy of Music, and connected therewith by a covered way over Montague street, a temporary structure			4,000
Room for Heavy Goods and Machinery, a temporary structure, adjoining the New England Kitchen			6,000
Total area provided for the Fair—Square feet			45,500

CONTRIBUTIONS THROUGH THE BOOT AND SHOE, LEATHER HAT AND CAP AND CLOTHING COMMITTEE.

Aaron Healy	$750 00	O. M. Lapham	$100 00
C. S. Parsons & Sons	600 00	Samuel T. Keese	100 00
L. H. Brigham	300 00	Thos. Kirk	50 00
H. S. Benedict	500 00	Frederick Haas	10 00
C. B. Camp	250 00	New York, cash	10 00
Isaac Hyde, Jr.	300 00	R. Grimshaw	50 00
John C. Southwick	200 00	W. Rhodes	25 00
C. H. Caldwell	200 00	B. Ruston	25 00
Nathan Southwick	200 00	Jno. O. Whitehouse	500 00
James McGregor	100 00	Aaron Claflin	500 00
W. M. Newall	100 00	Jno. T. Martin	500 00
M. S. Kerregan	100 00	James H. Prentice	500 00
John Coffey	25 00	J. W. Mason	300 00
A. W. Godfrey	10 00	East N. Y. Shoe Manuf'g Co.	100 00
Pickard & Anderson	10 00	Alanson Trask	250 00
Wm. Sherwood	50 00	F. A. Gale	50 00
Devlin & Co.	200 00	H. O. Bell	100 00
James M. Bart & Bros.	300 00	B. Mayberry	50 00
Shrather & Nichols	550 00	C. C. Warren	100 00
Geo. Dickerson	150 00	G. C. Treadwell	200 00
H. O. Lapham	100 00	James Van Name	10 00

Loeschick & Wesendonck & Co.	$100 00
H. Schlesinger	50 00
Augustus Studwell	25 00
Alexander Studwell	100 00
J. T. Whitehouse	200 00
Charles W. Brain	25 00
Thos. Clarendon	50 00
Josiah Brooks & Co.	25 00
Cash	5 00
C. H. C., 12 doz. Caps	100 00
Young, Schultz & Co.	300 00
David Wesson	100 00
John R. Ford	100 00
Stephen H. Powers	25 00
Sutton, Smith & Co.	200 00
John Roughts	30 00
Cash	$1 00
Thos. S. Dale & Co.	25 00
Christ, Jay & Co.	50 00
Granville Whittlesey	100 00
Williams & Whittlesey	100 00
J. D. Mattison	50 00
H. C. Southwick	50 00
Pearce & Brush	200 00
John Ballard	500 00
Geo. H. Studwell	25 00
Thos. Garner	25 00
Journeymen Morocco Manufact'y.	15 00
G. N. Osborn	25 00
Total	**$11,[illegible] 00**

All but a small amount of the above subscriptions are cash.

W. M. NEWELL, **Chairman.**

CONTRIBUTIONS THROUGH THE COMMITTEE ON BENEFITS, ENTERTAINMENTS, Etc.

Mrs. S. B. Chittenden, Parlor and Musical Entertainments	$480 00
Mrs. H. L. Packer, Parlor and Musical Entertainments	520 00
Mrs. A. S. Barnes, Parlor and Musical Entertainments	480 00
Mrs. Jane P. Torrey, Parlor and Musical Entertainments	805 00
Nicholas Luquer and friends, Musical Entertainments	240 00
Miss Lizzie C. Comstock, Grace A. Bowen, and Nellie A. Bowen	111 00
Miss Sarah E. Connor and Miss A. C. Smith	150 00
"Little Girls," 77 Henry street	12 00
South Brooklyn Savings Institution, per Jno. D. Cox, Esq.	2,150 00
Wm. Bagley, Esq.	50 00
Jno. B. Hutchinson, Esq.	175 00
Thirteenth Regiment N. Y. S. N. G., Col. Woodward	4,011 00
Students of Collegiate and Polytechnic Institute	1,078 25
Public School Exhibition, W. D.	1,178 10
Public School Exhibition, E. D.	285 14
Tableau at Athenæum, per Mrs. E. Anthony	1,563 00
Tableau Eastern District, per Mrs. C. Coles	308 00
"Five Little Girls"	5 00
Brooklyn Athenæum and Reading Room	$160 00
Brooklyn City Railroad Co.	1,985 64
Broadway Railroad Co.	100 00
Directors of Railroad, per H. A. Kent, Esq.	700 00
Burnham's Gymnasium	600 45
Germania Society	226 00
Skating Pond	96 85
Social Singing Society First Ref. Dutch Church, E. D., per Jno. A. Gray, Esq.	35 80
South Ninth st. Cong. Church, E. D., per Philip A. Myers, Esq.	614 51
Capitoline Association	175 00
Total	$16,[illegible] 78
Received for sale of Admission Tickets	$30,571 [illegible]
Received for sale of Admission Tickets for Benefit of Soldiers' Families	1,614 50
Lafayette Avenue Presb. Church, cash paid Treasurer for goods sold ... $1,685 60; Do. subscriptions ... 1,[illegible] 57; Do. Refresh't Com. ... 81 00; Refreshment do. ... 175 15	2,978 30

EDWARD A. LAMBERT, Chairman.

REPORT OF THE COMMITTEE ON MUSIC.

The Committee on Music of the Brooklyn and Long Island Fair, in aid of the U. S. Sanitary Commission, respectfully report:

That the multiplicity of public and private entertainments of all kinds, which were given in behalf of the Fair during their official existence, rendered it inadvisable to tax much further the already surfeited appetite of the people, by adding to the number.

Besides this, the Committee found their province preoccupied, and their action forestalled on every side by other committees whose jurisdiction was so nearly coincident with their own that the field of their duty was reduced to very narrow limits.

The following list comprises all the entertainments which the Committee were able to avail themselves of, with the several sums accruing therefrom to the cause, viz.:

Concert of the Philharmonic Society	$[illegible] 00
Advertising and Printing for the same, expense defrayed by A. V. Blake, Esq.	150 00
Two Entertainments by Hooley's Minstrels	[illegible] 00
Parlor Entertainment by Miss Rebecca W. Poole	80 00
Oratorio given in the Eastern District under the direction of Ph. A. Mayer, Esq., member of the Committee	614 51
Two Parlor Entertainments given by the late Pupils of P. K. Weizel, Esq., under his direction, at the house of E. W. Dunham, Esq.	$[illegible] 00
The entire expense of the Band for the first week of the Fair, defrayed by Messrs. P. K. Weizel, L. B. Wyman, J. P. Meyoen, and Pickering Clark, members of the Committee	628 00
Total	$2,[illegible] 18

L. B. WYMAN, Chairman.

CONTRIBUTIONS THROUGH THE PRODUCE COMMITTEE.

Sawyer, Wallace & Co.	$500 00
J. P. Wallace	500 00
Smith J. Eastman	300 00
Cur Adams	300 00
Various parties, collected by F. Sherwood	260 00
Wm. Beard	250 00
Curtis Noble	250 00
White & Douglass	250 00
Seymour Burrell	250 00
J. B. Leggett & Co.	250 00
Robert Thallon	250 00
S. Van Benschoten	250 00
J. P. Robinson	200 00
G. C. Robinson	200 00
F. D. Moulton	200 00
T. Woodruff	200 00
S. V. W. Carey	200 00
Parker, Brooks & Co	200 00
Clark, Clapp & Co.	$100 00
A. R. Kent & Co.	100 00
Cesar & Paull	100 00
Purdue & Ward	100 00
Prithaupt & Wilson	100 00
E. W. Dunham	100 00
P. Clark	100 00
C. H. Benedict	100 00
J. H. Holcomb	100 00
J. S. Robert & Son	50 00
A. Gamble	50 00
T. W. French	25 00
C. W. Wells	25 00
T. M. Brown & Son	25 00
Miller & Carr	25 00
Foster & Bros.	25 00
David W. Lewis	25 00
John F. Cook	25 00
D. Bower	25 00

Dotcher & Elberly	$[illegible] 00
J. W. Mason	150 00
B. K. Clark	126 00
Thomas & Benham	100 00
M. S. Nicholson	10 00
Isaac Crane	5 00
Sundry parties, through Mrs. P. Rice, 100 bbls. Flour	1,000 00
Archibald Baxter, 80 bbls. Flour	5[illegible] 00
Charles Taylor, 25 Hams	125 00
P. Vanderbilt, carting, etc	100 00
W. A. Work & Son, Hams	61 00
J. A. Ameling & Son, Hams	35 00
Robinson & Oviatt, Cleveland, O., 2 half bbls. family Beef	45 00
Alfred Benson	$20 00
Miller & Carpenter	25 00
Jones, Smith & Co	25 00
H. D. Peck	15 00
E. S. Philbrick, Beaufort, S. C., 1 bale Sea Island Cotton	304 00
B. F. Flanders, New Orleans, La., 1 bale Cotton, 1 hhd. Sugar, 1 hhd. Molasses	450 00
Citizens and U. S. Troops in Florida, 5 Turtles, transferred to the Restaurant, valued at	500 00
Total	$10,501 00

ARCHIBALD BAXTER, Chairman.

DONATIONS THROUGH THE COMMITTEE ON SCHOOLS AND SEMINARIES, IN GOODS AND MONEY.

Primary School No. 1	$5 00
" " 3	17 40
" " 4	2 00
Public " 4	[illegible] 00
" " 5	100 00
Primary " 5	11 80
" " 6	[illegible]
Public " 6	27 00
" " 7 8 bxs of articles not valued	
Public School No. 8	1 00
" " 9	28 00
" " 10	23 00
" " 11	100 00
" " 12	38 16
" " 13	120 00
" " 14	12 71
" " 15	830 08
Entertainment by Primary Dept. of Public School No. 15	$587 00
Public School No. 16	[illegible] 10
" " 17	65 74
" " 18	151 05
" " 19	[illegible]
" " 20	38 05
" " 21	5 00
" " 22	81 15
" " 24	68 50
" " 25	131 03
" " 26	30 00
Entm't by 600 children, P.S. No. 11	64 40
Exhibition of Public Schools, E.D.	165 91
Public School No. 8, New Utrecht	1 62
Dist. School No. 8, Greenfield, L. I.	[illegible]
Total from Public Schools	$1,[illegible]

PRIVATE SCHOOLS AND SEMINARIES.

Sidney Place Seminary	$7 00
Young Ladies, Mrs. Dunn's School in Columbia street	170 00
Pupils of Clinton Institute, Clinton street	35 00
Cole Grammar School	17 50
Juvenile High School, Washington street	41 00
Several Scholars, Mr. Simmons' School, Grand avenue	17 30
Young Ladies, Brooklyn Heights Seminary, Professor West	401 [illegible]
Young Ladies, Mrs. Osborne's School, Henry street	173 [illegible]
Mr. Bradbury's Seminary	30 00
Teachers and Pupils of Brooklyn Female Seminary, Clinton st.	85 00
South Brooklyn Female Seminary	$165 10
Entertainment Senior Class of Packer Collegiate Institute	148 [illegible]
Young Ladies of Packer Collegiate Institute	973 [illegible]
Pupils J. D. Clarke's School, Congress street	195 00
Collegiate and Polytechnic Institute	1,[illegible] 25
Madame Giraud's School	148 77
Misses Hooke's School, First Place	11 30
Mrs. Cooper's School, Clinton st.	53 11
School of Protestant Orphan Asylum	10 00
Total from Private Schools, etc.	$4,[illegible] 10
Bethel Mission Schools	123 91

Colored Union Sabbath School	$5 00
Plymouth Sabbath School	[illegible] 00
Sunday School of Fourth Universalist Society	47 25
Total	$[illegible] 18
Total Receipts from Schools	9,[illegible] 84

Mrs. H. L. PACKER, Chairman.

Other donations through Mrs. Packer not previously acknowledged: Proceeds of Musical Reception	$[illegible] 24
Box from Young Ladies of Corning, Steuben Co.	$11 25
Articles presented by Mrs. O. H. Gordon	[illegible] 00
From Flushing, through Miss A. S. Jones	16 00
Mrs. Hitchcock	8 00
Mrs. Culver	15 00
Mr. T. Rogers	1 00
	$[illegible] 64
	9,[illegible]
Grand total	$10,0[illegible]

THE LONG ISLAND CONTRIBUTIONS.

A full report of the contributions of Queens and Suffolk counties to the Fair has been published by Elias Lewis, Jr., Chairman of the Committee of these counties, from which we condense the following. The ladies in attendance at the Long Island tables were:

Astoria—Mrs. Blackwell, Mrs. Halsey, Misses Wyckoff, Carrington, Wilson, Mills, Blackwell, Mulligan, O'Reilley.

Newtown—Mrs. Wm. Knox, Mrs. Ayres, Misses Van Alst, Goldsmith, Palmer, Moe, Rapelyea, Mrs. Rapelyea.

Flushing and North Hempstead—Mrs. Cox, Misses Fuller, Darling, Hillyer, Wells, Van Zandt.

Glen Cove and Oyster Bay—Misses Coles, Craft, Moritt, Nellson, Emily Valentine, Susan Valentine, Mrs. E. Lewis, Jr.

Hempstead—Mrs. Harold, Erving, Misses Rushmore, Cortelyou, Clowes, Carman.

Jamaica—Mrs. Cogswell, Misses P. Hagner, Ludlam, Nichols, King, Andrews, Onderdonk, Crossman.

Stony Brook Suffolk County—Miss Oakes.

QUEENS COUNTY—CONTRIBUTIONS IN GOODS AND MONEY.

Newtown		$2,118 81
Flushing		1,780 11
District near Queens		146 50
Jamaica	$[illegible]	
Ladies of Queens	1[illegible] 45	
Ladies of Woodhaven	[illegible] 81	
		1,1[illegible] 15
Hempstead		1,870 85
Manhasset		1,119 44
Roslyn		120 16
Westbury		$[illegible]
Glen Cove		2,020 [illegible]
Oysterbay Village		[illegible] 41
Oysterbay Cove		287 64
Brookville		10[illegible] 00
Norwich		[illegible] 00
Farmingdale		119 50
Amityville		[illegible] 00
Total		$11,[illegible]

SUFFOLK COUNTY.

Huntingdon	$731 08
Babylon	163 00
Islip	40[illegible] 00
Patchogue	[illegible] 54
Smithtown	[illegible] 42
Stony Brook	100 00
Setauket	74 00
Port Jefferson	[illegible] 00
Miller's Place	112 0[illegible]
Riverhead	[illegible] 81
Mattituck	1[illegible]
Cutchogue	81 00
Southold	[illegible] 30
Greenport	180 00
Orient	[illegible]
Moriches	119 40
Quogue	[illegible] 75
Southampton Village	1,10[illegible] 00
Bridgehampton	[illegible] 44
East Hampton	[illegible] 67
Shelter Island	105 [illegible]
Sag Harbor	1,[illegible] 00
	$[illegible] 13
Miscellaneous	810 00
Total	$[illegible]

The Committee also state that liberal contributions had recently been forwarded to the Sanitary Commission from the numerous organizations of patriotic ladies throughout the Island, and they have reason to believe that the amount thus forwarded, for the year preceding the Great Fair, may be fairly estimated at $5,000.

It would thus appear that the Commission has received from the counties of Queens and Suffolk, (including $5,810 05 contributed to the Metropolitan Fair from Flushing,) in cash and hospital stores, during the time mentioned, nearly thirty-one thousand five hundred dollars, and that the good work is now pressed even more vigorously than before.

To the above should be added a large amount of clothing and hospital stores delivered to the Woman's Relief Association of Brooklyn.

AMOUNT OF CASH DONATED THROUGH THE COMMITTEE ON KINGS COUNTY TOWN CONTRIBUTIONS.

Town of New Lotts, by Rev. J. M. Van Buren	$171 50
Town of East New York, by Mrs. C. R. Miller	[illegible] 75
By Mrs. P. H. Hurd	41 75
Town of Gravesend, by Mrs. S. Gerretsen	23 30
Gravesend Neck	118 00
Town of Flatlands, by Rev. M. Doolittle	58 17
M. Magaw	820 00
Town of Flatbush, by John Lefferts	[illegible]
Windsor Terrace, by Miss Hudson	36 35
Greenfield, by Mrs. Clowe	18 55
St. Paul's Episcopal Church, by W. H. Matthews	$1,435 00
Town of New Utrecht, by Hardman Wright	47 50
Donations to New England Kitchen, from Flatbush	30 00
Sales at Kings County Tables	2,789 41
Articles belonging to Kings County, sold in other departments	140 00
St. Paul's Church, Flatbush, table	880 85
Goat—Flatbush	75 00
Total	$7,0[illegible]

JOHN LEFFERTS, Chairman.

CATALOGUE OF THE MUSEUM OF ART, RELICS AND CURIOSITIES.

NOTE.—All articles having D attached, were free gifts to the Fair.

C. R. Baxter—Model of Birthplace of Wm. Shakespeare, in 1564; Model of Birthplace of Wm. Shakespeare, in 1769; Model of the Grammar School, at Stratford-on-Avon; Model of Anne Hathaway's Cottage, at Stratford-on-Avon; Model of the Lodge in Charlecote Park; Model of the New Place, at Stratford; Model of the Globe Theatre, London; Model of the Smith's Forge, at Stratford; Model of English Castle; Model of English Castle with Watch Towers; 1 ditto ditto; Model of Front of Bath Abbey; Monstrous Horse's Bit, of 14th Century; Monstrous Horse's Bit, of 13th Century; Instrument of Warfare, of 9th Century; Instrument of Warfare, of 8th Century; Pipe made from the Elm Tree, from Holland; Stone Bottle, from the Great Fire in New York; Tooth of a Walrus; Snake, from China, of a poisonous nature. W. H. Mallory—Stalactite, from Cave of Bellamar, Cuba. Dr. R. C. Moffat—A Turtle's Skull. C. H. Baxter—A Basswood Shaving, 60 feet long; Curious Bean, from India; Japanese Dagger; Two Knights in Armor. Mrs. J. T. Howard—Vicksburg Newspaper (Rebel). H. Belden—Old Book, printed in 1477; Old Book, printed in 1520; A Volume of Sermons, printed in 1657; Latin Volume, printed in 1477. Mrs. J. Cooper—A Series of Continental Currency. Barnet Johnson—Map of Brooklyn, drawn by Jer. Johnson. J. H. Jackson—Continental Bills, State of New Jersey, 1780; Two Canes. Wilson G. Hunt—A Limb of Cotton-Plant, D. W. W. Wotherspoon—Landscape, D. J. C. Platt—Battle Scene, D. Granville Perkins—Water Scene, D. Ladies' Soldiers' Aid Association, Glen Cove—Brace of Pistols, in case, D. Ladies' Soldiers' Aid Association, Oyster Bay—Toilet Set, Japanese, D. Mrs. J. R. St. John—A Piece of the Album of Robert Burns, D. Mrs. Baigmann—An Oval for the Album.

Dr. J. T. Farley—Extract from Oration at Gettysburg, with Autograph of Edward Everett, D. C. M. St. John—A Copy of the Boston *Chronicle*, 1768, D. Mrs. Halmanno—Painting, Flowers. Mrs. St. John—Collection of Castes, D. Dr. Farley—Autograph Manuscript of Dr. Channing, D. Madam Ruthe—Autograph Letter of Louis Kossuth, D. Turkish Slippers; Persian Slippers; Chinese Slippers; Col. Philip's Circular to the Creek Indians; Sword presented by Gen. Washington to Gen. Lee. Mrs. R. W. Ripley—Piece of Tapestry from Holyrood Palace. Miss J. Cooper—Pistol used in the Revolutionary War; Petrified Cactus. Mrs. H. Pomroy—Bible Concordance, 225 years old. Lieut. Worden—Piece of Wood from the Merrimac, D. Miss J. Cooper—Revolutionary Camp Cup. Mrs. St. John—Autograph of Henry Clay, D. Miss J. Cooper—Petrified Sugar Cane. F. Bridges—3 Bronze Incense Burners. D. O. Kellogg—U. S. Naval Officer's Dagger, D; Court Dress Sword, D. A. P. Oswald—Instrument for Killing Buffaloes; Palmetto Leaf from Hilton Head. Mrs. W. M. Richards—Vase made from Wood of "Constitution." Albert Gray—Miniature Gun and Carriage, from Wood of Constitution, D. D. Crocker—Penknife Illustration on New Testament. J. L. Nathan—Portrait of Gen. Neal Dow; Letter, with Autograph of Lord Palmerston; Engraving, The Flight, by Kapp; Engraving, Morning. Alex. Muir—A pair of Washington Goblets. Mrs. J. R. St. John—Autograph of Andrew Jackson, D; Autograph of Eldridge Gerry, D; Autograph of Daniel Webster, D; Autograph of Josiah Quincy, D; Autograph of Samuel Lover, D; Autograph of L. H. Sigourney, D. W. E. Woodward—2 Swords, (no hilts) D. J. L. Latimer—Ancient Book. Mrs. St. John—Autograph of R. W. Emerson, D; Letter Press of Aaron Burr, D; Proclamation of Gov. Pratt, Md., D; Manuscripts of John G. Whittier, D; Autograph Letter of Wm. Ware, D; Autograph Letter of J. C. Calhoun, D; Calabash, or Indian Drinking Cup; Tongue of a Fish, from the Amazon. C. M. St. John—Resurrection Plant, brought from Egypt 40 years ago. Mrs. Richards—Mexican Drum. Ludovice—Case of Cuban Insects, Scorpions, etc. Mrs. J. O. Low—Venetian Chair. Ludovice—Buffalo Horns; Pair of Deer's Antlers; Matte Cup and Tube; Basque Shoes; South American Dress Poncho; South American Dress Pantalets; Bolas; Spurs; Stirrups; Whip; South American Stirrups; Horse Skin Shoes. D. O. Kellogg—Case of Coins, D. Allston Wilson—Port Fire used in the Revolutionary War, D. Christ Church—Water from the River Jordan, D; Shells strung by Monks of St. Athos, D. Mrs. Richards—Chinese Umbrella; Egyptian Sword. Dr. Farley—Autograph Letter of Washington Alston, D; Autograph Letter of Wm. Ellery, Signer of the Declaration of Independence, D; Autograph Letter of N. L. Frothingham, D.D., D. Mrs. Balmanno—Autograph Letter of Sir Thomas Lawrence, D; Autograph of Crofton Crocker, D; Bead Needle Case, D. G. Jones—Ship Candle Bracket, D. Mr. Peet—Pike from Fort Wagner. J. B. Waterbury—Root of Ancient Olive Tree; Vase of Old Frigate Constitution; Dairyman's Cottage. G. W. Dow—Laws of New York, 1752. H. Heaton—Rebel Dress from New Orleans. Mrs. J. O. Low—Bowie Knife from Camp Lovel; Bowie Knife from Chalmette Regiment; Salem *Gazette*, 1818; Malay Creese; Dirk, captured from Rebels; Rebel Spy-Glass. J. O. Low—Buffalo Head and Horns; "Apprentices Time Entertained." 200 years old. Chas. M. St. John—Rebel Gun. Mrs. J. O. Low—Balls, &c., from Waterloo; Rebel Sword, captured by Gen. Slaughter's Staff; Double barreled Gun and Sword Bayonet. Mrs. St. John—Sword Bayonet, captured at New Orleans. Mrs. J. O. Low—Turkish Shoes, 150 years old; Rebel Pistol; Japanese copy of Gospel of St. Matthew; Japanese Book, illustrated. J. O. Low—Indian Pants; Indian Moccasins. C. M. St. John—Pair Chinese Slippers; Autograph. Mad. Ruthe—The Color Ribbon of Kossuth's Battle Flag, carried through all his Campaigns. Mrs. J. R. St. John—Two Crayon Portraits, 1780, from Trieste; Landgrave Waldenholdt and his Wife. J. O. Low—Japanese Sword. C. H. Baxter—Chinese Idol. J. O. Low—Model of Chinese Sceptre. Mrs. Fulton—Brooch, of time of Louis XIV.; Piece of Lace. Mrs. J. D. Hurlbart—Old Dutch Bible; Old English Bible. R. W. Cushman—Old English Bible. Mrs. Crocker—Japanese Fish-Dish; Albatross Beak. M. P. Brown—Hair Necklace; 9 Indian Figures; Cingalese Spelling Book; Indian Money Pouch. Mrs. M. P. Brown—Kapa Cloth; Tamul Letter; Tobacco Pouch; Petrified Wood; Mar-

evances Watt. Mrs. Lyman Beecher—Old Jewelry; Infant's Wardrobe. Mrs. P. Brown—Model Sandwich Island House. James Ripley—Price Currents of 1786 and 1864. Mrs. J. R. St. John—Japanese Umbrella; Certificate, signed by Washington; Newspaper, containing death of Washington, 1800; 8 Chinese Maps; Pewter Platter, 150 years old. Mrs. Wm. M. St. John—Old Holland Bible, containing the family records of Abasuerus Turk—among the earliest Dutch Settlers; Chinese Map. Chas. M. St. John—Wine Press used by the Indians in Brazil; An Order of Society of Cincinnati. Mrs. Hastings—Roman Lamp; Turkish Slippers; Nubian Woman's Dress. Mrs. St. John—Certificate of Membership Society of Cincinnati. Mrs. M. A. Welch—Mayflower Chair. Miss Bradford—Gov. Bradford's Chair. Mrs. M. A. Welch—Copy of Miles Standish's Will; Rifle, Sabre, Shot. C. P. Storms—Cartridge box, from 1st Bull Run. Mrs. J. R. St. John—Pair Spectacles worn by Roger Williams; Grass Cloth, made by Creek Indians; Pair of Stirrup Cups, of 1778; Sword, Bayonet, and Rebel Uniform, taken at Battle New Orleans. Dr. Farley—Lines written for the Fair by J. G. Palfrey, D.D., LL.D., Autograph MS., D. Mrs. J. R. St. John—An African Ring, native work. Mrs. Dudley—African Idol, "Bashee, the Goddess of Thunder;" Bone of a Saw Fish; Instrument of Warfare, used by natives South Pacific Islands; Idol, from Java; Model of Chinese Lady's Foot; Specimen of Shell Rock, from St. Augustine, Fla.; Chinese Shoes. Brooklyn Yacht Club—11 Yacht Models. Thos. F. Knight—Group of Classical Figures, D. Mrs. Wm. Robinson—Vicksburg Newspaper. Mrs. M. S. Robinson—Curious Picture of Small. C. W. Morse—Sioux Indian Dress. Mrs. J. R. St. John—Old Book, Jewel of Contentment, 1650. C. W. Morse—7 pieces of the Town of Nankin. H. K. Cullen, Jr.—Sacred Book, from Buddhist Temple, Siam; Curious Plate, from Bankok, Siam; Water Proof Coat; Secesh Sabre, from Corinth. L. B. Wyman—Rebel Sabre, captured Hilton Head; Rebel Musket, captured near Bluffton; Rebel Flag, captured at Pocataligo; Rebel Knife, Pistol, and Coat, captured at do.; Skull found at Bluffton, S. C. Mrs. T. Messenger—Sword used in the War of 1812, by Captain Eagle; Prussian Sabre, captured by a British Officer; Sabre used in Battle of Danbury. Mrs. Richards—Carbine. Mrs. J. R. St. John—A Bracelet of Hungarian Coins, loaned by Mad. Rutka, sister of Kossuth; Collection of Bronze Gods. Charles M. St. John—A Rifle Musket, from battle Baton Rouge; Continental and Confederate Money. C. F. Hall—Group of Esquimaux; The Zabriskie Relics; Soup Canister, from Capt. McClintock; Canister of Beef, from Capt. McClintock; Canister of Carrots, from Capt. McClintock; Model of Esquimaux Canoe; Esquimaux Kyack; Esquimaux Woman's Ornament; Piece of Whale Skin; Esquimaux Tailor's Knife; Esquimaux Whalebone Ornament; Esquimaux Spear-head; Esquimaux Bone Relic; Esquimaux Reindeer Sinews; Cup from the Charter Oak. E. W. Shipman—Piece of the Charter Oak, D. J. Greenwood—Sword used in the Revolutionary War; Canister Shot and Piece of Shell from Wagner, D. Capt. W. H. Dunbar—Two pannels from J. C. Calhoun's House, D; Three pieces of Mantel-piece, D. Mrs. J. R. St. John—Piece of Cloth, woven in 1717. L. R. Reed—Pair Brogans, made in the South, previous to the Rebellion. Mrs. T. Messenger—Lamp from Pompeii. M. C. Robinson—Plaster from Napoleon's Tomb, St. Helena; Palm Leaf Book in the Balia Language. Mrs. Chase—Straw Slippers, D. Mrs. R. H. Jonsbery—Box of Minerals, D; 10 Loaves of Swedish Bread, D. Morris Wicket—Case of Assorted Coins; Continental Bill, Burlington, N. J. J. O. Lower—Powder Bucket, from Perry's Flag Ship at the Battle of Lake Erie—to be purchased and donated to L. I. Historical Society. H. S. Ogden—Sword, captured from Rebels, by H. D. White. Ed. Pell—Musket used in the Revolution; Musket and powder-horn. Chas. Parker—Powder-horn, found in tearing down old House in Roxbury. Mrs. Pollock—Box belonging to Mary, Queen of Scots. L. B. Wyman—5 Mounted Palmetto Canes, D; 10 Orange, Asia and Lemon Canes, D. Mrs. J. H. Prentice—Mosaic, of Lilly of Valley and Forget-me-Not. Capt. W. H. Dunbar—4 bundles Palmetto Stalks, D. H. H. Warden—A Chinese Idol. Sailors of Ship Oleo Clime—Pen Knife Model of Ship O. C., D. Capt. Radford—Old Venetian Time Piece. J. W. Hunter—Dutch Bible, date 1702. J. O. Low—Diary London's Register, 1708. Naval Lyceum—Limb of Tree incrusted with Salt, called by the sailors Lot's Wife's Arm. Francis Carass—Shrub of Myr-

ils incrusted. C. F. Hall—Esquimaux Lamp. Dr. Benerti—Shell Flowers in Glass Case. Mr. Ford—Portrait of Jane Brown, by Copley, 1755. J. Hall—Old Hoe, found in tearing down the first House of Miles Standish. J. B. Kirker—Rebel Sword, taken from the son of Lt. Brammes, at N. C., D. A. P. Oswald—Rebel Sword taken in Virginia; Indian Child, Bow and Arrow; Cavalry Sword from Hilton Head; Fragment Shell, from Hilton Head; Chinese Shield; Tomahawk used as a pipe of peace; Walking Stick of Cotton Tree; New Zealand War Club; Chinese Sun Umbrella; Two Japanese Brooms; Sample of Irish Bog Oak; Sandwich Island Canes; Domestic Implements of Indian Manufacture; Horse Pistol from Crimean War; Three Mexican Spurs; Knife Sheath and Tobacco Pouch; Fur Cap worn by North American Indians; Shell of a Tortoise, shot in Galveston; Chinese wooden Scale, Beam and Weight; Patagonian Spear, of wood; Gilt Lance used in Mexican War; Lance made by the natives of New Holland; Bow and Arrow from the Feejee Islands; Bow and Barbed Arrow, from the Feejee Islands. Mrs. T. Messenger—Book of Devotion, A. D., 1792, D; Cross and Bead, from Holy Land, D; Piece of Shell, from Sebastopol, D; Water from River Jordan, D; Piece of Charter Oak, D; Box, made from piece of first canal boat from Erie, with medal, D; Minnie Ball, from Sebastopol, D; Relic from Tomb of Abelard and Eloise, D; Bullet from Field of Waterloo, D; Relic from Tower of London, D; Cross made from Charter Oak, D; Relic from Church St. Saviour, Southwark, D; Indian Arrow-head, D; Stone, from Chatsworth, Devonshire, D. E. B. Spooner—Brooklyn Hall *Gazette*. U. S. Naval Lyceum—Case of Australian Birds. Franklin avenue P. Church—Japanese Tobacco Pouch, Matches and Tinder-box, D. Lieut. Nichols—Battle Flag. L. B. Wyman, Jr.—Esquimaux Seal Spear, from Dr. Hayes. Mr. Robinson, N. J.—Skull taken from the Grave of Red Jacket; Wallace Tree. Geo. Brown, Jr.—Piece of old London Bridge. G. O. White—Antique Proclamation. Mrs. Raymond—A Coat of Arms; A Pamphlet, by Nathaniel Taylor; A Powder-horn used in the French War 1758; Sea-weed, D. A. B. Young—Sea-weed, D. B. T. Frothingham—Orange Bough, with Fruit, D; Two Rebel Bayonets from Fort Wagner. Rev. F. Dellam—One Indian Vase; Stone Idol. J. T. Hildreth—Copper Marline-spike made from a bolt of steam frigate Fulton; Furlough given in the War of 1812. Ludovici—Indian Palm Leaf Fan; Burmese Sun Hat; Indian Hunting Hat; Cinnamon Stick, from Calcutta; Shark's Tooth, from India; Sword-fish's Sword; Petrified Wood, from Egypt; Himalayan Knife; Sword of Himalayan Chief; Two Calcutta Bottles and Glass-cooler; Egyptian Lantern; Ceylon Smoking Pipe; Himalayan Praying Machine; Two Burmese Hair-combs; Egyptian Cup; Egyptian Saucer; Raw Silk from India; A Figure of an East Indian; Indian Palankin. Mrs. Gracie—Old Chair from Holland, 200 years old. Rev. G. Jones, U. S. N.—Sailor's Candlestick, D; 2 Balls from battle at Gettysburg, D; 1 Cane from piece of Merrimac, D; Lot of pieces of Merrimac, D; 7-inch Shell from Merrimac, D. J. M. Taylor—Washington's Compass. Ludovici—7 Figures of Indians in Costume. J. H. Manning—1 Hair Frame. H. C. Spaulding—1 Engineer Drawing; 1 Map. C. H. Baxter—Japanese Image; Piece of Coral; Petrified Walnut. Mrs. J. O. Low—2 Dutch Tiles. Mrs. A. N. Littlejohn—Roman Lamp. Miss A. Whitney—Bass Relief Venus, D; 2 Goddesses of Liberty, D. Captain Radford—Chinese Opium Pipe; Japanese Travel Box; Tapa Cloth, used by South Sea Islanders; Chinese Visiting Card; Bell used in Mexico; Water Cup; Chinese Shoe, used by a lady of rank; Piece of Atlantic Cable; Part of an Elephant's Tooth; Chinese Lion, for guarding Temple. Mr. S. Prentice—Images; Charity and her Children; do. do.; Image. Mrs. S. T. Stranahan—2 Balls from Battle of Bull Run; Ball from Battle-field of Waterloo; Ball from Saratoga. Mrs. Rossiere—Psyche, in Bronze, D; Bust, bronze, D; The Muses, bronze, D; Card Stand, D. Mrs. Mall (Richards)—Lock of Napoleon's Hair. Thos. Messenger—Watch captured at Fort Pulaski. J. S. T. Stranahan—DeWitt Clinton; Proclamation. Mrs. H. F. Folsom—Hair Wreath. Mrs. Bradford—Hanging Baskets of Plants; do. do. Chauncey—Letter from Andre. R. D. Hurlbut—Gun from Malakoff Tower; Sword from Waterloo. Richards—Turkish Sword; Ornamental Sword. Dr. Jacobus—Cane from Mount of Olives. C. F. Leavitt—Pair of Shoes, 100 years old; Pair of Slippers; Stomacher, 130 years old. Mrs. St. John—Pilgrim Platter. Unknown—Photograph of

Rev. Jonas King, D; Pair of Bronze Flower-holders, D; 2 Pair Parian Vases, D; Fancy Case, D. Robert Tappan—Rev. Everardus Bogardus, portrait on glass, 200 years old. W. M. Richards—Flag captured at Hatteras by Commodore Stringham. Mrs. St. John—Two articles of Indian Warfare; Two Emblems of Authority—Indian. Unknown—Flora—a Parian Bust. C. M. St. John—Cotton in the Ball, D. N. P. Brown—Flesh Brush from Barring's Straits; 2 Chinese Idols. Mrs. Lawlie—Turkish Coffee-Pot and Cup; Chain made by Monks of St. Athos; Stockings worn by Greek Mountaineers; Albanian Tobacco Pouch; Pair of Shoes, 150 years old; Christmas Shoes, made in Germany. H. Dyke—Cavalry Sword, taken at surrender of Burgoyne. Mrs. Howell—Chinese Ladies Sack; Chinese Dress Coat and Vest; Chinese Dress; Chinese Robe; Chinese Lady's Robe; Seal and Rattlesnake Skins; Chinese Shoes; 2 Chinese Brooches. S. Simonson—Tecumseh's Pipe. Mrs. Paulding—Autograph Letter of Gen. Washington. J. L. Comlit—Book on Horsemanship, D. Mr. Paulding—Portrait of Gen. Greene; Powder-horn from Fort Donelson; Knife; Sabre; Sabre, cavalry. Mrs. Radford—Piece of Grand Mosque at Cairo; Dagger from Palace of Emperor of Chinese. F. Hubbard—Piece of Skirt of Dress; 1 Shoe, 1728. Capt. Meade—3 Rebel Shells, which struck the steamer Marblehead. Mrs. Edwards—Silver Cup, (Aaron Burr.) Mrs. St. John—Autograph of Aaron Burr. Mrs. Messenger—Double Guinea, 1738, D. Church of the Saviour—Painting. C. W. M., 81 S. Oxford st.—Dress of Yankton, Sioux Indian. Mrs. St. John—Letter from Aaron Burr; Continental Currency. Capt. Worden—Capt. Worden's Presentation Sword and Sash. Mrs. C. Congdon—Slipper, 1775. Mrs. J. O. Low—Antique Gold Watch. R. T. Banker—Check of the Bank of New York, 1794. Hunt—Picture; Hunt, Artist, D. J. L. B. Willard—Relics of Miles Standish; Lock of Gen. and Mrs. Washington's Hair. Mrs. McClaney—Japanese Model Boat. Mr. Chas. Christmas—Silver Pipe, D. Mrs. McClaney—Japanese Waiter; do. Bird-Cage; do. Waiter; do. Dinner-Set; do. Temple; do. Writing-Case, 2 pieces; do. Gentleman's Dressing Case. R. T. Banker—Fancy Shell work. A. Thomas—1 Mayflower Skillet; 1 Ancient Spoon Mould; 1 Chinese Scarf Pin, carved; 1 Petrified Bird, on Nest; 1 piece of Sandwich Island Cloth; 2 Coins; 1 piece Continental Currency; 1 piece Currency, 1815-16; Indian Arrow-Head; 1 Coin, 1591; 1 Old Book, 1678; 1 Extra Newspaper, 1815; 1 Wonderful Piece of Carving, by Soldier at Vicksburg. E. W. K. Lasell—Turkish Slippers. Mrs. A. Northam—Raphael. Gen. Hy. Storms—Original Letter of Washington to Major Tallmadge. Young Ladies Society, Westminster Church—3 packages Autumn Leaves, D. Mrs. Littlejohn—MSS. Tamill Language. R. T. Banker—Colonial Currency. Mrs. A. A. Costa—Lock of Henry Clay's Hair. Mrs. Messenger—Basket by a Madeira Christian Exile. Com. McCluney—Japanese Dog, made of Wood; do. Cup; do. Vase; do. Cup; do. Fruit; do. Cup and Saucer. York street M. E. Church—Chinese Idol, D. A. A. Low—Piece of old Government House in Florida, D; Fac Simile of Declaration of Independence. Rev. Mr. Thorne—Painting, The Annunciation. B. F. Stevens—2 Old German Bibles, from Hanover; Blunderbuss; Prussian Bayonet from Bull Run (1st) Battle-field. H. E. Pierrepont—Robe of Chief Justice Jay, 1790; Court Sword of Chief Justice Jay, 1794; Hunting Sword Aug. Jay, 1680; Dress Epaulettes of Aug. Jay, 1794; Tea Kettle given to Mrs. Jay by Benjamin Franklin, 1783; Embr'd Chair, worked by Madame Lafayette for Mrs. Jay; Velvet Dress Coat of J. Jay, 1794; Spanish Court Vest of J. Jay, 1779; Commission for Gov. Colden to John Constable, 1762; Photograph of J. Jay's House at Passy, France, 1783; Old Pincushion, from the first ship captured in 1776; Portrait of Chief Justice Jay in Robes; Relics from Frigate Hussar, sunk at Hell Gate, 1777; Robert Morris's Mourning Ring; Five Ancient Mourning Rings; Ancient Atlas of 1687; Plan of Forts at Governor's Island, 1798; Deed of Pierrepont Estate written and witnessed by W. Irving; J. Jay's English Waistcoat, 1794; J. Jay's Small Clothes; Pledge Cup of King William's adherents; 2 Crosses of wood from Mt. Olivet; J. Jay's Commission as Minister to Spain, 1779; J. Jay's Commission as Minister to England, '94; Algerine Dagger; John Hancock's Vest, D; Officer's Sword, dug up in Pierrepont street, near Sterling Fort; Patent of Alexander Macomb, 3,816,960 acres; Deed of Robert Benson, Pierrepont Estate; Chinese Ear Instruments; Buttons of Aug. Jay, 1680; Patent to Alex. Macomb of 1,920,000 acres; Deed from Alex. Macomb to W. Constable; Model of Chinese Foot and Slipper; Sugar Bowl of Louis Phillippe; Mummied Ibis from Thebes; Old Cavalry Pistol; Map of Brooklyn, 1836; Portfolio of Graham Art Association, D. Rev. Mr. DeHaas—Portrait of Dred Scott, D; Indian Stone Battle-Axe; Stone Peace Pipe. Geo. B. Moffat—Pair Stirrups. M. J. Lock, Esq.—Impression from Tomb of Washington's G. G. Grandfather. M. C. Tappan—Washington's Punch Bowl, from which Lafayette, Clinton, and others drank. Herbert Reed—Piece of Steamer "Planter," captured by Robert Small, D; Piece of Coquina, from St. Augustine. Mrs. Mumford—Old Papers, D. Stranahan—3 boxes Jewelry. A. V. Dike—Ethan Allen. Mrs. Peter Rice—Sacrifice of Isaac, D. Hempstead—Antique Satin Slipper, D. Brierstedt—Indian Dresses. Mrs. Van Zandt—China Plate, 100 years old; Wm. Bradford, Cream-Pot; do. Coffee-Pot; do. Tea-Pot; do. Cup and Saucer; do. Tea-Caddy. Rev. G. Jones—Lithograph U. S. Frigate; 2 Models, Merrimac and Monitor, in tub. W. C. Steele, 9 Court st.—Sword worn at Bunker Hill; Certificate of Member of Cincinnati. F. B. Reed—Sword captured at Battle of L. I.; Powder-horn, 1765. C. W. Leavitt—Flag carried by Capt. Kane. Mrs. C. F. Leavitt—5 Relics. Mrs. Whitcomb—Japanese Candy; Family Monument, D. Mrs. C. F. Leavitt—St. Joseph and Infant Saviour; After the Crucifixion; Head of St. Francis; St. Bartemas. S. C. Stringham—A Bottle of Snakes, (Swedish). P. V. Schoonmaker—A Pewter Platter, 100 years old; Pepper-Box from Holland, 1694; Powder-horn, from British Frigate Macedonian; Fashion of 1799 (picture). Louis Congdon—Sword of Sword-Fish. Francis Moore—Mortar given by an Indian to Dr. Francis. J. H. Frothingham—Slave Whip; Dirk taken from a Savannah Woman; Dirk captured at Roanoke Island; Arkansas Toothpick; Edgar Forman—Powder-horn made in 1776. L. B. Wyman—Female Head, (crayon) D; Photograph, with Nut Frame. Lydia Bradford—Autograph Letter of Gen. Washington, D. H. H. Worden—4 Japanese Swords; 1 Japanese Tea-Kettle. Dr. Farley—Fragment of Flag-Staff from Fort Sumter. J. S. Pearson—Book of English Signatures of Distinguished Men; Pay-Roll, dated 1777; New York *Post* of 1795. F. S. Lincoln—Ship made from piece of Gen. Magruder's Headquarters. Mrs. Pollock—French Damask Linen Towel of 1678. J. W. Wood—Piece of Plank bored by worms, 1676, D. Jas. Hall—6 Wills and 6 Plans of House of M. Standish. Mrs. Schoonmaker—Old Chair 100 years old. Mrs. H. Ullman—6 cards Indian Arrow-Heads, D. H. E. Pierrepont—Old Pierrepont House, Brooklyn Heights, front; Old Pierrepont House, Brooklyn Heights, rear. J. M. Falconer—Scottish Broad Sword. B. T. Frothingham—Palmetto Basket made by Minorcans, St. Augustine; 2 Napkin Rings; 1 Watch Case. Mr. Howard—Japanese Medicine Box; A Sphere of Rock Crystal. J. W. Hunter—Rebel Sword, captured in Department of the Gulf. J. W. Taylor—Washington's Compass. Geo. Jones—Chilian Stirrups. Dr. Swift—Dictionary of Ambrose Calepinus, and Languages, 1609. Jos. Hale—Photograph of Clothes Wringer. State street Cong. Church—Basket Wax Flowers, with Stand, D. Meyer—Case of Butterflies, D. M. F. Association—2 Framed Autographs; 1 Bill Lading; Japanese Opium Pipe; Cane made from the Trunk of Tea Tree. Mrs. Chauncey—Napkin of Louis XV. Mrs. Richards—Bowie-Knife and piece of Sword-Fish. Mrs. Wilson—Sword from Bull Run. C. B. Collins—Bracelet and Copy of Cameo. Miss Chittenden—Classic Hussey, D; Amulet worn by People of Hebron, D; Napkin Rings made of Wood of Mount Olives, D; Frankincense from Church of the Holy Sepulchre, D. J. J. Reed—3 Cases of Coins. Wm. Post—2 Boat models. S. Caldwell—Gobelin Tapestry. Miss J. Cooper—Communion Cup of the Oldest Ch. on L. I. Herbert Reed—Japanese Broom, D. L. B. Page—Lemon, preserved from Mount Vernon; Orange, preserved from Mount Vernon. Miss Eaton—A Manuscript Journal of the Revolutionary War. Chauncey—Sword worn by a British Officer. Mrs. H. L. Huntington—Fuller's Holy War. Mrs. J. F. Greene—9 Pictures of Autumn Leaves. Mrs. Pollock—Napkin, Woven and Spun in 1671; Pocket Dictionary of 1730; French Napkin of Curious Device, time of Louis XIV. A. P. Oswald—Implements captured from a Malay Proa. Mr. Carvey, N. J.—Inlaid Battle-Axe from India; 8 Badges of Office from India. D. E. Crosby—N. Y. *Evening Post*, bound volume. Hafferty & McCue—Swiss Scene, (cork); [illegible] Pipes, (cork). D. McGregor—Sword used at Bunker Hill; Old Iron Slaves' Whip;

Tortoise Case; A Chip from Hancock House; Iron Hook, from Rebel Steamer Atlanta. J. S. Farron—Map of United Colonies. Wm. Rimble—Fac Similie of Major Andre's Papers. Mr. Noyes—3 Valuable Autographs. C. M. St. John—Bark of Tree, worn as Cap by Amazons; China Plate and Wine Glass of the Pilgrims. Mrs. Fish—Chinese Purse and Coin; Lace from the Oldest Convent in Portugal; Japanese Umbrella and Window Shade. W. R. Woodward, Boston—Antique Furnace from Herculaneum, D; 10 Bibles, captured from Blockade Runner Minna, etc., D; 11 Testaments, do., D.; 12 Testaments with Psalms, do., D.; 8 sets of the Four Gospels, do., D.; 5 Psalters, do., D.; 2 Prayer Books, do., D.; 5 Com. Letter Writers, do., D.; Wm. Penn Documents, do.; 6 Trays of Medals and Coins. Mrs Burroughs—Paper Weights; Card Shell. A Draper, 187 Carlton avenue—Japanese Crystal. Mrs. Archer—2 Old Books, 1 Continental Atlas; 1 Elbow Cuff. Thos. U. Hooker—Paper Matrices, D. J. H. Frothingham—Leaves from Tomb of Keats and Shelley, D. E. S. Mills—Illustrated Copy of the Bible. Mrs. Meyer—Specimen of Hair Work. R. W. Hubbard—2 Gov. Saltonstall's China Plates; 1 do. Silver Mug; 1 Ring, with Miniature of Mad. Winthrop. Chas. W. Copland—Drawing of Steamer Paragon, N. R.; Drawing by Robert Fulton, of Ferry Boat; Drawing by do. of Bridge; Drawing by do. of Engine to N. R. Steamer; Drawing by do. of Engine to War Steamer; Drawing by do. of First N. R. Steamer; Drawing by do. for Steamer Pacific. Mrs. A. R. McClane—Pencil Drawing, Grapes, D. T. C. Farrar—Pen and Ink Sketch, D. J. W. Hall—Water Color Drawings, 8 D. O. J. Vining—Lithograph Portrait of J. Patchen, D., Old Map of New York, D. Wm. M. St. John—Ivory Type, by T. H. Lane, D. Sag Harbor—Permit of Ship Hamilton, by Andrew Jackson. Abel Denison—Check of Gen. Washington. J. D. Steele—Shield of Charter Oak, to be sold for the L. I. Historical Society. Miss Tuckett—2 Water Color Sketches, D; 1 do. do. Major J. P. Horton—War-Club from Marquesas Island, D. Southampton, L. I.—4 Whalebone Canes, D. Mrs. T. J. Payne—Washington Relics; Needle-Work. W. H. Slipper—1 Colt's Revolver, captured by W. H. S.; Balls from Malvern Hill; Private Signal from British Navy, 1755. Wm. Jones, 66 Duffield street—Life of Cardinal Wolsey. J. H. Frothingham—Japanese Dressing Gown, D. J. M. Falconer—Pallette used by Thos. Cole. Miss Mary Sands, Sands street—Pair Ear-Rings and Ring, from Tyranno; Pair of Shoes, worn by M. Sands, 1770; Knife and Fork used by H. Sands in the Sugar-House Prison. D. A. Taylor—Rainbow Opal Button. Josiah Rogers—Antique Emb'd Bed Curtains, D., Rebel Flag, from Steamer Chesapeake; Old Cup and Saucer, 85 years old. Mrs. Fulton—Bell from Cathedral of Mexico; Copy of Star Spangled Banner. A. C. Richards—Relics from Fort Washington. Rev. T. C. Trowbridge—Lot of Stamps from Constantinople, D. Mrs. Fish—Native Cloth from Sandwich Islands; Chinese Stand for Tablet; Piece of Stone from Fort Erie; A Pair of Mitts, 80 years old. Geo. Hall—Likeness of Jacob Patchen. J. & E. Woodbridge, 184 Hicks street—Letter of Mrs. J. Edwards, 1753. S. B. Chittenden—Ivory Ornaments, Carved by Soldiers, D. Miss Chittenden—A Morning in the Tropics, D; Noon on the Sea-Shore, D. Rev. Geo. Jones—A Broken Rebel Musket from Gettysburg, D; Rebel Bayonet. J. D. McKenzie—Autograph of David Crockett, D. P. E. Bogert—A Bolt from Prow of the Merrimac, D. S. H. Deshon—Fragment of Shell from Fort Wagner, D. W. C. Conant—Cartridge and Bullet from the Revolutionary War, D. J. Morey—Revolutionary Canister Shot from Fort Stanwix, D. Mrs. E. W. House—Bullet taken from Hougoumont, Waterloo, D. W. A. Martin—Chinese Painting on Glass. Merwin Bros., 223 Broadway—Ballard's Patent Infantry Rifle; Ballard's Patent Mounted Rifle; Ballard's Patent Sporting Rifle; Ballard's Patent Army Carbine. Bigelow & Co.—1 Stuffed Coon; 1 Stuffed Fox. Officers 56th Regiment, N. Y. S. M.—Model of Block House, D. Mrs M. F. Odell—4 Photographic Views of Pontoon Bridge, D; 1 Wagon, loaded with Pontoon Bridge, D; 1 Chasse Wagon, with Chasse, D. 8 Pontoons in Bridge, equipped, D. F. E. Church—1 Butterfly from New Grenada. C. W. Wemple—Printing for the Blind, D; 2 Figures in Turkish Dress, D. John D. Rose, M. D.—1 Indian Axe, found in digging, D. John Harold—Old Sermon; Syrian Glass Rings, etc., in box, D. Mr Chas. J. Smith—Dancing Belt of Shells, and War Belt of Human and Monkey's Teeth, worn by an Indian Chief, of the Amazon River territory. Mrs. Smalley—1 Box of

Relics, 6 articles; Chinese Lady's Skirt. S. L. Vanderveer—Amusement in the Country; Laws of New York, 1753; Acts of Assembly of New York, 1691. John Harrold—Pair of Cornets, 100 years old, D. Mrs. M. C. Robinson—A Variety of Siamese Curiosities. H. R. Pease—Cannon Powder for a 300-lb. Parrot Gun, D. Miss Post, S. I.—Pine Burr Cross, D. Miss F. Shepherd, S. I.—Pine Burr Corner Ornaments, D. Miss Laura Shepherd, S. I.—Pine Burr Corner Ornaments, D. Mr Henry Heaton—Rebel Belt, taken at New Orleans; Rebel Bayonet, taken at New Orleans. Mrs. C. F. Loomis—Table-Cloth from the May Flower. A. Dyke—4 Confederate Flags.

ARTICLES IN THE JAPANESE ROOM.

Those Donated, marked "D"—Those Loaned, with an "L"—affixed.

Mrs. F. Griffing—Japanese Work-Box, L; do. Straw and Gilt Box, L; do. Large Cabinet, L; do. Looking-Glass, L, do. Two Story House, L; do. Bird Cage, L; do. Trays, L, do. Wine-Stand, L; do. Seven Cups, L; do. Skull Cap Basket, L; do. Umbrella, L; do. Silk Wadding, L; do. Sword, L; do. Hat, L; do Tea Pot, L; do. Tea Box, L; do. Stand, L; do. Dishes, L; do. Fruit Basket, L; California Pearl Shells, L; do. Bear Skin, L; do. Bark of a Large Tree, L; do. Cone of a Large Tree, L; do. Wood of a Large Tree, L; do Moss, L, do. Corn Broom, L, do. Laurel Wood, L; do. Lot of Quartz Jewelry, L; Feather Brush from Chili, L; Sandal Wood Glove Box, L; Table Cloth used at a Fête given by Alexander of Russia, L, Guaymas Table Cloth, L; do. Piece of Molten Silver, L. Mrs. A. C Brownell—Chinese Painting on Glass, of the Resurrection of a Holy Mother and her Children, L, Picture Wrought on Satin (1818) of Hector and Andromache, L. Mrs. W Greenough, of Boston—An Apron Embroidered on White Satin, worn by the Hancock Family, L. An Old Porcelain Plate belonging to the Hancock, D. Mrs. John D. Gibson—Chinese Cap, L, do. Dress and Shoes, L, Japanese Work Box, L. Mr. B. F. Stephens—African Bread, L; Tile from the Dining-Room of the Convent of Pacho Heronimo, Spain, L; Tile of St. Paul, Seville, Spain, L, Silver Jewel worn by a descendant of Mahomet, L; Shoes worn by Soldiers, Valencia, Spain, L; Andalusian Tooth Pick, Seville, L; A Discipline Whip, used in the Church of Spain, L; Andalusian Leggins from Cordova, Spain, L; Cane made of an Olive Branch, consecrated by the Pope, L; Wine Flask from Seville, Spain, L; Badges made by Nuns and worn during Holy Week in Seville, Spain, L; A Collection of German Seals, D; Holy Wax from a Cathedral in Seville, D; Piece of Charter Oak, D; Veneer taken from a Window Blind, D, Monastery of Escurial, Spain, D, Olive Branch taken from the High Altar of the Cathedral of Seville, D; Sand from the Desert of Sahara, D; Water from the Bay of Biscay, D. Mrs. A. A. Ridner—Chinese Souchong Cup, D; do. Card Case, (Silver), D; do. Wedding Card, D; do. Pillow, D Mrs. William D. Lewis—Three Chinese Opium Boxes, Pipes and Implements, D; Five Chinese Cigar Cases, D; Chinese Steamboat, D; do. Tea-Caddy, D; do. Checker-Board, D. Mr. J. T Howard—Japanese Medicine Box, L; A Sphere of Rock Crystal, L. Mrs. M. A. Fish Chinese Embroidered Piano Cover, L; do Carved Ivory Pleasure Boat, L; do. do. do. Cigar Case, L; Work-Box from Bombay, Ivory and Silver Inlaid, L; Japanese House and Pleasure Grounds, L; Japanese Embroidery, D; Japanese Slippers, D. Mrs Stoddard—Two Chinese Marble Tables, L, Two Chinese Marble Seats, L; Landscape Marble, L; Inlaid Chinese Tables, L; Mermaid, L. Mrs. John Norton—An Ancient Illuminated Book, L. Mrs. J. H. St. John—Chinese Maps, L. Mrs. J. A. Low—Chinese Portrait, L. Mrs. J. C. Bogart—100 Japanese Photographs, D. Mrs. Com McCluney—Japanese Bird-Cage, L; do. Lunch-Box, L, do. Boat, L; do. Temple, L; do. Trays, D.

Articles Loaned by Mr. Charles Congdon and Mrs. Dr. Smith of the Navy Yard will be found on Mr. Fisher's Books.

PAINTINGS, ETC., CONTRIBUTED FOR SALE.

R. W. Ropes—Landscape, by Rondel. E. S. Mills—Landscape, by Gifford. Mrs. S. B. Chittenden—Natural Flowers, pressed. Mrs. Salmano—Flowers mentioned by Shakespeare. E. S. Mills—Coast Scene, by Kensett. A Chappel Equestrian Portrait of Washington. Granville Perkins—Marine View. J. W. Paller—Peaches. J. T. Howard—Farm Yard, by Giradet. R. W. Ropes—Landscape, by Rondel. H. Balling—Portrait of Ericsson. Co. H, 18th Regiment—Picket Duty. Charles Parsons—Marine View, by Moran. G. G. White—A Calm, by Lane. S. J. Eastman—Flemish Market, by Wouverman. South Congregational Church—Catskill. Dr. J. Barker—Flowers, Wisteria, Williamson. Chas. A. Townsend—Swiss Landscape. South Congregational Church—Cottage Scene. C. M. St. John—Ivory Type, by T. H. Lane. Lake Scene. R. Craig—Fruit Piece. Christ's Church—Water Color Fruit. John Rhodes—View on Lake George. E. N. York—The Inconvenience of Single Life. Windsor Terrace—Landscape; Landscape; Landscape. Mrs. J. C. Henshaw—Oranges; Landscape, with Villa. L. B. Wyman—Copy of Rembrandt. Miss J. E. Wesson—Portrait of Sir Joshua Reynolds; Landscape and Waterfall. S. J. Eastman—Highland Landscape. F. G. Conn—Mount Vernon. J. D. Barrow—Beach Scene. Mrs. A. N. Littlejohn—Autumn Leaves; Beatrice Cenci; Landscape. L. P. Smith—Landscape. Dr. Elmendorf—Scene in Venice. Fanny Grey—Conway Valley. H. Turner—Fruit and Glass of Wine. H. Allen—Melon, by Williamson. W. P. Whitlock—Fort Washington, by Annelli. Cyrus Butler—Landscape, by Jerome Thompson. G. S. Stephenson—Flowers, by G. H. Hall. Home Ins. Co.—Mount Mansfield, by Nichols. S. J. Eastman—Flowers, by G. H. Hall. Shirk Bros.—Landscape, by Carmiencke. W. H. Millen—Landscape, by Rondel. G. G. White—Marine View, by Lane; Lilies, by G. H. Hall. Christ's Church—Water Colored Flowers; 2 Landscapes; Landscape, (no frame); Niagara, (no frame.) Morand—Rev. Dr. Cutler, (no frame); Dead Game. C. H. Baxter, Concord, New Hampshire. Morand—Swiss Lake and Chalet. D. O. Kellogg—Winter Scene. J. C. Platt—Battle Scene; Mount Vesuvius; Landscape; Landscape, a Study. S. J. Eastman—Sweet Peas, by Williamson. Witherspoon—Lake Nemi, near Rome. S. J. Eastman—Female Head, by W. Page; The Pet. Dr. J. Barker—Sunset, by Williamson. F. A. Farley, D. D.—Pastel, Fruit by F. Grube. W. S. Mount—Little Girl, by Mount. A. Fisher—Peaches. S. J. Eastman—Duke De'Urbino after Titian. H. W. Beecher—Landscape, by Inness; A Pair of Crayon Heads. P. P. Ryder—Female Head. R. J. Powell—Landscape. William E. Oddie—Landscape, by W. M. Oddie. Townsend—Farm Yard. J. R. Murray—Young Quails, by Tait; Dred Scott; Isabel. Christ Church—Angel, by Bashfield; Mount Tom; Wm. Tell's Chappell; Recruiting in Dixie. S. Walters—Landscape, by Carr. Mrs. Balmano—Marine View. Max Sand—Columbia; Raphael. Ackerman—Young Irish Girl, Landscape, Flower Girl, Virgin, Water Colored Flowers. G. O. Fish—Blue and Gold. Miss H. White—Home from the War. Mrs. E. S. Mills—Union Refugees, (a caste.) Miss Homan—View of Montauk, by Miss Homan. Miss Ripley—Picture on Ivory. A. F. Tait—Goat and Ducks, by Tait, Strawberries and Flowers; Young Chickens, by Tait; do. by Tait. William Hart—Landscape, by William Hart; View in Ulster County, New York. C. H. Baxter—Bay of Naples; Pro Patria, (caste.) Miss Annie Whiting—Venus, Bass Relief; Portrait; View in Holland; Landscape. Mr. Robert Balmano—Painting, all the *Flowers* mentioned in Shakespear's Writings. D. O. Kellogg—Winter.

CATALOGUE OF ENGRAVINGS EXHIBITED IN THE MUSEUM OF ARTS, RELICS AND CURIOSITIES.

NOTE.—All those marked * were donated for sale.

SUBJECT.	PAINTER.	ENGRAVER.	EXHIBITOR.
1 Robert Dundas	Raeburn,	Sharp,	C. Burt.
2 Twelfth Night	E. Landseer,	J. H. Robinson,	"
3 Princess Victoria	Westall,	E. Finden,	"
4*Nell Gwynne and the Courtiers	C. Landseer,	L. Stocks,	W. H. Swan.
5 The Chief's return from Deer Stalking	E. Landseer,	Willmore,	H. W. Beecher.
6*Battle of Trafalgar	Stansfields,	Miller,	W. H. Swan.
7*Happy as a King	Collins,	E. Finden,	"
8*Battle of Waterloo	G. Jones	Willmore,	"

SUBJECT.	PAINTER.	ENGRAVER.	EXHIBITOR.
9*Rustic Hospitality	Collins,	Outrim,	W. H. Swan.
10 The Laughing Girl	Reynolds,	English Sch'l,	H. W. Beecher.
11 Nature	Lawrence,	Do.,	J. M. Falconer.
12*The Coquette	Reynolds,	Humphrey's,	W. H. Swan.
13*Behold the Lamb of God	Uwins,	Outrim,	"
14*Descent of the Holy Spirit	Murillo,	Bridoux,	"
15 The Doctors of the Church	Guido Reni,	Sharp,	H. W. Beecher.
16 The School	Wilkie,	Burnet,	J. M. Falconer.
17*John Knox and Queen Mary	A. E. Chalon	Roden,	W. H. Swan.
18 The Spinning-Wheel	Topham,	Hall,	J. M. Falconer.
19 The Prayer of Innocence	Uwins,	Sangster,	"
20 Minna Troil	Drummond,	Do.,	"
21*Deliverance of St. Peter	Hilton,	Portbury,	W. H. Swan.
22 Harvest in the Highlands	E. Landseer & Calcott,	Willmore,	H. W. Beecher.
23*Lear and Cordelia	Newton,	Hatfield,	W. H. Swan.
24*Christening Procession	Williams,	Stock,	"
25*Othello relating his adventures	Cowper,	E. Finden,	"
26*Escape of Novello	Eastlake,	Bacon,	"
27*Sir Roger deCoverly and Gypsies	Leslie,	Rolls,	"
28*Sunset after Storm	Danby,	Miller,	"
29*The Escape	Witherington,	Fisher,	"
30*City of Ancient Greece	Linton,	Appleton,	"
31*Neapolitan Peasants	Uwins,	Sangster,	"
32*Mercy Interceding, etc	Etty,	Do.,	"
33 Bolton Abbey in olden time	E. Landseer,	Cousens,	S. P. Avery.
34*Sickness and Health	Webster,	W. Finden,	W. H. Swan.
35*Highland Cottage	E. Landseer,	"	"
36*The Young Brood	J. Linnell,	Outrim,	"
37 The Shipwreck	Turner,	Fielding,	S. P. Avery.
38*Ruins of Carthage	Linton,	Willmore,	W. H. Swan.
39 Spanish Officer	Rubens,	Fittler,	C. Burt.
40 Cupid	Vanloo,	Strange,	J. M. Falconer.
41*Benj. West	Newton,	Heath,	W. H. Swan.
42 Magdalen	Batoni,	Pichler,	H. W. Beecher.
43 Derby Day	Frith,	Lemon,	S. B. Caldwell.
44 Death of the Fox	Gilpin,	Scott,	H. W. Beecher.
45 Charles the I	Vandyck,	Mandel,	"
46 Mignon Aspiring	Scheffer,	Louis,	J. M. Falconer.
47 Dido and Aeneas	Jones,	Woolett,	H. W. Beecher.
48 Morning	Swanevelt,	"	"
49 Game at Draughts	Burnet,	Burnet,	C. Burt.
50 Mignon regretting	Scheffer,	Louis,	J. M. Falconer.
51 Children of the Mist	E. Landseer,	T. Landseer,	H. W. Beecher.
52 Lost Children	Scheffer,	T. Johannot,	C. Burt.
53 Waffles for Sale	Ostade,	Mille,	"
54 The Orphans	Scheffer,	A. Johannot,	"
55 Alcides, (front view,)	Canova,	Foto,	H. W. Beecher.
56 " (back view,)	"	"	"
57*Margaret going to Church	Kaulbach,	Photograph,	E. Seitz.
58 Solitude—Etching	Calame,	Calame,	S. P. Avery.
59*Margaret at the Shrine	Kaulbach,	Photograph,	E. Seitz.
60 Reading the Bible, etc	Harvey,	Graves,	J. M. Falconer.

	SUBJECT.	PAINTER.	ENGRAVER.	EXHIBITOR.
61	Highlander's Home	E. Landseer,	Gibbon,	J. M. Falconer.
62	Golden Bough	Turner,	Willmore,	H. W. Beecher.
63	Greenwich Pensioners	Burnet,	Burnet,	J. M. Falconer.
64	John Knox Preaching	Wilkie,	Doo,	"
65	Horses at the Fountain	E. Landseer,	Watt,	"
66	Temple of Jupiter	Turner,	Pye.	
67	Highlander's Return	Wilkie,	Finden,	J. M. Falconer.
68	Hastings	Turner,	Willmore,	H. W. Beecher.
69	St. Agatha	Parmigiano,	Toschi,	"
70	St. George	"	"	"
71	Camera di. S. Paolo, No. 16	Corregio,	"	"
72	The Dead Christ	Canova,	"	"
73	Virgin of the Rocks	De Vinci,	Desnoyer,	"
74	Camera di. S. Paolo, No. 8	Corregio,	Toschi,	"
75	" " " " 7	"	"	"
76	Vittorio Pullione	Reggio,	Bernard,	C. Burt.
77	Moses	Campagne,	Edelinck,	H. W. Beecher.
78	Camera di. S. Paolo, No. 9	Corregio,	Toschi,	"
79	" " " " 11	"	"	"
80	St. Lucia and Appolonia	Parmegiano	"	"
81	Two Deacons	"	"	"
82	Camera di. S. Paolo, No. 9	Corregio,	"	"
83	St. Luke	"	"	"
84	St. John	"	"	"
85	Quarto gruppi di Apostoli	"	"	"
86*	Rembrandt	Rembrandt,	Longhi,	W. H. Swan.
87*	M. Angelo	Longhi,	"	"
88	Madonna del Sacca	Del Sarto,	Bartolozzi,	H. W. Beecher.
89	Madonna della Scalla	Corregio,	Toschi,	"
90	Marriage of the Virgin	Raphael,	Longhi,	"
91	Christus consolator	Scheffer,	Blanchard,	"
92	St. John, Evangelist	Corregio,	Toschi,	"
93	St. John, Evangelist	Domenichino,	Muller,	"
94	St. Mark	Corregio,	Toschi,	"
95	St. Matthew	"	"	"
96	Second gruppi di Apostoli	"	"	"
97	Marathon	Rottmann,	Wurthel,	"
98	St. Vincent de Paul preaching	Delaroche,	Prevost,	J. M. Falconer.
99	St. Cecilia	Von Begas,	Knolle.	H. W. Beecher.
100	Virgin and child	Murillo,	Graves,	"
101	St. Marguerite	Raffaelle.	Desnoyers,	"
102	Napoleon	Delaroche,	Louis,	"
103	Charles I. in Guard Room	"	Martinet,	J. M. Falconer.
104	St. Cecilia	"	Forster,	"
105	Belisarius	Gerard,	Desnoyer,	H. W. Beecher.
106	St. Catharine	Muche,	Felsing.	"
107	Assumption	Murillo,	Bridoux,	"
108	Vierge au bas-relief	Davinci.	Forster.	"
109	The Peasant's rest	Lepicie,	Hervie,	"
111	Faust, the Seduction	Scheffer,	Blanchard,	"
112	Good Dame of Normandy	P. A. Wille,	J. G. Wille.	J. M. Falconer.
113	The two Ways		Beauvarlet,	H. W. Beecher.
114	Angel's Head	Guido Reni,	Strange,	J. M. Falconer.

SUBJECT.	PAINTER.	ENGRAVER.	EXHIBITOR.
115 Aalis	Rothman,	Worthat,	H. W. Beecher.
116 Tomimia	Mieris,	Wille,	C. Burt.
117 L'Incoronata	Corregio,	Toschi,	H. W. Beecher.
118 W. A. Mozart	Tischbein,	Sichling,	C. Burt.
119 G. E. Lessing	Graff,	"	"
120 The Piper	Wilkie,	E. Smith,	J. M. Falconer.
121 Holy Family	Raffaelle,	Rivera,	H. W. Beecher.
122 St. Thomas	Corregio,	Toschi,	"
123 St. Sebastian	"	Lefevre,	"
124 Battle of the Huns	Kaulbach,	Thaeter,	"
125 Flight into Egypt	Corregio,	Toschi,	"
126 Magdalen	"	Longhi,	"
127 Brigand's Wife	Robert,		"
128 St. Maria	Guido,	Gandolfi,	C. Burt.
129 Portrait	Largilliere,	Desplaces,	"
130 Chev'r de Coite	Rigaud,	Drevet,	"
131 Jean de Troy	F. D. Troy.	Vallee,	"
132 Venice	Turner,	Miller,	H. W. Beecher.
133 First Ear-ring	Wilkie,	Chevalier,	J. M. Falconer.
134 Sterne and the Grisette	Newton,	Doo,	"
135 Camera di S. Paolo—No. 1	Corregio,	Toschi,	H. W. Beecher.
136 " " " " 2	"	"	"
137 Modern Italy	Turner,	Miller,	"
138 Napoleon and the Pope	Wilkie,	Robinson,	J. M. Falconer.
139 Venice	Harding,	Lucas,	H. W. Beecher.
140 Madonna and Child	Raffaelle,	Mandel,	"
141 Marguerite and Faust	Scheffer,	Blanchard,	J. M. Falconer.
142 Dover	Turner,	Wallis,	H. W. Beecher.
143 Innocence	Greuze,	Louis,	"
144 Messiah	Raffaelle,	Doo,	J. M. Falconer.
145 Gentle Shepherd	Wilkie,	Stewart,	"
146		Beauvarlet,	H. W. Beecher.
147 Death of Wolfe	West,	Woolett,	J. M. Falconer.
148 Venice	Prout,	LeKeux,	H. W. Beecher.
149 Pan and Music	Kloeber,	Olderman,	"
150 Robert Burns	Nasmyth,	Walker & Cousins,	"
151 Sibyl	Huntington,	Casilear,	S. P. Avery.
152 Mount Washington	Kensett,	Smillie,	C. Burt.
153 Dream of Arcadia	Cole,	"	"
154 Stag Hunt		Lauri,	H. W. Beecher.
155 Interior and Figure	Lefevre,	Chaplin,	C. Burt.
156 The Jig	Nichols,	Bell,	"
157 Isaac Bronson	Inman,	Burt,	"
158 Sibyl (early stage)	Huntington,	Casilear,	J. W. Casilear.
159 Distraction	Diaz,	George Wray,	C. Burt.
160 Slave Traffic	Biard,	Wagstaff,	H. W. Beecher.
161 Cartoon of Pisa	M. Angelo,	Schiavonetti,	J. M. Falconer.
162* Madonna and Child	Raffaelle,	Thouvenin,	W. H. Swan.
163 Uncle Toby and Widow Wadman	Leslie,	Danforth,	J. M. Falconer.
164 The Prison	Loutherburg,	Romanet,	"
165 J. G. Wille	P. A. Wille,	Ingolf,	C. Burt.
166 The Melody	Nichols,	Bell,	"
167 J. Fenimore Cooper	Elliott,	Burt,	"

SUBJECT.	PAINTER.	ENGRAVER.	EXHIBITOR.
168 Sparking	Edmonds,	Jones,	C. Burt.
169* Correggio	Asioli,	Asioli,	W. H. Swan.
170 Joan of Arragon	Raffaelle,	Lefevre,	H. W. Beecher.
171 W. E. Channing	Harding,	Hoogland,	J. M. Falconer.
172 Dr. Chalmers	Claudet,	Hall,	C. Burt,
173 Harvesting	Cropsey,	Smillie,	"
174 Meditation	Lauri,	Lauri,	H. W. Beecher.
175 Old '76 and Young '48	Woodville,	Pease,	C. Burt.
176 Louis de Boulonghe	Mathieu,	Surugue,	"
177 Tennyson	Watts,	Stephenson,	H. W. Beecher.
178 M. Angelo	M. Angelo,	François,	"
179 Titian	Titian,	"	"
180 Escape of the Mouse	Burnet,	Burnet,	J. M. Falconer.
181 The Dancing Dolls	"	"	"
182* John Calvin			W. H. Swan.
183 Anne Page, Slender and Shallow	Leslie,	Burt,	C. Burt.
184 The Present | Paper Money	American Bank Note Co.,		
185 Wood Engraving	Menzel,	Kretschmar,	S. P. Avery.
186 Faust and Guttenberg	"	Thompson,	"
187* Taming the Shrew	Leslie,	Rolls,	W. H. Swan.
188 Andrew Jackson	Vanderlyn,	Durand,	J. M. Falconer.
189 Legion of Honor	Leutze,	Burt,	C. Burt.
190 The Last Supper	Da Vinci,	"	"
191 Ariadne	Vanderlyn.	Durand,	S. P. Avery.
192* Triumph of Patriotism	Darley,	Ritchie,	A. H. Ritchie.
193* Madonna della Sedia	Raffaelle,	Petersen,	W. H. Swan,
194 Anne Page, etc., Proof in progress	Leslie,	Burt,	C. Burt.
195 Walter Scott	Raeburn,	Walker,	H. W. Beecher.
196 Sebastian del Piombo		Mandel,	"
197 Paper Money | the Past	Wood Engrav'g A. D.,		
198 Commemoration of Washington	Barralet,	Barralet,	J. M. Falconer.
199 Baptism of Pocahontas	Chapman,	Am. Bank Note Company.	
200* Deer Stalking	Cooper,	Shenton,	W. H. Swan.
201 White Plume	Ingham,	Durand,	J. M. Falconer.
202 David Crockett	De Rose,	"	"
203 J. Trumbull	Waldo & Jewett	"	"
204 Rembrandt	Rembrandt,	Turner,	H. W. Beecher,
205 Rubens	Rubens,		"
206 Satin Gown	Terburg,	Wille,	C. Burt,
207* Virgin of the Rocks	Da Vinci,	Desnoyer,	W. H. Swan.
208* Titian	Titian,	Mandel,	"
209* Lord Byron	Phillips,	Graves,	"
210* First Day of Oysters	Fraser,	Greatbach.	"
211* Trout in Tyrol	Calcott,	Allen,	"
212* Contadina Prisoners	Eastlake,	E. Smith,	"
213* Beggars' Opera	Newton,	Tinden,	"
214* Greek Fugitives	Eastlake,	Goodyear,	"
215 Albert Durer	Albert Durer,	Forster,	H. W. Beecher.
216 Andrea del Sarto		St. Eve,	"
217 Francesca de Rimini	Scheffer,	Calamatta,	"
218 Pope Pius VII	Lawrence,	Cousins,	J. M. Falconer
219 Vandyck	Van Dyck.	Mandel,	H. W. Beecher.
220 Erminia and Peasant	Vanloo,	Porporati.	C. Burt.

SUBJECT.	PAINTER.	ENGRAVER.	EXHIBITOR.
221* Holy Family	Raffaelle,	Richomme,	W. H. Swan.
222 Coronation Mary de Medicis	Rubens,	Douglass,	C. Burt,
223* Murillo	Murillo,	Blanchard,	W. H. Swan
224* Garrick as Richard III	Hogarth,	Hogarth,	"
225* St. Marguerite	Raffaelle,	Desnoyers,	"
226* Van Dyck	Van Dyck,	Mandel,	"
227* Virgin of the Rock	Raffaelle,	Richomme,	"
228* Helena Forman	Rubens,	Rollo,	"
229* Da Vinci	Da Vinci,	Cattino,	"
230* Virgin Child and St. John	Raffaelle,	Tompkins,	"
231* Salvator Rosa	Salvat'r Rosa,	Neagle,	"
232* Madame Vestris	Paris,	Bacon,	"
233* Holy Family	Marratti,	Sherman.	"
234* Mater Amabili	Attori,	Bettilini,	"
235* Raffaelle	Raffaelle,	Schroeder.	"
236* Hogarth	Hogarth,	Freeman,	"
237* Charles V	Fac simile,		"
238* Poussin	Poussin,	Pouncey,	"
239* Lavater	Johnson,	Blake,	"
240* Portfolio of Sundry Prints	Prints,	Various,	H. S. Cutter.
241 Spring	Harvey,		C. H. Baxter.
242 Summer	"		"
243 Autumn	"		"
244 Winter	"		"
245* Set of Engravers Working, proofs in progress, Old '76 and Young '48,	Woodville,		J. I. Pease.
246* Penns' Treaty	West,	Hall,	J. C. Brevoort.

DEPARTMENT OF ART, CURIOSITIES AND RELICS—RECAPITULATION OF PROCEEDS.

Proceeds Reception, (say)	$1,700
Sales and Admission at Museum and at Auction, (say)	10,000
Due from Treasurer of B. & L. I. Fair for Admissions to Picture Gallery	6,000
Artists Sketches, including Cabinet and Stand	5,000
Sale of Catalogues, at Picture Gallery	500
Amateur Concert by Miss Chittenden	200
Amateur Album	500
Other items, (say)	1,100
	$25,000

AUXILIARY ENTERTAINMENTS IN BEHALF OF THE FAIR.

During the inception of the Fair, numerous entertainments, both public and private, were given, showing the wide and generous interest which was felt in the work among all classes of our citizens. We note briefly here the entertainments alluded to, returns from which will be found duly credited in the Treasurer's report. It is possible that the list may not be perfectly complete, as there were a number of parlor entertainments given of which no public notice was made.

TABLEAUX VIVANTS.

Of these there were a number of exhibitions, chief among which was a series of three given at the Athenæum, on the evenings of February 22, 23 and 24, under the direction of a Sub-committee on Tableaux of the Committee on Benefits, Entertainments, Etc. This was an entertainment of marked excellence and brilliant success.

An excellent series of three Tableaux Vivants was given by the pupils of Mrs. Van Deusen's School, on the Heights, the last being on the evening of February 9.

An exhibition of Tableaux was also given at Williamsburgh, under the direction of Miss C. Coles.

MUSICAL AND DRAMATIC ENTERTAINMENTS.

The young ladies of Packer Institute gave two brilliant and unique musical and dramatic exhibitions, on the evenings of January [illegible] and [illegible], entitled: "The Women of History."

Hooley's Minstrels played on the evenings of January 27 and 28, for the benefit of the Fair.

Two spirited amateur dramatic entertainments were given at the Athenæum on the evenings of February 3 and 4, under the management of Dr. Hull.

A private soirée musicale was given, February 4, at the residence of Mrs. Robert Murray, Jr., Clinton avenue, by Miss Mary Judd, soprano, assisted by Mr. George Simpson, tenor, Mr. J. R. Thompson, baritone, and Mr. G. W. Colby, pianist.

A grand concert was given by the Philharmonic Society on Saturday evening, February 6, at the Academy of Music, under the direction of the Committee on Music.

A private musical reception was given at the Athenæum, on Monday evening, Feb. 8, by Mrs. Terry, at which a programme of remarkable merit was gone through with. Mrs. and the Misses Terry, Miss Mary Post, Miss Georgia Post, Miss Eunice Norton, Miss Lillie Wheeler, Miss Fanny Cushman, and Miss Emily Barber, were the performers.

On the evening of Tuesday, February 9, the young ladies of Brooklyn Heights Seminary gave a concert of vocal and instrumental music in aid of the Sanitary Fund.

The young ladies of the South Brooklyn Female Seminary gave a capital concert on Thursday evening, February 11, which was so successful that it was repeated the following evening.

On Saturday evening, February 13, the pupils of the Primary Department of Public School No. 15 gave an exhibition entertainment at the Academy of Music.

The "[illegible] Association" gave a highly successful entertainment at the Athenæum on the evening of February 15.

A mammoth concert was given at the Academy of Music on Monday evening, February 15, by five hundred pupils of the public schools of Brooklyn.

On Tuesday evening, February 16, a public entertainment was given at Washington Hall, in Williamsburgh.

The Thirteenth Regiment, N. Y. S. M., gave a brilliant Promenade Concert at the Academy on Tuesday evening, February 16, and the Forty-Seventh Regiment gave a similar entertainment at the Odeon Armory, Fifth street.

The public schools of the Eastern District united on Thursday evening, February 18, in a grand exhibition entertainment at the Lee Avenue Church, for the benefit of the Fair.

On Friday evening, February 19, the "Germania Verein," one of our largest and best musical and dramatic societies, gave a superb musical entertainment, at their rooms on Atlantic street.

On Wednesday evening, February 24, a very pleasant parlor entertainment was given at the residence of Mr. Jeremiah Mundell, by Misses Conner and Smith, assisted by Mrs. Abbot, Mrs. Rogers, Mr. Bulkley, Mr. Abbot, Miss Rogers and Miss Gleason.

On Thursday evening, February 25, a parlor entertainment was given at the residence of Mr. H. C. Bowen, consisting of choice music and readings, in which Miss Mathews, Mrs. Comstock, Miss Dargon, Miss Blanche Carpenter, Mr. B. F. McIntosh, Mr. Comstock, and Mr. Pomeroy took part. The Committee of young ladies who prepared this entertainment are Misses Lizzie S. Comstock, Grace A. Bowen, Edwina H. Richards, Emily A. Cowling, Mary M. Baxter, Jennie S. Howe, Mary A. Bowen, Susie Grierson, Juliet S. Gibson, Amelia C. Daniels, Emma B. Beach, and Nellie A. Bowen.

A series of three very pleasant parlor entertainments was given at the house of Mrs. A. S. Barnes, Clinton avenue, in which Mr. and Mrs. Ely, the Misses Olney, of Stratford, Ct., Misses Chapin and Spinner, of Bridgeport, Ct., Messrs. Alfred and Moses S. Beach, were prominently interested.

On Thursday evening, March 3, the Social Singing Society of Rev. Dr. Porter's Church, in Williamsburgh, gave their third Annual Concert, the proceeds of which were applied to the funds of the Sanitary Commission.

A successful parlor entertainment was also given at the residence of Mr. S. B. Chittenden, No. 18 Pierrepont street.

AUXILIARY FAIRS.

The Young Ladies' Loyal League of South Brooklyn held a Fair at the Athenæum near the close of December, the funds resulting from which were handed over to the Commission.

On the 29th and 30th of December the children of Public School, District No. 3, held a Fair in Greenfield, L. I., in aid of the Brooklyn and Long Island Fair.

Lucia B. Hazen, Fannie C. Hodges, Josephine Lewis, Lizzie Sharpe, Minnie Welch, Hattie Burgess, Edith Burgess, Ella McCollum, Anna Blashfield, and "tiny little Mary Wing"—ten little girls of South Brooklyn, thought they would try what they could do for the soldiers, and they did a truly noble work. Mr. John H. Lewis gave them the use of the cottage No. 149 President street, which they fitted up, and held a Fair, from which the very handsome sum of $164 was netted to the Sanitary Commission.

LECTURES.

On Monday evening, January 18, Rev. A. A. Willetts lectured in aid of the New England Kitchen, at the Hanson Place Church on "Sunshine, or the Secret of Happiness."

On Friday evening, February 5, Mr. B. L. Baugher lectured on the Battle of Gettysburg, before the Long Island Historical Society, in behalf of the Fair

OTHER ENTERTAINMENTS.

Tuesday evening, February 10, the members of Burnham's Gymnasium gave an exhibition at the Academy of Music, in aid of the Fair.

The Managers of the Washington Skating Pond gave a benefit festival to the Sanitary Commission, which yielded $58.

Presents to the President of the United States.

Several of the most noteworthy articles exhibited in the Fair were sent as presents to President Lincoln. Among these were the elegantly drawn Proclamation of Emancipation of Mr. Paine, described in the History of the New England Kitchen, and a superb silk bed-spread, the gift of Mrs. Margaret E. Dodge, a lady eighty-one years of age. The correspondence attending the presentation of this latter gift is given below:

BROOKLYN, March 7, 1864.

To the President of the United States:—

DEAR SIR:—A few of your fellow-citizens have the honor of offering for your acceptance herewith, a silk "Bed Spread," formed of the National Colors, and emblazoned with the Stars and Stripes and the National Eagle. It may interest you to know, that this fine specimen of needle-work is from the hands of a venerable and loyal woman, Mrs. Margaret E. Dodge, who has reached the age of eighty-one years; while the painting is the work of her equally loyal son, J. W. Dodge, a Union Refugee from Tennessee, whose property in the South has been put in jeopardy, if not already confiscated by the Rebel power. We know no depository for a household article thus designed and prepared with the noble purpose of aiding our Great National Charity, so appropriate as the Executive Mansion; were it may endure to the use of him who now holds the highest office in the nation; to whose charge the People have entrusted the Fortunes of the Republic when imminently threatened; and in whose wisdom and firmness, devout reliance on God, and honest devotion to the country, they confidingly rest.

In behalf of Two Hundred Subscribers limited to One Dollar each.

I remain, with the highest personal respect,

Your friend and fellow-citizen,

FREDERICK A. FARLEY, D. D.,

Corresponding Secretary of the Brooklyn and Long Island Fair

EXECUTIVE MANSION, WASHINGTON, April 1, 1864.

Reverend and Dear Sir:—

Permit me to return my most cordial thanks for the beautiful present transmitted by you, and for the kind and graceful manner in which it was conveyed.

I am very truly yours,

A. LINCOLN.

REVEREND FREDERICK A. FARLEY, D. D.

A Post-Office Letter.

We select for publication the following letter sent through the Post Office of the Fair to the Corresponding Secretary, not because it was the best of the many capital missives which passed through that pleasant channel, but because of its ingenious and happy interweaving of the names of so many gentlemen prominently connected with the Fair:

Dear Doctor:—

I've got your prospectus,
  And am very sorry to learn
That the enterprise you're engaged in
  Is such a *Low* concern.

Not only the Chair, but the body
  Must be every one "Mud-Sills,"
Or at least but greasy mechanics,
  For they all depend on *Mills*.

The *Lott* are decidedly common,
  Their names have a mercantile ring,
But still to save them from ruin
  I'm glad to observe one *King*.

That some are *Wilde* is no wonder,
  That some are a *Burden* not strange,
But I suppose that's no matter,
  As long as they're good on 'Change.

I see you've got *Hill* and *Brown*,
  May they sustain your hopes—
But whatever scheme you think on,
  Be sure you know the *Ropes*.

The *Brooks* are at your service,
  Where the *Archer* his tired feet laves,
You command both *Woods* and *Waters*,
  And your *Blossoms* hide your *Graves*.

Beside the *Ford* your *Huntress*
  Its *Fairbanks* leaves for you,
The *Fish* and *Eells* are swimming,
  Their loyal part to do.

The *Swan* leaves the *Lake*, and hastens,
  The *Crane* from the Marsh doth fly,
And *Hope* like a *Starr* goes before you,
  And *Knight* and *Ryder* draw nigh.

But I'm sure *I* don't approve
  Such mixed society,
On your list are a *Sawyer* and *[illegible]*,
  With a *Prince* and *Earle*, I see.

But I'm glad for your sake, Doctor,
  And the sake of your noble cause,
That the *Miller* and all the *Fellows*,
  Bring such abundant *[illegible]*.

I wish I could come to your Fair
  Without harming my dignity,
But I hope for the sake of the ladies,
  Fair-Weather it may be,

Yours truly,
Hon. AUUUSTUS FITZ NOODLE.

PHILADELPHIA, February [illegible]th, [illegible].

ADDENDUM.

Not included in any of the above reports is Vernon, Batting & Co., cash donation $200 00
Paper.. 80 50

Total.. $280 50

FINAL CORRESPONDENCE

WITH THE

UNITED STATES SANITARY COMMISSION,

IN RELATION TO THE DISPOSITION OF THE FUNDS REALIZED FROM THE

FAIR.

U. S. SANITARY COMMISSION, 823 BROADWAY, N. Y.,
MARCH, 22, 1864.

To Messrs. Dwight Johnson, J. S. T. Stranahan, George S. Stephenson, Committee of Brooklyn and L. I. Fair:

GENTLEMEN:—Having learned from your Committee that the proceeds of your brilliant Fair are likely to amount to the surprising sum of four hundred thousand dollars, I have the honor to make you the following proposition: Assuming that these funds are all to accrue to the benefit of the U. S. Sanitary Commission—for the sake of which your zeal and patience have created them—it has occurred to us that it might save you from embarrassment to indicate our wish that one quarter of the sum realized by your Fair should reach us not directly in the form of money, but in the shape of supplies, to be created by the admirable association of Brooklyn women so largely contributing to our dépôt of stores for the last two years. The Woman's Relief Association of Brooklyn is so zealous, methodical, and persistent, that we feel confident it will expend a hundred thousand dollars, through its regular machinery, in a manner even more for our benefit than if the money were in our own hands

I can lose no opportunity of repeating the expression of the admiration and gratitude the Commission feel for Brooklyn's abundant labors, and unwearied because principled exertions, in support of our cause. The Fair has been only the flower of a plant you have abundantly tended and watered and sunned for two years. I hope and believe the noble root will not, like the aloe, die of the magnificent bloom it has produced. May it live to your honor and praise as long as the war lasts.

Most gratefully and faithfully yours,

(Signed) HENRY W. BELLOWS,
President.

BROOKLYN AND L. I. FAIR IN AID OF THE U. S. SANITARY COMMISSION, BROOKLYN, March 28, 1864.

To Henry W. Bellows, D. D., President of the U. S. Sanitary Commission:

DEAR SIR:—Your note of the 22d instant, addressed to Messrs. Johnson, Stranahan, and Stephenson, was duly communicated by them to the Joint Executive Committee *ad interim*, in whose behalf and by whose appointment they had called on you. The undersigned were immediately instructed by the above-named committee to reply that your proposition gives them great satisfaction, and that they adopt it to the full. Accordingly, and at the same time, they authorized and directed our Treasurer, Mr. James H. Frothingham, to pay over to the Treasurer of your noble Commission, Mr. Strong, the sum, in cash, of three hundred thousand dollars ($300,000) as the first instalment of the Fair held in this city for its aid. In so unhesitatingly allowing us to reserve the balance, or one hundred thousand dollars ($100,000), for the purpose of having it accounted for from time to time to the Commission in the shape of supplies, to be as rapidly furnished through the agency of our Woman's Relief Association, as the exigencies of the service may require, we are glad to recognize only a merited compliment to the ever active, judicious, efficient, and unwearied efforts of the women of Brooklyn.

The plant to which your refer will not be allowed to die in the hands which have reared it. It has struck its roots deep in loyal soil; and the patriotic love and zeal which have thus far tended and nourished it are by no means exhausted. While the war lasts they will last, and the fruitage be renewed and reproduced in constantly ripening fullness, according to the needs of the hour and of our heroic and suffering men in field or hospital.

With truest regard, we are, dear Sir, faithfully yours,

(Signed) A. A. LOW,
President.

(Signed) FREDERICK A. FARLEY,
Corresponding Secretary.

BROOKLYN, March 29, 1864.

George T. Strong, Esq., Treasurer U. S. Sanitary Commission:

DEAR SIR:—In conformity with a resolution of the Joint Sub-Executive Committee of the Brooklyn and Long Island Fair in aid of the United States Sanitary Commission, I have the honor to pay over to you the sum of three hundred thousand dollars on account of the proceeds of the Fair.

Herewith I beg to enclose my check for that amount on the Nassau Bank of Brooklyn, to your order; which be good enough to acknowledge at your convenience.

With great respect, yours very truly,

(Signed) JAMES H. FROTHINGHAM,
Treasurer.

No. 68 Wall Street, New York,
March 28, 1864.

My Dear Sir:—I have the honor to acknowledge the receipt of your favor of the 26th instant, and of the sum of three hundred thousand dollars on account of the proceeds of the Brooklyn and Long Island Fair.

I beg leave to return to the committees of patriotic and public-spirited citizens by whom this Great Fair has been conducted with so much discretion, energy, and success, the sincere thanks of the United States Sanitary Commission for this most munificent contribution to its Treasury; and also to congratulate yourself and your associates in this work on the fact, that its results are nearly double what has been raised for army relief by like agencies in any other city of the Union.

I am very respectfully and truly,
Your obedient servant,

(Signed) GEORGE T. STRONG,
Treasurer United States Sanitary Commission.

JAS. H. FROTHINGHAM, Esq.,
Treasurer, &c.

United States Sanitary Commission,
New York Agency, 823 Broadway,
New York, March 29, 1864.

A. A. Low, Esq., President, and F. A. Farley, D. D., Cor. Sec., of the Brooklyn and Long Island Fair.

Gentlemen:—Your favor of yesterday is just received, and I rejoice that our action is approved by your committee. Since my last communication to your Board, our Treasurer informs me that he has received your Treasurer's check for three hundred thousand dollars, being the first instalment of the total amount of $400,000 realized from your Fair. As this is by far *the largest amount ever put into our Treasury at one time by any community*, I feel that it deserves the most marked expression of our gratitude and wonder. We really know not which sentiment prevails—amazement at your prodigious success, or satisfaction that our Commission was the object for which you labored so hard and so victoriously!

Whatever New York or Philadelphia may hereafter do for us, they cannot take away your honorable claim as the shining example which has raised their standard and stimulated their efforts. Brooklyn, by the only thoroughly approvable kind of secession, has henceforth declared her independence of New York. She has vindicated her right and power to lead; and we shall no longer hear her spoken of as an appendix to the Metropolis. She is at least entitled to be the second volume of that great work, the Commercial Capital, of which New York is the first. Rather may I not say that

New York and Brooklyn form a binary star; and that if our magnitude is greater, the lustre just exhibited in yours is brighter. With the heartiest wishes for the growth, prosperity and repute of Brooklyn, and with profound thanks for the noble, persistent support given the U. S. Sanitary Commission by its citizens, I remain, gentlemen, with the warmest personal regard your obliged friend and servant,

HENRY W. BELLOWS,

President U. S. Sanitary Commission.

www.ingramcontent.com/pod-product-compliance
Lightning Source LLC
Chambersburg PA
CBHW020829190426
43197CB00037B/1057

* 9 7 8 3 7 4 1 1 4 4 4 5 5 *